A Game Well Played

# A GAME
# WELL PLAYED

## A History of Cricket
## in Norfolk

Keir Hounsome

First published in Great Britain in 2015 by the author

Copyright Keir Hounsome 2015

Keir Hounsome has asserted his right under the Copyright, Designs and Patents Act 1988 to be identified as the author of this work.

A catalogue record for this book is available from the British Library.

ISBN 978-0-9932296-0-2

Typesetting and design: Ben Cracknell Studios

Printed by www.printondemand-worldwide.com

# About the Author

Keir Hounsome was born in Bishop's Stortford in 1952 but spent his early years in Lincolnshire. He moved to Norwich in 1984 to take up a post as a solicitor with Norfolk County Council. Now retired, he divides his time mainly between chairing the Norfolk Cricket Board, various church activities and working for voluntary organisations un-associated with cricket.

# Contents

# Introduction and Acknowledgements

In 1960 my family moved to Sleaford in Lincolnshire where our first home was 200 yards or so from the town's cricket ground. From the age of eight, I was a regular visitor during the summer months: watching, scoring and in due course playing for their emerging youth team and then, occasionally, with the adult weekend sides.

Sleaford were then, as now, one of the strongest clubs in the county and regularly hosted county games. More than that, though, they were a club with a strong social side, many 'characters' and, importantly, an ethos that combined enjoyment, encouragement and a wish to be successful. I look back on my years there with affection.

Following my further education I moved to Lincoln where, in a club of lesser status but a similar approach to the game, I spent ten happy years before moving to Norfolk in 1984. I was doubtful that my enjoyment on and off the cricket field could possibly be repeated and I was ready to drop out of cricket altogether. However, through Tom Harris, the Secretary of the Norfolk Cricket Association, I was introduced to Hellesdon Cricket Club and have remained involved in local cricket ever since in a range of roles and getting more enjoyment than I could ever have imagined. I am extremely grateful to Norfolk cricket for these last 30 years and hope that in a small way this book can be regarded as a 'thank you'.

When at Sleaford I was constantly attracted to the impressive board at the entrance to their ground that announced that the Club was 'formed prior to 1834'. These words intrigued me and looking back I guess they helped to kindle a life-long interest in cricket history, including a latent wish to write a book of my own. Well, here it is. It would, however, be wrong to say that it has been a piece of cake. The scores and scores of hours spent in local libraries, particularly the Millennium Library in Norwich, whilst a most pleasant setting, tested my powers of endurance. Fortunately, I was not alone: Dr Stephen Musk, Mike Davage and Alex Evans were writing their own books on aspects of Norfolk cricket at the same time and in this context their encouragement has been invaluable. It was also good to see other familiar faces there.

David Armstrong has written an excellent history on the County Club and whilst I have obviously drawn on it I was keen that this book should cover all aspects of cricket in Norfolk. That said, the County Club has for nearly 200 years been an important and pivotal part of the game in Norfolk and I have therefore devoted a substantial part of this book to it. I also decided, for the sake of easiness, to separate the chapters on the County Club from those on the development of cricket generally in the county. This is not to suggest that they are unrelated; indeed today there is a closeness between the County Club and the Norfolk Cricket Board that is the envy of other counties.

I also felt it important to recognise the contributions and careers of that most famous of Norfolk cricket families, the Edriches. This is not to minimise those other Norfolk-born cricketers who have played the game at the highest level but rather to highlight their unique position in Norfolk cricket. In addition, I felt that a chapter on the matches played by national touring sides in Norfolk would be appropriate to include.

That said, the chapters which proved the most interesting, and time-consuming, to research were those on the development of cricket in Norfolk from the first recorded match at Stoke Ferry in 1745. My involvement with the Norfolk Cricket League and, more recently, the Norfolk Cricket Board derives from my interest in the organisation of the game. Equally, I believe that one cannot fully understand how the game has developed, either in Norfolk or more generally, without recognising the social and economic context in which it is set. In a very simple way, I have tried to illustrate this. Similarly, one cannot view trends in Norfolk cricket without understanding the changes generally taking place in cricket in this country. Most of all, however, I hope you find these chapters as fascinating to read as I did to research.

This is a book about cricket in Norfolk. In this respect, I am very conscious that clubs from the Waveney Valley – Lowestoft, Bungay and Beccles in particular – have played their part in Norfolk cricket over the years. I have tried to recognise this in the text but have deliberately not woven those clubs into the book in the way I have done for Norfolk teams. No slight is intended.

Lastly, and most importantly in this Introduction, I come to my acknowledgements. I have already referred to my visits to the Millennium Library in Norwich. In addition, I made use of the newspapers held at Great Yarmouth and King's Lynn libraries, and in all of them the staff were incredibly helpful. As an aside, we have been fortunate in Norfolk to have had over the years a County Council that values what public libraries offer. Similarly, I thank the Norfolk Record Office and the Swaffham Museum for their help as well as the staff at the MCC Library who on my visit there ensured prompt access to material stored away in their basement. (I should incidentally record that unattributed quotes in the text generally derive from local newspapers).

I have also already referred to Dr Stephen Musk and Mike Davage. Both were unfailingly prompt in replying to my many queries on the county club and their players. Mike's book *Knights in Whites, Major Men* was published at a most convenient time for me and I am grateful to him for the opportunity to use information in it. Stephen was also generous in his assistance with the statistical section and both he and John Chilvers made helpful comments on the text for which I am also grateful. Having recognised their substantial support, I must stress that any mistakes of fact and typography are wholly mine.

I was very fortunate that my wife was happy to carry out the major task of proof reading the final draft. I am also grateful to Linda for the use of her office at home: it can now be returned to her. Well, sort of!

Kieron Tuck and Kevin Denmark kindly checked some of the more recent parts of this history. Together with Godfrey Batley before them, Norfolk cricket has been fortunate to have such able people driving the development of cricket in the county. I also thank Stephen Skinner for making available so many county handbooks. Paul Ingram helpfully shared with me his own substantial researches into cup cricket in years gone by and into grounds long since abandoned and teams long since folded. His list of contacts eased my task of finding out about the nature of village cricket in the middle of the 20th century.

Kit Hesketh-Harvey and Brian Harrison were both invaluable in helping me to identify the site of that first recorded game at Stoke Ferry. More generally, my thanks go to so many people who shared their knowledge and reminiscences with me: David Armstrong, Dave Bowker, Colin Brassett, David Childs, Ted Childs, Mick Coe, Eric Craske, Maurice Crow, Kevin Denmark, Kevin Fisher (from West Norfolk), Brian Harvey, Frank Haverson, Paul Hooton, Ray Hubbard, Richard Key, Russell Knights, Colin King, Jack King, Arthur Lawrence, Terry Moore, Nigel Rudd, Tim Smith, Derek Tooley, David Tubby, David Turner, Aubrey Webb, David Wells and Graeme Wilton.

I am also grateful to David Armstrong, Kevin Denmark, Paul Ingram, Roger Mann, Steve Phoenix and Philip Yaxley for the many photographs they provided and to the Archant Group and the County Club for permission to use others. Their help in this regard has been greatly appreciated.

Finally, my thanks go to Ben Cracknell without whose professional help and advice this book would never have been published.

To you all and anyone I have missed, thank you.


Keir Hounsome
Norwich
March 2015

# Explanatory Notes

## Monetary comparisons

The *Measuringworth* website identifies a number of ways to compute the relative value of UK money, and two are relevant to historic sums referred to in this book. I have applied the one that uses a converter based on the Retail Price Index, that is, a converter that updates to the present day the price of household commodities, and therefore indicates the spending power for the average household.

## British Summer Time

British Summer Time was introduced in 1916. Therefore, references to time before then are in effect an hour earlier than they would be today. For example, where wickets were pitched at ten o'clock in the morning for a game in the 18th century that would now equate to 11 am.

## Geographical boundaries

In the last 40 years, the geographical boundaries of a number of counties have significantly altered and this can be relevant to a county history. In Norfolk's case, the only changes were in 1974 when the parishes of Belton, Bradwell, Burgh Castle, Fritton and Hopton and parts of Corton and Herringfleet parishes transferred into Norfolk from the former administrative area of East Suffolk.

## Balls per over

Until 1884 the Laws of Cricket in this country only provided for four-ball overs. In one-day matches, five or six-ball overs were introduced from that date; six or eight- ball overs from 1947; and just six-ball overs from 2000 although it is open to competitions to agree a different number. In matches played over two or three days, five-ball overs were introduced in 1889, six-ball overs in 1900, and for 1939 only overs comprised eight balls.

## Results in one-day games

Until 1947 the Laws of Cricket provided for one-day games, including therefore almost all the inter-club matches referred to in this book to that date, to be decided on first innings unless 'played out'. From then until 2000 there was specific provision in the Laws for a one innings match to be continued if, after the completion of the first innings of each side, there was in the remaining time available a prospect of carrying it on 'to a further issue' ie a result based on two innings per side. With the advent of League cricket and the increasing ability of sides to bat for 'half an afternoon' in friendly matches the two innings per side one-day game has long since disappeared.

## Over-arm bowling

Originally, all bowling was under-arm. Round-arm bowling was legalised to elbow height in 1828 and to shoulder height in 1835. Over-arm bowling was legalised in 1864. However, and particularly in local cricket, it was not uncommon even after 1864 for bowlers to deliver the ball underhand or with a round arm ie at about waist level.

## First (given) names

I struggled at times with the use of first names. I was keen to avoid formality (on the one hand) and over-familiarity (on the other). I have generally avoided nicknames except in a very few cases where otherwise confusion may have arisen or it seemed appropriate to use them. I have also tried, when introducing a player for the first time, to use the given name by which they were generally known, and I was disappointed when my researches and enquiries drew a blank.

## Great Yarmouth

Although, of course, the town is called Great Yarmouth the senior club based there has more usually been referred to in the press simply as 'Yarmouth' and for the sake of consistency, I have therefore always referred to the club as such.

Keir Hounsome

# PART ONE

# The Development
# of Cricket in Norfolk

# CHAPTER 1

# Early Days
# of Norfolk Cricket

It is unlikely that we will ever now know exactly where and how the game of cricket originated. Sports historians in the past have picked up on references in mediaeval documents to suggest that cricket was being played in this country by the end of the 13th century and in France in the late 15th century. However, neither reference is considered now to relate the game of cricket, even in its embryonic form.

Rather, the first reliable reference to cricket dates from 1598. In a court case in Guildford concerning an argument over a piece of land one of the witnesses, a John Derrick, testified that he and his friends had, as schoolboys, played 'cricket' and other games on the land some 50 years previously. This, then, dates the game from at least as early as the middle of the 16th century, that is from about the end of the reign of Henry VIII.

The next documented references also tend to be concerned with court cases, an indication that at the time very little other written material existed. Certainly, books were rarely written for entertainment or even educational purposes. Newspapers, too, were a thing of the future. The court cases themselves covered a miscellany of legal litigation: playing cricket on a Sunday, playing in a churchyard, damage to a window, and an assault with a cricket bat, or 'cricket staffe' as it was called. There is also a reference to an inquest on a certain Jasper Vinall (from West Horsley in Sussex) accidentally hit with a cricket bat whilst trying to catch the ball.

So, by the early 17th century, there is clear evidence that cricket was being played, most often by boys and apparently in an unorganised and spontaneous way. Perhaps the first reference that hints at a more organised form of the game comes in 1646 when there was another court case which involved betting on cricket. Later, in 1668, there is a reference to the sale of drink at cricket matches.

It is relevant to note here that all the earliest recorded games of cricket took place in the south-east of England – in Surrey, Kent and Sussex. Indeed, there are no records of cricket being played in other parts of the country for some while afterwards although that is not to deny that cricket in some form was developing elsewhere. And we know that for whatever the reasons, and cricket historians do not wholly agree on this, the period following the restoration of the monarchy in 1660 saw the 'adoption' of the game by the landed gentry. Similarly with horse racing as both, crucially, became an avenue for gambling, particularly amongst the rich.

It was inevitable that with the active support of major estate owners cricket would spread away from its roots in the South East. In 1710, there is mention of cricket at Cambridge University and later there are references to matches in Gloucestershire (1729), Buckinghamshire (1730), Essex (1731), Hertfordshire (1737), Bedfordshire and Northamptonshire (1741) and Suffolk (1743). And, then, in 1745, in Norfolk, the most northerly reference at that time.

This is not to say that cricket was unheard of in Norfolk before that date. *The Cricketer* magazine in September 1927 referred to a report in the *Norwich Gazette* for 10–17 June 1723 of a game played by 14 'old men' from the town of Cranbrook in Kent. Those interested in the early days of cricket in the county are indebted to a comprehensive piece of research written by J.S. Penny in 1979 which details all the cricketing references in a range of Norwich-based newspapers from 1701 to 1800. (Curiously, he does not include that 1723 reference and enquiries of those libraries most likely to have a copy of the newspaper have drawn a blank). Not all of these newspapers would be recognisable as such today but they help to provide an informative and fascinating picture of the early days of cricket in Norfolk. The first references identified by Mr Penny can be found in the *Norwich Gazette* for 6 September 1729. They related to games in Kent and London and it is unlikely that they would have been included if the game was not already broadly familiar to the paper's readership, albeit that these readers would have been drawn largely from the wealthier, more educated, members of society. Then, between 1730 and 1737, there are nine references in the *Norwich Mercury* and *Norwich Gazette* to matches in London and the South East, including two in which the then Prince of Wales appeared. And, in 1743, the *Norwich Mercury* carried an advertisement for prints obtainable from W. Chase, a bookseller in Norwich, Mrs Samuel of Lynn and Mr Haliday of Yarmouth, one of these prints being titled 'Cricket Match'.

*The Cricketer* magazine in August 1924 also contained an item relevant to this history. In 1744, an actor by the name of G.A. Stevens – not of course to be confused with the famous Norfolk cricketer of the same name and initials – appeared at a Norwich theatre in the character of a cricketer and recited some lines on the game as 'desired by the Gentlemen cricketers of Barrow'. They contained the following

> 'The sight how glorious when the bat we wield,
> Dressed plainly, elegant, and spread the field.
> At distance wait, to break the striker's force,
> And catch the mounted ball, or stop its course'.

So, it was clear that by the 1730s, at the latest, the game was known in Norfolk and it is also possible that by then cricket had begun to be played in the county. This is not, though, to say that the game at that time in Norfolk, or any other one area, was played in exactly the same form as in another part of the country.

However, before reviewing the recorded matches in Norfolk in the 18th century, it is important to look at the county as a whole at this time. By 1700, Norwich was, after London, the second largest city in England and had a thriving economy centred on the cloth trade but also including other industries such as leatherworking and brewing. Great Yarmouth and King's Lynn, for their part, were prosperous and flourishing ports and, as today, there were a number of smaller market towns. However, most of the county's population lived away from these three major centres, in the rural parts of Norfolk which were to be in the forefront of the Agricultural Revolution as more and more fields were enclosed and new farming techniques introduced. The major road network was broadly as it is today except that, obviously, it was far less busy and of a much lower state of repair. The 'Railway Age' was still a century away; instead, coaches, horseback and foot were the means of transport. Generally people did not travel far, certainly not for sport and recreation. Indeed, except for the well-off, the long hours of work meant there was little opportunity for social recreation.

It was against this social and economic background that references to cricket in Norfolk began to appear. The first was an advertisement in the *Norwich Mercury* for 4–11 May 1745. It was addressed to 'All Lovers of CRICKET' and encouraged them to meet at Gray's Coffee-house on Friday 17 May at 6 o'clock in the evening in order to 'settle Rules for that Manly Diversion'. It is not stated to whom and in which games the rules were to apply and the outcome of the meeting is not recorded. However, it was a recognition that if cricket was to be played in anything other than a disorganised way it needed rules, not least because of the heavy gambling and significant prize money then associated with the game. This was at a time when there were no generally applied Laws of Cricket although the first known full 'Laws' had been drawn up in London in the previous year by the Royal Artillery Company and representatives of clubs in that area.

And so to the first reference to a cricket match in Norfolk. The notice which appeared in the *Ipswich Journal* on 18 May 1745 stated that on Tuesday 28 May 'there will be played for at Cricket at the Crown Inn, Stoke Ferry, Norfolk, by any gamesters that please, 11 pair of buckskin gloves of 2 guineas value, every gamester to put in 1/-'. The 'gamesters' were asked to bring 'batts and balls, there being none good to be had in the place'. The venue of the first recorded match in Norfolk was not therefore Lakenham or any current home of cricket but at an Inn in the far west of the county. The outcome of the match is unknown but the site can be identified with some certainty as land a short distance to the rear of a 14th century building on the old Lynn road passing through the village that is now a private residence but which at the time was the Crown Inn.

The Crown Inn, Stoke Ferry. *Now a private residence, the long since closed Crown Inn in Stoke Ferry was in 1745 the site of the first recorded cricket match in Norfolk. More specifically, the match was played on land behind the Inn.*

The next reference to the game in Norfolk is in an advertisement that appeared in the *Norwich Mercury* in the Spring of 1747. It addressed itself to 'ALL Gentlemen who are Lovers of the Game of CRICKET' and informed them that they could now subscribe their names, either at Gray's or the Union coffee-houses in the Market Place in Norwich for the ensuing season. 'Batts, balls etc' would be provided together with a 'very commodious piece of ground'. The cricket was to begin on the following Tuesday at 4 pm and 'to continue as long as the Weather will permit every Tuesday and Friday' but only subscribers would be allowed to play. Dogs were prohibited with the warning, partly it seems because there were sheep on the land, that they would 'certainly be kill'd on the Spot'. It is significant here to note the references to a 'season' of cricket, that there was an identified ground (although its location is not recorded) and that kit was provided. Cricket in Norwich was starting to be organised.

In 1751 there appeared for the first time in a Norfolk newspaper, the *Norwich Mercury*, the full 'scorecard' of a game although it was played outside of the county on Newmarket Heath between the teams of the Earl of Sandwich and Lord March, these being two of a number of the nobility who put together teams to play, not least for the high wagers involved. Indeed, Lord March's side is grandly called 'All England'.

The next reference to a match being played in Norfolk was in 1755. This time, the *Norwich Mercury* reported on 7 June that on the previous Friday a 'great Cricket Match' was played at Hempton Green (near Fakenham) between Colonel Townsend and Lord Orford, which the latter won 'with great ease'. On the following day there was another, five-a-side, match between the two gentlemen 'for five Guineas a Man at single Wicket'. On this occasion, the Colonel's side won easily with the Colonel himself scoring 21 'notches', as runs were then called, in one innings off his own bat.

There are no Norfolk cricketing references at all between 1756 and 1763, this probably connected to the fact that this period coincided with the Seven Years War in which Britain was actively involved against the French. However, they then start to appear with greater frequency and, as with the match at Stoke Ferry, not necessarily in places one might expect today.

On 28 July 1764 the *Norwich Gazette* announced that the 'Gentlemen Cricket Players' of Diss had laid down a challenge to any other town in Norfolk or Suffolk 'for Guineas or Half-Guineas per Man, on a Fortnight's Notice; to meet Halfway, or play Home and Home'. That the challenge was taken up is clear because on 23 August a 'grand cricket match' was played at Bury between Sir Charles Bunbury and the neighbouring gentlemen and the 'cricketing players' of Diss which Diss won. A second match, this time played at Diss, followed on 3 September and on this occasion the side now described in the *Norwich Gazette* as 'the gentlemen of Suffolk' prevailed.

However, before these two games were played the *Norwich Mercury* advertised a cricket match to be played at Blackmore Row Common in Shipdham on 11 August 1764. The game was to be eleven-a-side and the prize for the winners was given as eleven pairs of 'neat Buckskin Gloves, of a Crown Value'. The advertisement explained that all disputes would be prevented or decided by 'two joint Persons, under the Direction of the well-known Laws of the Game' and also carried a challenge from Shipdham to any town in Norfolk 'at the same Time and Place', on the face of it an indication that a match would only take place if the challenge was taken up.

Also in September 1764, the *Ipswich Journal* carried a report of two 'grand Cricket-Matches' played on Scole Common between the Gentlemen of Norfolk and Suffolk, both easily won by the latter. The report goes on to say that for the first game the bets were five to one against Suffolk but that 'each day the Knowing-ones were taken in'.

The next reference in the local newspapers is to a game at Long Stratton in September 1767 between the Gentlemen of Diss and the Gentlemen of Norwich, the first time one reads of the city having a side. Norwich won 'with great ease'. In the following year the Gentlemen of Diss entertained the Gentlemen of Eye and beat them easily and a few days later, in a match played at Tharston Green, they gained revenge over the Norwich Gentlemen, winning with '11 men and 19 notches to spare'; an innings and 19 runs in today's language.

May 1769 saw an advertisement in the *Norwich Mercury* from a William Hilling of Norwich, described in other advertisements around that time as a muffin baker. Addressed to gentlemen cricket players and others, it announced that at 4 pm every Monday, Thursday and Saturday he would be on Mousehold, near the Old Bowling Green, with bats and balls 'etc'. The same advertisement also gave notice of a game to be played there for 12 handkerchiefs with a value of 40 shillings for any two Elevens that chose to play for that prize. It is not clear what would happen if more than two sides turned up to play!

In August of the same year there is a report in the *Norfolk Chronicle* of another game, again referred to as a 'grand Cricket Match', and this time between Shipdham and Swaffham. The venue was the raceground at Swaffham and the home side were victorious, the second time in that year that they had beaten their opponents. However, what made the report unusual was that it contained the comment that Shipdham attributed Swaffham's success to their superior skill in freemasonry, with many of their side belonging to various lodges. As a result, the report ran, Swaffham were 'better judges of Right Lines, Angles, and Distances, with the only true method and secret how to level a wicket, or cut the horizontal bale'.

A week later, the same paper reported on another 'great cricket match', on this occasion between the 'gentlemen of Norwich and Yarmouth', which Norwich won. The last two reports from 1769 are of further games between Swaffham and Shipdham, both played in September and both won easily by

Shipdham. The second of these games, and the third between the two sides that year, was described as 'the Victory Match', presumably for the reason that each had won one of the first two games. The report highlighted the considerable betting on the game and described the teams as 'Cricket Heroes'.

Perhaps buoyed by their successes against Swaffham, in 1770 Shipdham issued a challenge against 'any Company now residing in any one Town in the County of Norfolk, to play Home and Home, for any sum not less than two Guineas, nor more than five each Man'. A similar advertisement appeared later in the summer but with a much-reduced stake. Presumably, the first challenge had not been taken up but the second appears to have been because at the end of August notice was given of a match between Shipdham (described as a town in the notice) and the cricket players of the towns of 'Swaffham, Ashill, Fakenham, Rudham, Rainham, Necton etc'. Shipdham must have been some side! The result, though, is unknown.

The apparent pre-eminence of Shipdham at this time is confirmed by a report that appeared in the *Norfolk Chronicle* in July 1771 about a challenge laid down by them against 'all Norfolk', to be played either home or away or halfway. The stake was given as between half a guinea and one guinea. There are no subsequent match reports, so probably the challenge was not taken up. Similarly, there is no report of the outcome of a challenge issued in 1772 by the 'Gentlemen of the CRICKET SOCIETY in Great Yarmouth' to play any single team in Norfolk or Suffolk. In each case the address for replies to this and the Shipdham challenges was an Inn, helping to confirm the role of licensees in setting up these more significant matches.

In June 1775, Shipdham broadened its challenge to Suffolk. It was presumably in response to this challenge that at the end of September notice appeared of a match to be played at East Harling on 3 October between Shipdham and Eye and the neighbouring towns in Suffolk. A 'considerable sum of money' was at stake in a match with an advertised start time of 9 o'clock. The match report explained that the opposition comprised the cricket players of Eye, Botesdale, Stowmarket, Walsham, Bramford, Ipswich and Diss. Unsurprisingly, perhaps, Shipdham lost. They also lost a match in 1777 played at Hempton Green against the gentlemen of Docking and Burnham.

The high proportion of references to Shipdham does not necessarily mean that they were the only side playing regularly in Norfolk at that time.

It may simply have been that their publicity was better than other teams. However, we do know that the game was not then universally popular in the county because in February 1775 the *Norwich Mercury* referred to a court case which decreed that Chapelfield in Norwich was the private property of that city's Corporation and was <u>not</u> to be used for a range of sporting activities, including cricket.

This is an appropriate place to review the development of the game elsewhere in the country. By the 1780s cricket had spread to Nottinghamshire (first reference in 1748), Berkshire, Somerset, Warwickshire and Yorkshire (all 1751), Derbyshire (1757), Northumberland (1766), Wiltshire (1769), Huntingdonshire (1775), Dorset and Leicestershire (1776) and Cheshire and Lancashire (both 1781). The first reference to a cricket match in Hampshire was in 1749 and it was there that the first great club became established, at Hambledon close to the Sussex border. Founded in the 1760s, and with a ground next to the famous Bat and Ball Inn with which the Club will always be associated, it attracted some of the outstanding cricketers in the South East and for the next 20 years they would compete with the best in England. The club's success also added to the image of cricket as essentially a rural activity.

As may be gathered from some of the Norfolk references, cricket was still associated with gambling and was a game played, to a large extent but by no means exclusively, by 'gentlemen'. Indeed, the social historian, G.M. Trevelyan, was to write that if the French nobility had been capable of playing cricket with their peasants their chateaux would not have been burnt.

In many respects, the game was played in a way that would be recognised today. The more important games were normally eleven-a-side, and there were umpires and scorers, although scoring was by notches cut on sticks rather than in scorebooks. The wickets were 22 yards apart and there was a popping crease. All the main ways of being dismissed existed by 1774, and byes and no balls were recognised, though not leg byes and wides. Three stumps, rather than two, followed by the use of two bails rather than one, had been introduced by about 1775, albeit not universally. The width of a cricket bat, originally unrestricted, was limited to four and a quarter inches in 1774 and by then was beginning to resemble the cricket bat of today. At the same time, the weight of a cricket ball was restricted to between five and a half and five and three quarter ounces. On the other hand, runs were still called notches and perhaps the two biggest differences compared with the game today were that bowling was under-arm (and would remain so for another 50 years) and that protective equipment was basic and minimal. Shirts might be white but the convention of wearing cricket whites was a long way in the future.

Against this background, the rest of the 18th century saw a steady increase in the number of recorded matches in Norfolk and in the spread of teams. The next reference, though, is to a meeting of the 'Cricket Society' in March 1781 at Back's Bowling Green in Norwich. Addressed to 'all LOVERS of MANLY EXERCISE' the notice in the *Norfolk Chronicle* expressed the hope that all gentlemen fond of cricket would either meet or write to the meeting place with a view to joining the Society. There is no conclusive evidence of games played by the Society but later in 1781 notice was given of two matches to be played at Dickleburgh Moor between the Gentlemen of Norfolk and Suffolk. The winners in the first match received 11 half-crowns, the losers 'eleven Shillings worth of Liquor'; the victors in the second game were rewarded with eleven pairs of gloves each valued at two shillings. For the spectators 'Good Liquors and Eatables' were provided.

At the same time, the *Norfolk Chronicle* reported a match played between the Gentlemen of Lynn and the Docking Eleven at Gaywood that was won by the latter by ten wickets and described as 'the grandest match of cricket ever known in this county'. The newspaper report also included the names of the umpires for the first time – John Godbold for Docking and a Mr Stanley for Lynn.

There was also scheduled in 1781 a match between a team drawn from a regiment of Dragoons quartered in Norwich against a party of Essex militia encamped at Hopton. The stake was to be the princely sum of one hundred guineas (approximately £10,000 in today's money) but the Essex side called off and paid an unspecified forfeit.

The first reference to cricket in Downham Market appeared in 1783. The match in question was described as being between the 'young gentlemen of Wisbech' and a company of men from Methwold. In fact, as the report continued, two matches were played in both of which Methwold were victorious. The first, a two-innings game, was won by an innings and 1 run and the second, just one innings per side, by ten wickets. The scores were low, with Wisbech's three innings amounting to 42, 41 and 45.

In the next year, the *Norfolk Chronicle* carried the scores of a contest between Wells and the combined settlements of Holt and Brinton, won easily by the latter. There was also a game at Brandon when the hosts' 'young men' overcame the 'noted cricket players of Thetford'. Lastly, in 1784, the *Bury and Norwich Post* reported a match in which the gentlemen of Yarmouth travelled to, and beat, the Bungay club by the convincing margin of 136 notches. However, it seems that the Yarmouth victory was due to their including two players 'who did not belong to them'. One, a Mr Edwards, scored 98 notches and the other, Mr Barrett, 57.

1785 saw just one local report, of two matches between the gentlemen of Harleston and the neighbouring towns and the Bungay Society. Bungay won both games, by 56 notches and an innings and 20 notches. In the next year there is also only one report, this time of a match at Hempton Green played for a 'considerable bet' between the Brinton and Holt Club and the Lexham and Castle Acre Club. The advance notice referred to the wickets being pitched at eight o'clock and the match report recorded that it lasted for eight hours. Brinton and Holt won by three runs in a two-innings game – 61 and 70 to 72 and 56.

In the following year, there are reports of matches played at Swaffham – apparently on the racecourse – and at Gaywood, on Sayers Marsh. In the second of these games the gentlemen of Lynn beat those of the 'adjacent villages' and according to the *Norwich Mercury* displayed a perfect knowledge of the game. The 'knowing ones' were said to be 'deeply taken in'.

The most intriguing reference, though, in 1787 was to a game played in Blickling Park between a team from Blickling and a side described by the *Norwich Mercury* as 'the party who practise on Mousehold Heath'. Blickling were the clear winners, scoring 84 and 59 in their two innings as against the 31 and 11 mustered by the visitors. The detailed report refers to a large crowd that had travelled great distances to see a match between two first-rate sides, with bets running high. It also stated that the Blickling side acknowledged the excellence of their opponents and that they were even superior in some important elements of play. However, there was some controversy because the Norwich side had been led to believe that their opponents would only include Blickling players whereas they were considerably strengthened with two from Gunton.

If the level of local newspaper reporting is a true indicator then 1788 saw a significant increase in the amount of cricket played in the county. The following are recorded

- a victory at Swaffham for the gentlemen of Northwold over the gentlemen of Swaffham – with a prize of 20 guineas
- again at Swaffham, a win for Shipdham's gentlemen over the towns of Northwold and Methwold – this time played for 50 guineas a side
- a proposed match between the gentlemen from the East Dereham and Shipdham clubs, at East Dereham – much betting was involved and 'much diversion' expected from 'the known activity and agility of the parties'
- a victory on Sayers Marsh for the gentlemen of Downham over the gentlemen of Lynn
- a game on Yarmouth Denes between the gentlemen of Norwich and Yarmouth which the home side won by 11 runs and where the playing area was described as a 'circle of 200 yards diameter which, much to the credit of the numerous spectators, was kept perfectly clear'
- a match played at Brisley Green between the gentlemen from the parishes of Brinton and Shipdham – with a 9 o'clock start and a prize of 20 guineas
- a return fixture at Downham Market between gentlemen from the Downham and Castle Acre clubs – for a prize of 22 guineas with the report for this game suggesting that the two clubs were the best in the county
- a game on Swaffham racecourse in which West Lexham beat Downham by an innings.

Occasionally, contests were arranged on different lines. In July, a game took place at Brinton between the single men and the married men from the parishes of Brinton and Holt which the former won by 27 notches after seven hours of play. At Foulsham, after a 'severe contest of five hours', the single men of the parish overcame the married men by seven wickets. Also in July, the *Ipswich Journal* carried a report of a game on Bungay Common described as being between 'Mr Barrett of the Norwich Theatre' and three others named as Thomas Scarfe, Mr Freeston (both from Bungay) and William Gooch (from Woodton). In fact, the match report shows that Mr Scarfe partnered Mr Barrett and that they won a very low scoring two-innings game by four notches and so claimed the ten guineas prize.

Mr Barrett's name also appeared in the report of the game at Yarmouth Denes referred to above when he was described as assisting the Norwich side. There are detailed reports of that game which was said to have involved 'much good play'. There was a large crowd and much betting, with fortunes going from side to side. A return match was arranged to be played in Norwich, either on Mousehold Heath or Magdalen Fairstead. However, the Yarmouth side withdrew in circumstances that involved some disagreement. They clearly blamed the Norwich Club and this led to the latter placing a long advertisement in the *Norfolk Chronicle* and *Norwich Mercury* in particular as an explanation to those spectators who had travelled some distance to watch the contest. The substance of the advertisement was that the aforesaid Mr Barrett had appointed himself as the manager for the game contrary to the opinion of everyone else present. His own side agreed that he should not manage or, in the words of the advertisement, 'mismanage' any longer and as a result he withdrew. The Norwich side then asked for permission to have a substitute, to field but not to bat or bowl, but with one of the Norwich team batting twice. Yarmouth objected, taking the line that it was Norwich's problem that Mr Barrett had withdrawn and making it clear that if Norwich changed their eleven they would be taken as forfeiting the match. According to the advertisement the Norwich Club backed down and agreed to play with ten players as against Yarmouth's eleven at Mousehold Heath on the following day. However, having assembled on the next day, and the pitch marked out, the Yarmouth team then forfeited, in one report because their umpires were concerned about the bad state of the ground. Norwich felt that it was never their opponents' intention to play and they concluded their advertisement by stating that they would not respond to any subsequent comments on the matter.

The advertisement prompted a response from a correspondent calling himself 'Fair Play' and describing himself as an 'indifferent spectator'. 'Fair Play' supported Norwich's account of the dispute with Mr Barrett. However, he went on to say that the visitors had been unable to give a positive response immediately to the proposal to play the game on the next day because not all their players were present. He continued that it had originally been intended to play the match not at Mousehold but at Magdalen Fairstead and that this was the match that should have been played. According to 'Fair Play' the reason for Yarmouth's withdrawal was that Norwich had changed the venue. He also refuted the suggestion that Yarmouth had no intention in the first place of fulfilling the fixture. The tone of the response was highly critical of the Norwich Club and suggested that 'Fair Play' may not have been an indifferent spectator after all.

Over the next few years there are records of a range of matches in the county which together help to confirm the spread of the game locally. In 1789 we can read of

- two matches between the Castle Acre and Docking Clubs, both won by the former. The report of the second match stated that for many years Docking had been 'the champions of the county'
- a game between the gentlemen of Foulsham and the gentlemen of North Elmham, won by the latter
- a game between the gentlemen of Castle Acre and the gentlemen of Brinton, won easily by Brinton. The advertisement referred to the wickets being pitched as early as eight o'clock and the two sides being the two premier clubs in the county. (A return game was initially postponed because of illness and when it did eventually take place in October it ended in dispute and with Castle Acre alleging that Brinton were afraid to play them. This led to Brinton issuing a challenge either to Castle Acre or the whole of Norfolk for 50 guineas a side, the match to be played on Hempton Green. However, there is no record of this match taking place)
- a match to be played on 19 October on Hempton Green between the Castle Acre and Docking Clubs, again with wickets pitched at eight o'clock.

In 1790, there are references to

- 'the annual match' between 'the married and single of Harleston'
- two matches between the gentlemen of Swaffham and Sporle and adjacent villages, both won by Swaffham
- two games between the gentlemen of East Dereham and gentlemen chosen from the Castle Acre, Brinton and Elmham clubs. East Dereham won both
- a contest in which Castle Acre defeated the united clubs of Swaffham and Sporle
- a proposed match on Mousehold Heath in Norwich between the gentlemen of Norwich and Taverham for which the latter were the favourites.

In the following year, local newspapers only mentioned two games, in which Sporle twice defeated Swaffham. In 1792, there were games at Attleborough (in which Hingham triumphed over the home side); at Aylsham (where in a match between married men and 'youths not pubescent' the 'rising generation' won after 'a strong and furious contest'); and at Brinton (against Walsingham). 1793 saw a game on Hardingham Common where the 'cricket players' of Attleborough easily beat those of Hingham (but note the reference to 'players' rather than the more usual 'gentlemen', probably an indication of the social standing of the participants). In the same year, Downham Market twice defeated Wisbech.

In 1794, there is recorded a game at Palgrave in which Diss beat Finningham and another in which Longham lost to Brisley and which was accompanied by a single wicket contest between a John Garwood of Brisley and Robert Peck of Gressenhall convincingly won by the former. The newspapers included nothing in 1795 but in the next year there are matches between Swaffham and Brinton, Walsingham and Fakenham, Walsingham and Wells, Litcham and Tittleshall, Bungay and Norwich, and Wells and Holkham.

One further game in 1796 was between Swaffham and Shipdham. At the end of August, Shipdham had placed a challenge in the *Norfolk Chronicle* which referred to suggestions that they had refused to play Swaffham, and offering to play any single parish in Norfolk for one guinea a man (or more, if required), but nothing less than that. Any gentleman wishing to play on this basis was asked to respond to the Post Office in Shipdham. There was a footnote that 'No Company need apply that have not resided together in one parish for these six months last past', a clear message against 'team strengthening'. Whether or not as a response to this advertisement, at the end of September the gentlemen of Swaffham and Shipdham contested a game at Necton, which Swaffham won by one wicket.

In July of the following year, the gentlemen of Lyng and Elsing defeated the gentlemen of Aylsham, Blickling, Aldborough and Thurgarton, and in the same month there also took place at Swaffham two matches that up to that point were the most important played in Norfolk.


Nationally, cricket was developing towards the end of the 18th century, albeit not with the same special or revolutionary fervour as some other aspects of society. As it had been since it began to be played in any organised form, the game was still under the control of the gentry. Witness, for instance, the number of matches in Norfolk played between the 'gentlemen' of particular towns or villages. In addition, cricket teams in many areas continued to be sponsored to a significant degree by 'patrons', that is, wealthy landowners who put together sides of the best players in the area, some of whom they might employ in another role such as a gardener. The great patrons of the game, such as the second Duke of Richmond and the third Duke of Dorset, were based in the counties of Kent, Surrey, Sussex and Hampshire and played their games in that part of the country, but elsewhere landowners generally were promoting the game, for example at Burghley Park near Stamford and Burley on the Hill in Rutland, the country residence from 1769 of the Earl of Winchilsea. That in itself illustrated that the game was generally spreading northwards from its historic base in the South East. Reference has already been made to the first recorded matches in many counties north of London, and in addition clubs were starting to be formed in the industrial centres of the north. However, these clubs were not the playthings or gambling tools of the nobility but were generally formed by working men, sometimes under the management of a local publican.

Whereas the former would tend to play their cricket on private estates the latter would more likely play on common land.

Perhaps the most significant cricketing development in the later part of the 18th century was the formation of the Marylebone Cricket Club. The MCC had started life a few years earlier as the Star and Garter Club – and then re-named as the White Conduit Club – but by 1788 it was known as it is today. It was in 1788 that the Club updated the Laws of Cricket originally produced in 1744 and first revised in 1774. The 1788 changes were relatively minor but they served to create a role for the MCC as guardians of the Laws of Cricket that, the Regulations of the International Cricket Council notwithstanding, survives to this day.

The other comment to make here about the MCC relates to its ground. Thomas Lord originally came from Thirsk in North Yorkshire but whilst he was still a boy his family moved to Diss. It is just possible that as an eight year-old living there in 1764 he was a spectator at the game between Diss and Sir Charles Bunbury's side, and it is most likely that he would have learned something about the game of cricket whilst in Diss. Moving to London in his twenties, he was employed by the White Conduit Club and, being a reasonable cricketer himself, he was asked by representatives of that Club, including the aforementioned Earl of Winchilsea, to lay out a cricket ground for the Club to use as its own. Thomas Lord was also involved in the wine trade and he took the opportunity to lease not only the ground itself but also a public house adjoining it. As London developed, Lord twice had to move his ground until it came to its present site in St John's Wood in 1814.

The most comprehensive record of the more important games played in the 18th and much of the 19th centuries was compiled by Arthur Haygarth in 14 volumes of match scores titled *Scores and Biographies* and published between 1862 and 1895. These books also included potted biographies of a great number of the players involved in those games. The first part of the first volume is dominated by the matches played by the famous Hambledon Club, particularly against Kent and Surrey and even 'England'. Also included, particularly from about 1780, are matches between clubs under the names of the major patrons such as Sir Horace Mann and the Earl of Winchilsea and between counties in the South East. Generally, these matches were 11-a-side but occasionally there are included contests between teams of fewer players – perhaps five or six – and even single wicket games are included. Until 1800, at least, almost all of these recorded matches were played in and around the Home Counties, increasingly at Lord's ground wherever it was at the time. Occasionally, though, Haygarth records games further afield, in places such as Nottingham and Burghley Park. Then, in July 1797, at Swaffham, he details matches between, firstly, Norfolk and England and, secondly, the sides of the Earl of Winchilsea and Lord Beauclerk.

Notice first appeared in the *Norwich Mercury* and *Norfolk Chronicle* on 22 April 1797 advertising a match to be played in July between Norfolk and All England. It told readers that the 'First General Meeting will be held at Hempton Green on Friday, April 28, 1797' with a note that all gentlemen wanting to play in this match should attend the meeting or inform a Mr Meadows of Necton of their wish. The notice also announced that the match was to be played for 500 guineas (approximately £45,000 in today's money). On 13 May, the same newspapers carried a second advertisement along similar lines except that on this occasion the next general meeting would be at Brinton on 19 May. Further advertisements appeared on 3 and 24 June with the general meetings to be at Swaffham and Hempton Green on 9 and 30 June respectively. The second of these advertisements stated that the wickets for the game on 30 June would be pitched at ten o'clock, an indication that these gatherings were more than just meetings but rather 'trial' or practice matches. These notices and the preparations illustrate the importance locally of the first Swaffham match. The *Norfolk Chronicle* on 24 June also informed its readers that on 26 June there would be a meeting of 'the Norfolk Cricket players' at Brinton for the purpose of selecting the players for the game against All England.

On 8 July, the *Norwich Mercury* and *Norfolk Chronicle* reported that the Norfolk v All England game would be played on 17 July and warned that a very great crowd was anticipated with a heavy demand on accommodation in the inns and private dwellings in the town. In particular, many members of the nobility were expected from London and elsewhere.

Not mentioned in the newspapers but asserted by G.B. Buckley in his 1935 work entitled *'Fresh Light on 18th Century Cricket'* was that the match had been arranged as early as October 1796 and that the backer was a Mr Robert Denn. In addition, it was said to have been arranged following a comment made by Lord Beauclerk that England could beat 33 of Norfolk that then led to a challenge from the 'Norfolk party', presumably Mr Denn.

The venue, as already noted, was at Swaffham. In 1910 *Cricket: A Weekly Record of the Game* referred to a 'tradition' that there was a cricket club in Swaffham as early as 1700 which, if true, would make it easily the earliest recorded reference to cricket in Norfolk. However, there is no independent evidence to support this and it is difficult to reconcile with the chronology of the development of cricket referred to earlier. The precise venue for the 1797 games was the Racecourse Ground situated to the south-west of the town on what more recently has been known as Swaffham Heath. It has long since ceased to be used for cricket.

And so to the players. Norfolk played with 33, all of whom fielded. None of their names are familiar, perhaps not surprisingly given that up to that time the Norfolk papers had not given the details of those playing in local matches. On the other hand, the England Eleven contained many of the great cricketers of the day. In batting order they were

**Tom Walker** (born 1762) – renowned as a defensive batsman and as a very slow runner between wickets. He is reputed on one occasion to have received 170 balls from one of the great early bowlers, David Harris, in a single-wicket match and scored just one run. Not for nothing was he known as 'Old Everlasting'.

**Lord Frederick Beauclerk** (born 1773) – involved in major cricket for over 35 years he was perhaps the best batsman of his day and also the greatest amateur single-wicket player. He was also well known for his uncontrollable temper and autocratic nature.

**Hon. John Tufton** (born 1773) – a wicketkeeper who was also believed to be a right-handed batsman and bowler. He was at the time of this match the Member of Parliament for Appleby in Westmorland.

**Andrew Freemantle** (born circa 1768) – a left-hander described as a 'good hitter', he was also a reliable fieldsman away from the wicket.

**John Hammond** (born 1769) – another left-handed batsman and a powerful hitter, he also bowled and was a wicket keeper of the highest standard.

**Robert Robinson** (born 1765) – also a hard-hitting left-handed batsman. As a boy he lost two fingers, and his bat handle had to be specially adapted to fit the deformity. In later life he returned to Norfolk to take up employment as a gamekeeper at Dereham.

**John Small junior** (born 1765) – whilst not as famous or prolific as his father he was nevertheless an accomplished batsman.

**William Beldham** (born 1766) – known as 'Silver Billy' his career in major cricket stretched from 1787 to 1821. He was a batsman of the very highest standard who bowled, for an underarm bowler, at medium pace.

**Harry Walker** (born circa 1760) – he was a tall aggressive left-handed batsman and somewhat more entertaining than his brother, Tom. He was an early exponent of the cut shot.

**William Fennex** (born circa 1764) – he was a leading exponent of forward play and going out to meet the pitch of the ball. He was better known as a single-wicket player.

**John Wells** (born 1759) – a right-handed batsman and fast under-arm bowler.

This Eleven were a mixture of gentlemen and professionals. Six had played for Hambledon; all represented All England on other occasions.

And now to the match itself, played on 17–20 July 1797 in front of a crowd described as 'an immense number of spectators from all parts of the kingdom'. The scorecard confirms an easy win for the England Eleven, by an innings and 14 runs. What is less clear, as with a number of matches in the early days of cricket in Norfolk, is who batted first. Given that, until 1835, a side did not follow on unless more than 100 runs behind on first innings one might assume that it was Norfolk. However, all the accounts of the game indicate that it was England who took the first innings, in which case Norfolk must have followed on by agreement. Whatever the true position, Lord Beauclerk was proved correct in his assertion that England would prevail.

The scorecard as it appears in *Scores and Biographies*, although other versions show differences both in the names of the local players and the individual scores and dismissals, reads

## THIRTY-THREE OF NORFOLK

| | 1st Inn. | | 2nd Inn. | |
|---|---|---|---|---|
| _ Brown, | b T. Walker .... | 6 | st. Hammond.... | 0 |
| _ Sculfer, | run out........ | 1 | c H. Walker ..... | 2 |
| M. Raven, | c Fennex ...... | 3 | c H. Walker ..... | 1 |
| R. Harmer, | c Hammond.... | 0 | b Beauclerk ..... | 9 |
| James Fuller, | c Beauclerk..... | 7 | b Beauclerk ..... | 0 |
| _ Jackson, | c Freemantle ... | 1 | b Beauclerk ..... | 0 |
| John Stibbard, | st Hammond ... | 0 | b Fennex ....... | 9 |
| _ Allen, | b Wellls ....... | 5 | b Fennex ....... | 2 |
| John Fuller, | c Beldham ..... | 6 | run out........ | 1 |
| _ Archer, | b Wells........ | 9 | b Wells......... | 9 |
| (Little) Raven, | c H. Walker .... | 0 | c H. Walker ..... | 1 |
| _ Cox, | b Beauclerk .... | 1 | c Beauclerk...... | 7 |
| James Withers, | c Hammond.... | 0 | b Wells......... | 0 |
| _ Brooks, | b Wells........ | 0 | st Hammond .... | 0 |
| _ Rust, | c Beldham ..... | 1 | b Wells......... | 3 |
| G. Withers, | c Beldham ..... | 0 | st Hammond .... | 4 |
| Ben. Fuller, | c Hammond.... | 0 | c Wells......... | 0 |
| R. Rainer, | b Beauclerk .... | 0 | c H. Walker ..... | 0 |
| _ Curtis, | c Small........ | 0 | c Fennex ....... | 8 |
| T. Rumball, | c Fennex ...... | 0 | b Fennex ....... | 0 |
| _ Bennett, | c Hammond.... | 0 | st Hammond .... | 3 |
| _ Hulph, | b Beauclerk .... | 0 | c Hammond..... | 0 |
| _ Shirley, | b Wells........ | 1 | c Hammond..... | 0 |
| _ Paul, | st Hammond ... | 2 | b Fennex ....... | 0 |
| _ Scott, | b Beauclerk .... | 0 | b Beauclerk ..... | 0 |
| _ Watling, | c Beldham ..... | 0 | c H. Walker ..... | 1 |
| _ Milligan, | b Beauclerk .... | 6 | lbw............ | 0 |
| _ Mitchell, | b Beauclerk .... | 0 | b Wells......... | 14 |
| Ben. Fuller, | b Beauclerk .... | 1 | c Small......... | 0 |
| _ Glasscock, | not out ........ | 0 | b Wells......... | 0 |
| _ Cushing, | run out........ | 0 | c Fennex ....... | 0 |
| J. Emmerson, | b Beauclerk .... | 0 | not out ......... | 0 |
| _ Warner, | b Beauclerk .... | 0 | c Wells......... | 1 |
| | Byes .......... | 0 | Byes .......... | 5 |
| | | **50** | | **80** |

## ALL ENGLAND

|  |  | 1st Inn. |
|---|---|---|
| T. Walker, | c Scott . . . . . . . . | 55 |
| Lord F.Beauclerk, | c Emmerson. . . . | 39 |
| Hon. J. Tufton, | c. Archer . . . . . . | 19 |
| A. Freemantle, | b G. Withers . . . | 4 |
| J. Hammond, | c J. Fuller . . . . . . | 10 |
| R. Robinson, | c Rainer . . . . . . . | 2 |
| J. Small, jun., | c Sculfer. . . . . . . | 2 |
| W. Beldham, | not out . . . . . . . . | 6 |
| H. Walker, | b B. Fuller . . . . . | 0 |
| W. Fennex, | b Milligan. . . . . . | 4 |
| John Wells, | c Warner . . . . . . | 3 |
|  | Byes . . . . . . . . . . | 0 |
|  |  | 144 |

An engraving of the 1797 match at Swaffham between Thirty-Three of Norfolk and All England. *This match was played on the Racecourse Ground in Swaffham, now part of Swaffham Heath.*

That, though, was not the end of the cricket entertainment that week in Swaffham. This first match finished on the Thursday, and on the following day there began a two-day, 11-a-side, game between sides led by Lord Frederick Beauclerk (or, according to some accounts, by the Honourable Colonel Lennox, another leading amateur of the day) and the Earl of Winchilsea and including, in one team or the other, nine of the players who had just played for the England Eleven. It will be seen from the scorecard below that Thomas Lord also appeared, this being his only appearance in a major match in Norfolk.

Brief references have already been made to the Earl of Winchilsea. He was tremendously influential in cricket at the time and perhaps more than anyone else was responsible for moving the centre of cricket in this country to London and to the MCC in particular. Although autocratic, he was broadly benevolent and public spirited. And he loved his cricket. The match itself was played for 1000 guineas (approximately £90,000 in today's money) with the participants being described as 'noblemen and gentlemen', mostly from the Marylebone Club. The local newspapers also referred to the game giving much satisfaction to the spectators who had 'never seen the game played in such superior style'.

As the match details now show the Earl of Winchilsea's side won by 27 runs:

## EARL OF WINCHILSEA'S SIDE

| | | 1st Inn. | | 2nd Inn. |
|---|---|---|---|---|
| John Wells, | c Fennex | 6 | c Lennox | 26 |
| Hon. J. Tufton, | c Hammond | 13 | c Upton | 15 |
| T. Walker, | b Hammond | 24 | b Fennex | 4 |
| _ Ray, | b Hammond | 17 | c Hammond | 2 |
| Earl of Dalkeith, | b Hammond | 0 | b Beauclerk | 0 |
| Earl of Winchilsea, | st Hammond | 6 | c Hammond | 4 |
| W. Beldham, | st Hammond | 75 | st Hammond | 18 |
| _ Wilson, | c Lennox | 0 | not out | 0 |
| _ Rice, | c Lennox | 1 | b Fennex | 0 |
| T. Mellish, Esq., | c Fennex | 4 | run out | 0 |
| _ Sylvester, | not out | 0 | c Fennex | 4 |
| | Byes | 3 | Byes | 3 |
| | | 149 | | 76 |

## LORD F. BEAUCLERK'S SIDE.

| | | 1st Inn. | | 2nd Inn. |
|---|---|---|---|---|
| J. Small, jun., | b Walker . . . . . . | 4 | c Ray . . . . . . . . . | 9 |
| J. Hammond, | run out. . . . . . . . | 21 | c Beldham . . . . . | 13 |
| Lord F.Beauclerk, | c Ray . . . . . . . . . | 37 | b Wells. . . . . . . . | 0 |
| W. Fennex, | b Wells. . . . . . . . | 12 | b Walker . . . . . . | 40 |
| _ Graham, | c Wells. . . . . . . . | 15 | c Wells. . . . . . . . | 6 |
| Hon. A. Upton, | b Beldham . . . . . | 4 | c Beldham . . . . . | 1 |
| T. Lord, | run out. . . . . . . . | 0 | not out . . . . . . . . | 1 |
| _ Brown, | b Wells. . . . . . . . | 1 | c Beldham . . . . . | 0 |
| _ Courtney, Esq., | lbw. . . . . . . . . . | 1 | b Walker . . . . . . | 0 |
| _ Cooper, | not out . . . . . . . . | 0 | c Ray . . . . . . . . . | 0 |
| Hon. Colonel Lennox | c Ray . . . . . . . . . | 25 | b Beldham . . . . . | 4 |
| | Byes | 2 | Byes | 2 |
| | | 122 | | 76 |

And, so, Swaffham's 'festival of cricket' came to an end.

# CHAPTER 2

# The Age of
# Fuller Pilch

By the end of the 18th century the Agricultural Revolution had been under way for over 50 years. New farming techniques were well established and the practice of enclosure, whereby open fields and common land were by means of parish-specific legislation divided up amongst a limited number of landowners, was spreading particularly quickly. However, the economic prosperity that followed the improvement in agriculture had a downside: an increase in the number of jobless labourers.

The Agricultural Revolution was quickly followed by the Industrial Revolution. The second half of the 18th century saw major changes in the nation's manufacturing practices – particularly in the production of coal and iron and textiles. The full fruits of the Industrial Revolution would not be realised until the 19th century but the foundations, and more, were in place by 1800 as the country's manufacturing industries began to develop radically.

The two Revolutions largely fed off one another, and both were a response to the need to sustain and employ a population which was growing more quickly than ever before, mainly due to improved medical conditions. One significant consequence of these dramatic social changes was the increasing migration from rural villages into urban areas, particularly the industrialised towns where the factories, and therefore work, could be found. By 1800 this urbanisation had begun in earnest, and was fuelled by the growth of London and other cities as centres of commercial trading, not least with the rest of the world. The need for professional services such as insurance, law and banking grew as a result.

The quality of the road network was improving not least in order to support these social changes, although railways were still at least a generation away. Canals were also being built, and rivers improved, in order to facilitate the transport of goods and materials.

These developments inevitably impacted on Norfolk. The county was one of those most affected by the enclosure of its open fields with the newspapers of the time regularly including formal notices about the enclosure legislation for this or that parish. It was estimated that by 1796 two-thirds of Norfolk was used for arable farming of which three-quarters was enclosed. The Agricultural Revolution had many of its roots in Norfolk and it was inevitable that as a consequence of these social and economic influences many of those living in the countryside moved into Norwich or the towns. However, it was still the case that at the end of the 18th century less than a quarter of the county's population lived in the three urban centres of Norwich, King's Lynn and Great Yarmouth. Into the 19th century, the move away from the countryside to the urban areas continued such that, as the county's population as a whole grew from 274,000 to 413,000 between 1801 and 1850, it was these three settlements where the growth was most marked; in Norwich alone, the population almost doubled in this 50-year period.

This is not to say that Norfolk was industrialising at the same rate as in the north of England. Indeed, because of the competition from elsewhere, the textile industry in Norwich had begun to decline. On the other hand, leather working and brewing were expanding, both having a clear link to agriculture. The ports at Great Yarmouth and King's Lynn flourished, bringing prosperity to those towns.

Communication within the county, as elsewhere, was improving although turnpike roads, for instance, did not develop as quickly in Norfolk as in many other places. There was less pressure to improve roads compared with the more industrialised parts of the country. Stagecoaches were introduced in the late 18th century and could travel up to ten miles an hour on the better roads in the county. Norwich was the focal point of local services with daily runs to King's Lynn and Great Yarmouth and less frequent journeys to smaller towns in the county although those longer services might stop there.

Across the English Channel, the French Revolution had led to the rise of Napoleon and by 1800 Europe was in the grip of war. A consequence of the Napoleonic War, in which Britain was involved from the end of the century, and its demands on human resources, was a reduction in the amount of cricket played in England. Whilst not an absolutely reliable barometer, Haygarth's *Scores and Biographies* contain 220 pages of what generally were the more important matches between 1786 and 1800 but only 101 between 1801 and 1815. Peter Wynne-Thomas in his *History of Cricket from the Weald to the World* also attributes the apparent decline in the game to the impact of the Industrial Revolution with its long working hours in the factories and to the need to restrict people's rights in the light of the threats from France. The resurgence, when it came in the 1820s and 1830s, was largely due to interest taken in the game within the universities, public schools, army and clergy.

Norfolk's newspapers were still the main record of cricket played in the county and they paint a similar picture with limited references to the game in the first decade of the new century. To a degree, this was because the local papers of the day still comprised only a very few pages – generally no more than four – and in the early part of the century these were dominated by news from the War and Parliament together with reports of court cases and notices of auctions, Inclosure legislation and general sales. (In addition to reports in the local newspapers, there was published in 1844 'The Register of Cricket for Hingham' by 'An Old Player'. The writer was Thomas Driver, and his book serves as a rare record of a village club in the first half of the 19th century).

This is not to say that there were no reports of matches in Norfolk in the early years of the 19th century. For example, in 1805 the Gentlemen of Reepham, Hackford, Whitwell and Corpusty featured in two matches with the Gentlemen of Foulsham with the second being played as late as 21 October. In the same year, Blickling were host to the Norwich Club. Later, in 1811, the Gentlemen of Swaffham's victory over the Gentlemen of Terrington brought the comment that 'a better match was never played in Norfolk'. And in the same year, a game took place at the Town Close ground in the city between the Norwich Club and 'the two new ones united', although it is not clear who those two new clubs were. A year later, Norwich beat the combined team of Bungay and Beccles by an innings. There were also matches involving army regiments stationed in the county.

Some contests took a surprising form. In 1806, two players from Hilborough took on 25 from Thetford. A year later, there was a single wicket match at Mundford between D. Bowd of Ickburgh and John Spinks of Hilborough – not unusual on the face of it except that Bowd was 80 years old and his opponent half that age. In the following year, one member of the Swaffham Club played and beat six players of 'professed celebrity' in that town. More generally, single-wicket games were quite common. And it was not unknown for the two competing sides to have a different number of players as when seven players of Norwich played 11 of the Wiltshire Regiment of Militia in 1807.

It was still common, and would remain so for some years, for the more important games of the day to be played for high stakes. Even in Norfolk, there might be a reward for the winners, albeit of a relatively modest scale, as when the Swaffham and Shipdham Gentlemen competed for 50 guineas (over £3,400 today) in 1808 and Norwich played Bungay for 100 guineas in 1813. More unusually, in 1811, Mulbarton played Ashwellthorpe on Mulbarton Common for 22 bottles of cider and 22 pounds of cherries! This was not enough to inspire Mulbarton who were dismissed for 14 and 22 and lost heavily. Later, in 1827, Frettenham and Hainford competed for 'a barrel of Hawes fine ale'.

However, cricket around this time was not universally appreciated. For instance, in 1812 there were reports of 'idle men' playing cricket in Chapelfield in Norwich and 'using abusive language to the annoyance of those who frequent that pleasant promenade'. Five years later, a number of people were convicted and fined by the magistrate at Larlingford for playing on the village green in Old Buckenham on a Sunday in October. It seems from the reports that those convicted had been persistent offenders.

1815 brought with it a return to peace although perhaps the Eleven of Fakenham, Walsingham and Hempton wished they had not hosted, on

Hempton Green, a fixture in July of that year against an Eleven drawn from Litcham, Dunham and Brisley. They were dismissed for 0 with contemporary reports suggesting, probably incorrectly, that this was the first occasion on which a side had been all out without registering a single run. Elsewhere that year, Yarmouth played Bungay for £100, and there were also games involving teams from Downham, Litcham and Castle Acre, as well as the Holt Club of whom as early as 1811 it was written that 'they will soon be able to challenge any side in England'.

By 1815, it was clear from both the press and Driver's book, that the game's popularity was growing, particularly in Norwich, Thetford, Fakenham, Swaffham, Downham, Great Yarmouth, Attleborough, Hingham and Shipdham (described by Driver in 1810 as having stood 'foremost in notoriety in Norfolk'), and many smaller settlements. In some cases, a formal club existed; in other places, the arrangements for playing cricket were less structured. 'Reconstitution' of a club was certainly not unknown; Hingham re-formed in 1814 after an interval of three years and following the recruitment of new players.

1816 sees reports of wins for Hingham over Shipdham – with the comment that for many years the latter had been victors over all who had opposed them – Attleborough over Banham (who forfeited the return match and paid a financial penalty as a result), Emneth over Wisbech in all three games between them that year and Litcham over Holt.

In the following year, one can read of games between Swaffham and Hingham, the first of which was played for 22 guineas a side and described by Driver as 'by far the most important match' Hingham had been involved in both as to the sum played for and 'the anxiety of the public to witness it'; Thetford and Newmarket; and Aylsham and the combined forces of Aldborough, Matlaske, Baconsthorpe and Bessingham and surrounding parishes. In the last of these games, won by Aylsham by one wicket, the report referred to the batting being 'much superior to what could be expected', the ball being 'handled with dexterity' and the 'scouting' – that is, the fielding – being 'well supported on both sides'. And in that same year, there was a single-wicket game in Chapelfield, Norwich, involving two players from Sussex and Hertfordshire as early as the beginning of March. 1818 also saw Lynn taking on Marham for five guineas a side and winning by two wickets (with, as was common, all four innings completed in the day); they also earned the comment that they were considered unrivalled within a 15-mile radius. That year, there were also games in which East Dereham twice defeated a Lyng and Elsing side and Harling had two fixtures with Hingham. Generally, these games continued to be described as being between the Gentlemen of the towns or villages in question.

The years that followed the end of the Napoleonic Wars saw the confirmation of a new force in Norfolk cricket. Undefeated throughout 1818, the first references to Holt in *Scores and Biographies* are in that year when they featured in games against Cambridge Town, Newmarket and Bungay, all played away and all won very convincingly. The Bungay match was in fact played with only ten men batting (but 11 fielding) each team having objected to the other including a particular player. One may suspect that these objections were made because the considerable sum of £132 was at stake and that each side was seeking to include players not otherwise associated with them. (It was not the first time this had happened; five years earlier, Bungay had refused to allow 'three expert cricketers' to play for the Norwich Club, a stance which drew a sarcastic comment from the *Norfolk Chronicle*.) The two 1819 fixtures between these same clubs also had their share of controversy with more disputes over team strengthening and the questioning of the Holt umpire's impartiality. Things went more smoothly in the match between Holt and the Cambridge Club in the same year notwithstanding the high stakes of £500 (over £30,000 today). All this apart, Driver was able to write in that year that the Holt Club was considered to be the best side in Norfolk, Suffolk and Cambridgeshire.

Appearing for Holt in these games were the brothers Nathaniel and William Pilch. Nathaniel was primarily a batsman; William more a slow bowling allrounder whom Driver credited as introducing round-arm bowling to Norfolk. Both were tailors by trade, although William also made bats in later life. They both appeared in a match played at Lord's in July 1820 against the MCC, a contest notable for a number of reasons. To begin with, it was the first recorded game involving a side with the name of Norfolk since the first Swaffham match of 1797, although clearly this was not the County Club the formation of which was still six years in the future. Indeed, it is now accepted that the fixture was contested by the

Holt Club. The match itself resulted in an overwhelming victory for the hosts – by 417 runs – after the MCC had posted a first innings score of 473, one of the highest team totals recorded to that date and including a massive individual innings of 278 from William Ward and 82 not out from Lord Frederick Beauclerk. Ward's innings was the first double-century ever made in a major match and remained the highest individual score at Lord's until 1925. Being played before bowling figures were first recorded, it is not known which bowlers suffered most at the hands of Ward and his team-mates. Ward himself was a successful businessman as well as a very capable batsman and it was this that enabled him to make his finest contribution to cricket when in 1825 he bought the lease to Lord's from Thomas Lord at a time when the latter was proposing to develop a large part of the ground with housing. Turning back to the 1820 fixture, Holt were strengthened by the inclusion of three 'guest' players, one of whom was the accomplished all-rounder Edward Budd, although clearly their inclusion was to no avail. Indeed, in their second innings the other two 'guests' were, together with one other Norfolk player, recorded as absent.

The game also marked the debut in 'big' cricket of Nathaniel and William's younger brother, Fuller Pilch. Aged only 17, he performed inauspiciously, with scores of 0 and 2, although he did take four wickets. In due course he would come to be recognised as a batsman of the highest class. Indeed, following the close of his career in the 1850s Haygarth wrote that 'considering the fine bowling and fielding he had to contend against, Pilch has proved himself to have been the *best* batsman that has ever yet played'. William Dennison in his *Sketches of Players* would write that within a few years of his debut he would 'stand forth as the finest batsman of his time'. Even William Ward noted on the occasion of that first match in 1820 that 'if that young Pilch goes on in his play there is much promise in him'. The reasons for his predominance in the years that followed appear to result from his style. Standing at just over six feet tall, he had a long reach that enabled him to develop his forward play, that is, on the front foot. This was particularly useful in mastering round-arm bowling which was increasingly common in the early part of the 19th century before it made way for the over-arm bowling we can recognise today. He was also a bowler in his younger days, and a fine fielder, particularly at mid wicket or cover point.

Fuller Pilch. *By the 1830s, Fuller was considered the best batsman in England.*

In due course, Fuller Pilch would be lost to Norfolk cricket but at this stage in his career he was very much part of the Holt Club. However, whilst very successful locally, they were convincingly beaten by Nottingham in two fixtures in 1821 and 1822. The Midlands side themselves fielded in William Clarke a player who later became a major influence on the development of the game. The 1821 match at Holt was clearly a major affair with the ground being filled with lots of booths and marquees; the turf was also described as 'beautifully prepared'.

Norfolk cricket in the 1820s was not just about Holt and Fuller Pilch. Indeed, in the late 1820s he played out of the county with the Bury St Edmunds Club before moving in 1831 to Norwich where he took on the licence of the Anchor and Hope Tavern and pleasure grounds on Bracondale Hill as well as the lease of the Norwich cricket ground in the management of which he was assisted by his brother William. Rather, here in Norfolk, one reads of matches across the county. They tended to follow a reasonably common pattern with games still generally featuring teams of 'Gentlemen', a term that continued to be used in describing town and village teams until the 1850s, albeit with decreasing frequency. In 1825, for instance, there were contests between 'Gentlemen' from East Rudham and Gatesend; Lynn and Grimston; Mileham and Bradenham; Swaffham and Dereham; and North Elmham and Litcham. Often, there were return matches and stakes to be played for; for instance, 20 guineas in the East Rudham v Gatesend contest. Also, matches, still normally comprising two innings a side, were most usually played in midweek, and occasionally spread over two days. In one contest, between East Dereham and Hingham in 1826, the first day's play was on Hardingham Common and the second at Dereham.

There is a hint in these fixtures that cricket was strongest in the middle of the county but it was by no means restricted to there. For instance, in 1825 there were return fixtures between Norwich Union and the Norwich Club, with the second match taking place on Mulbarton Common, as well as games involving Yarmouth and Harleston.

Newspaper reports, although generally brief, often used language that helped to promote the game. For instance, the 1825 match between Yarmouth and Beccles was said to be 'likely to excite considerable interest'; and another, between North Elmham and Litcham, was described as 'a very pleasant and friendly game'. In the 1826 game between Hingham and Dereham referred to above the latter won 'after a most brilliant display of the above science by each party to the great gratification of many of the lovers of the noble game'.

Cricket etiquette of the day was apparent in the comment in 1825 that Bradenham allowed Mileham to include 'three picked men from other parishes', and this practice was not uncommon. For instance, in 1830 eleven of Mattishall took on nine of Cossey – that is, Costessey – together with a player from each of New Buckenham and Hingham. On the other hand, as the Holt versus Bungay games illustrate, disputes sometimes arose when one side included players not ordinarily associated with their club. The practice also drew the comment from Driver that Hingham 'in all her matches played with residents of the town except where a special agreement was made for a given player'.

If Holt were the leading side in Norfolk at the beginning of the 1820s they were not without rivals. For instance, 'the old established club of Aldborough' were reported in 1826 as having played 19 games without defeat (including a victory over Holt) before losing by two runs to the same opposition. Hingham, Dereham, Litcham and Swaffham were also strong. And to demonstrate their ambition Dereham hired a professional from Lord's in the early 1820s by the name of Robinson to coach their players, this drawing the comment from Driver that a 'new era' was commencing in Norfolk cricket.

The Norwich Club were also beginning to emerge as a force and in 1827 they took a lease of a field at Lakenham for use as their ground. In the same year, they strengthened their side for the home match against Hingham by including well-known players Henry Bentley (who laid out the Lakenham ground) and William Caldecourt, described as 'two men of high repute'. Notice of that match also referred to admission being sixpence to the lower part of the ground and one shilling to the upper part where tents and seats would be available. However, dogs were not allowed. In the following year, they played a game for the benefit of the Norfolk and Norwich Hospital and the School for the Indigent Blind although bad weather and a poor attendance restricted the takings at the gate to just under £10. The ground was not just used for cricket and in 1831 it was the venue for a 'camping match' between Norwich and Blofield. The latter 'gave up' and neither the camping (that is, camp football, a crude form of the sport for which this is the last record in Norwich) or the wrestling that followed were said to be well-contested; and in the following year, it hosted a dinner for two thousand people to celebrate the passing of the Reform Bill. Fuller and William Pilch were also members of the Norwich Club around this time when it was strong enough to visit Lord's and defeat an MCC Eleven.

A new ground was provided in Great Yarmouth in 1829 but generally grounds were laid out for cricket on a more *ad hoc* basis. For instance, the 1828 fixture between Fakenham and Wells was reported as being played on a pasture belonging to a Mr Blomfield of Warham, and this would not have been unusual.

Increasingly, stakes were not involved. Similarly, references to betting on the outcome of matches became much rarer although the 1838 fixture between Attleborough and Great Ellingham is an exception. Indeed, the 1845 Gambling Act hastened the end of betting on matches by providing that a wager was unenforceable as a legal contract. It also made it an offence to win money at sports and games by cheating.

Around this time references to youth games began to appear. In 1823, Hingham Youth – described by Driver as 'the second or junior side' – beat the apparently adult eleven of Barnham Broom; and a year later, Dereham Youths easily defeated the Gentlemen of Fakenham. Then, in 1830, a 'juvenile' match was played between 12 of Litcham and 12 drawn from 'the neighbourhood'. Driver also reminisced on how in earlier times Hingham Fairstead was regularly used by children and youths for the playing of cricket although at the time of his writing in the early 1840s this had fallen away.

More unusually, in 1823, in Hockwold-cum-Wilton, 11 married women defeated 11 single women in a game in which the players were dressed in jackets and trousers and decorated with ribbons. In February 1827, a game was played on the iced-over Mere at Diss in which the 'ardent cricketers of the district' playing a 'bona fide match on skates' in front of 1500 spectators. The game itself lasted from 10 in the morning until 5.30 in the evening and was played 'as far as possible according to the laws of cricket'. (There was also a similar game played on Scoulton Mere in 1840 between two selected elevens from Hingham. Some players wore 'skaits' and others stump shoes to prevent them from falling. The side batting first scored 66 and the other 170 'in the most slashing style hitting the ball quite off the ice in all directions').

In 1835, after the Ringstead Blue Club had travelled to, and beaten, the Lynn Junior Club, and at a time when the speed of transport was still slow, the result was conveyed back to Ringstead by means of a carrier pigeon which covered the 17 miles in 45 minutes. For those who were prepared to wait to read of results the local newspapers gave increasing prominence to match reports and scorecards.

A year earlier, the *Norfolk Chronicle* referred to the longest period of peace in living memory during which 'the game of cricket has grown into great repute and is very extensively adopted. It is a noble and manly exercise; it promotes the intercourse of distant societies, it excites a courteous and friendly contention' and continued by referring to the game as 'the image of war without its guilt'. Certainly, Haygarth felt it right to record a number of games played in the county in the 1830s, in addition to those played by Norfolk or the Gentlemen of Norfolk. These included fixtures involving Brinton (often including Fuller Pilch), Brisley and Litcham and, in 1838, East Norfolk versus West Norfolk. Driver also listed a number of games played by Hingham in the 1830s.

Later, in 1842, the *Norfolk Chronicle* referred to the revival of the game in Norwich following a few years of 'considerable fluctuation' when 'nothing appeared more probable than its extinction'. There therefore appears to have been a significant decline in interest in the game in Norfolk in the late 1830s due at least in part to Lord Suffield's death in a riding accident in 1835 and Fuller Pilch's departure to Kent in the same year.

Single wicket games were still common. A contest was staged at Dereham in 1831 between two sides of four players each, including Fuller Pilch, Herbert Jenner and William Lillywhite. Two years later, there were matches between Abraham Spinks of Mileham and William Wilkerson of Shipdham for £10 – when neither player scored a run in their two innings and Wilkerson won only by courtesy of a wide – and Robert Cowles of Hingham and William Brett of Shipdham. And in 1834, two of Hingham competed against two of Swaffham.

Pilch himself, as well as being firmly established as the premier batsman in England and a regular member of the 'England' Eleven, was dominant in single wicket matches. Famously, he featured in two such contests with the Yorkshire champion, Thomas Marsden, in 1833. In 1829, Marsden had challenged anyone in England to a single-wicket match, and this was accepted on Pilch's behalf by a Mr C.D. Leech of Bury. However, because of Pilch's ill-health at the time, the contest did not come about until four years later when the first match was played at Norwich in July. It was anticipated that the contest would stretch over several days but in the event it was completed in one. In a match in which there were no fielders Marsden was only able to score 7 runs (from 48 balls) in his two innings to which Pilch replied with 77 (from 131 balls and including extras) in his only innings. The reports also record that Pilch hit 113 of the balls he received. On the following day, the two players' backers themselves played, with Pilch's side emerging victorious due largely to his own innings of 87.

Financially, the games were a great success with £260 taken at the gates in sixpences and threepences. The return single-wicket match took place in Sheffield three weeks later when, over three days and in front of a total attendance of at least 20,000, Pilch confirmed his superiority by scoring 190 runs in his two innings, including a century in his second knock, to the 62 of his northern opponent. These performances caused the *Sporting Magazine* to write that

> 'Pilch's batting was of the finest description, and a better display of the art of cricket was never witnessed in any former match. This second victory places Pilch at once at the very top of the players of England. As a double wicket player he is allowed to be unrivalled, and as a single wicket player his second conquest over the man who was said to be the first, has at once given him the championship which we suppose no one will challenge'.

Pilch was now playing most of his cricket on the national stage, and in 1834 he scored 551 runs in first-class matches at an average of over 61, an overall total that remained a record until 1861. Figures such as this were unheard of at the time, and it was perhaps no surprise that in 1835 he received an offer to leave Norfolk and move to Town Malling in Kent where, for an annual salary of £100 (nearly £8,000 today), he managed a tavern and the cricket ground attached to it. In 1842 he moved to Canterbury to work for the newly-formed Kent Cricket Club and he remained as their groundsman until 1868, two years before his death. In later years he also returned to his original trade as a tailor, and was involved in a partnership making cricket bats. He also appeared occasionally in games in the county of his birth.

Back to Norfolk in the 1830s and the evidence points to teams continuing with fixture lists which were generally very limited in terms of games played and distances travelled, and often involved return matches. In some cases, they were referred to as clubs, whilst in others the inference is that the elevens were not so formalised. The reports indicate that the game was played across the whole county although not so much in the very east of

Norfolk. Matches continued to be over two innings and generally at this time there would be a positive result, even when, as was usual, the game was restricted to one day; starts as early as 10 o'clock in the morning no doubt facilitated this as did the poor wickets and consequent low scores. (These are extreme examples but in 1841 Brinton with scores of 14 and 14 for four beat Edgefield – 11 and 16 in their two innings – by six wickets; and in 1849 Old Buckenham's 29 and 19 for seven beat Rockland's 26 and 20). In contrast, individual centuries in Norfolk were virtually unheard of with Nathaniel Pilch's 112 for Brinton against Brisley in 1834 a rarity.

There is evidence, too, of clubs becoming more formalised with annual meetings, presentation of accounts and the adoption of Club rules; for example, the Lynn Club published a set in 1833 as did Thetford a few years later.

So what form did cricket equipment take around this time? Spring-handled bats did not appear until the 1840s; before then bats were made from one piece of wood. Cricket balls were hard and leather-bound and similar in size to those in use today. Until about 1840, pads were small and flimsy but from then on they began to resemble the modern version albeit of more rudimentary construction and reaching little above knee-height. Batting gloves with tubular finger padding were introduced a few years earlier; but until the 1860s wicketkeepers devised their own hand and leg protection. And personal protectors had yet to be introduced. Not that the equipment that had been invented would necessarily have found its way to rural Norfolk.

It was also around the 1840s that scoreboards, nets (of a sort) and rollers began to appear. Similarly, mowing machines did not come into regular use at major grounds until the early 1850s although the idea dated from the 1830s; until then, sheep were generally used to keep the grass short. Finally, sightscreens (as we broadly know them today) and the covering of pitches were not introduced until towards the end of the century. And in all cases, initially at least, these would rarely have been seen on grounds in Norfolk.

The absence of rollers and mowing machines of course contributed to the low scores that were a feature of the first half of the 19th century and as did the prohibition, in the 1820 Laws of Cricket, of any rolling, watering, covering, mowing or beating of the wicket during a match without the consent of the opposition. In addition, wicket preparation fell far short of today's standards. Indeed, there is a report of Fuller Pilch playing for Kent against Nottinghamshire at Trent Bridge in 1841 and, on going into bat, clearing the wicket 'of every little stone or encumbrance that might impede the ball or sight'. The presence of stones and gravel on the wicket was not unusual.

Cricket dress was somewhat different from the traditional 'whites'. In particular, at least at the higher levels, coloured shirts were the norm; it was only in the 1860s that white became the accepted colour. Until the 1830s, knee breeches were common, sometimes with silk stockings, but by the end of the decade they had given way to white trousers supported by braces or a belt. And until the 1860s boots were black, but might well be spiked. Finally, the most common headgear was a tall hat, black or white in colour, although this would soon be replaced by billy-cock hats and then caps. But what the occasional player in the villages of Norfolk wore is another matter; probably it would have been their day-to-day clothes. Photographs of such players from the end of the 19th century indicate some in whites but others in dark trousers often held up by braces.

As to an image of village cricket around this time, Charles Dickens gives us a clue in his description of a fictional game between Dingley Dell and All-Muggleton in *Pickwick Papers* first published, in serial form, in 1836 and 1837. But perhaps a better picture can be obtained from Mary Mitford's account contained in her stories of village life on the Hampshire / Berkshire border published from 1824. She makes it clear that, in doubting that there can be any scene in the world more animating or delightful than a cricket match, she is not referring to games played for money or even matches played by gentlemen. 'No', she writes,

> 'the cricket that I mean is a real solid old-fashioned match between
> neighbouring parishes, where each attacks the other for honour and
> a supper, glory, and half-a-crown man. If there be any gentleman
> amongst them, it is well – if not, it is so much the better. Your
> gentleman cricketer is in general rather an anomalous character.
> Elderly gentlemen are obviously good for nothing; and your beaux
> are, for the most part, hampered and trammelled by dress and habit;

the stiff cravat, the pinched-in waist, the dandy-walk – oh, they will never do for cricket! Now, our country lads, accustomed to the flail or the hammer (your blacksmiths are capital hitters) have the free use of their arms; they know how to move their shoulders; and they can move their feet too – they can run; then they are so much better made, so much more athletic; and yet so much lissomer . . . No! a village match is the thing – where our highest officer – our conductor (to borrow a musical term) is but a little farmer's second son; where a day-labourer is our bowler, and a blacksmith our long-stop; where the spectators consist of the retired cricketers, the veterans of the green, the careful mothers, the girls, and all the boys of the two parishes, together with a few amateurs, little above them in rank, and not at all in pretension; where laughing and shouting, and the very ecstasy of merriment and good-humour prevail'.

Not that all matches passed off in such an atmosphere. Disagreements still occurred such as in 1841 when the report of a return game between Diss and Bungay also stated that Bungay's account of the first game was not fair. This prompted a long letter from the Bungay umpire referring to a dispute over Diss's alleged inclusion of three players from outside of the town and immediate neighbourhood (contrary to Bungay's stipulation when the fixture was agreed). Then, in 1842, the *Norfolk Chronicle* firstly reported a nine-run win for Cawston over North Walsham and a fortnight later explained that the losers wanted to contradict the earlier statements about the score and Cawston claiming the match. Rather, the later report ran, it had been agreed to withdraw the stakes. Three years earlier, a letter had appeared in the *Norfolk Chronicle* from a correspondent calling himself 'A Lover of Fair Play' and referring to an incident in a match between Thetford and Mildenhall when one of the former's 'gentlemen' was given not out. Mildenhall disputed this and would not continue until the batsman retired and the two runs he had subsequently scored were 'given up'. He did, and they were, but the point was later decided in favour of Thetford who as a result won by one wicket. This was all the more curious because the original report had indicated that at the conclusion of the match the players had retired to the local inn and there spent the evening 'in great harmony'.

It was about this time that there occurred a technological development that would have a significant impact on the game: the coming of the railways. Previously, the fastest means of transport had been the horse with the result that travelling long distances was difficult and time consuming. However, the railway age would change all that. It opened up the countryside in a way never previously dreamed of and enabled much quicker communication between major settlements. The first Norfolk railway appeared in 1844 between Norwich and Great Yarmouth and by the following year the connection to London was finished. Within five more years, lines had been opened to Ipswich, Fakenham and King's Lynn. Travel was now not only quicker but also cheaper. Perhaps the biggest consequence for Norfolk was that it facilitated the emergence of the county as a major holiday destination but, as elsewhere, there were also consequences for cricket, most notably in the easier access the railways provided for the emerging touring and wandering elevens made up of professional cricketers. The first and most famous of these teams was the All England Eleven led and managed by William Clarke, by now well into his forties. He had the foresight to marry the widowed landlady of the Trent Bridge Inn in Nottingham and soon afterwards he enclosed and developed the adjoining field now known as the Trent Bridge Cricket Ground. He was an astute businessman as well as an accomplished bowler, and it was his entrepreneurial skills that led to him creating the All England Eleven in 1846. He collected together a group of professional cricketers and took them around the country playing mainly in cities and the emerging industrial towns, but also in market towns, against opponents comprising 14 or 18 or sometimes 22 mainly local players but often reinforced by one or two professional bowlers known as 'given men'. He made his money from these games – and a lot of it, too – by either requiring the hosts to guarantee a fixed payment (with the hosts keeping the gate receipts and other income) or keeping the gate receipts for himself but meeting the expenses. Either way, it was a great success with large crowds drawn by the opportunity to see the great players of the day. That, though, was a few years in the future for Norfolk.

Also in the 1840s, a wandering club by the name of I Zingari was formed by four Cambridge undergraduates. They had a somewhat different fixture list involving matches against public schools, university colleges, regimental clubs and teams of 'Gentlemen'. They, too, would soon appear in the county.

As early as the 18th century there were examples of country houses with cricket grounds but from the 1830s they became more common. Often the owner employed a professional during the summer months, not just to play but also to be a net bowler and coach. By the 1840s, Norfolk was not short of country-house estates and on some of these cricket grounds were laid out. An early example was Lord Suffield's estate at Gunton Park which became a venue for early county matches, a facility which his widow, the Dowager, continued to make available after his premature death in 1835. Lady Suffield also maintained a ground within Blickling Hall. Elsewhere, the Earl of Leicester's seat at Holkham Hall hosted important games from the 1840s; the Earl himself was a good enough batsman to play for Norfolk around the same time. These grounds and the clubs that played there featured regularly in newspaper reports for much of the 19th century, but one, at least, where cricket seems to have been short-lived was Spixworth Park in the 1840s. The teams based in these Parks would also be relatively strong with fixtures against one another and some of the stronger club sides of the day. Indeed, in 1847, Blickling defeated a Norfolk eleven. Holkham, too, were a force around this time, with James Grundy (see Chapter 6) engaged as the professional. For a short while, they were also able to field Walter Marcon, an Oxford Blue in 1843 and 1844, whom Haygarth described as 'one of the fastest, if not *the* fastest, bowler that has ever appeared'. Notwithstanding an action described as 'almost underhand', his pace was 'terrific always requiring two longstops, nor was a wicketkeeper of the slightest use' and he was rumoured on one occasion in his University days to have broken a man's leg when bowling to him. Like many of his contemporaries, his vocation was in the Church and in due course he became the Rector of Edgefield.

None of this is to say that the cricket teams based on the country estates were pre-eminent. Swaffham were still a major force, competing well with the likes of Bury, Cambridge Town and Newmarket in the early 1840s. Indeed, in 1843, they were strong enough to have defeated 'Suffolk', even though they were without a key player and their opponents had strengthened their side, and had the best of an unfinished game against a strong Norfolk Eleven. They also had regular games with Blickling, and this fixture list, and their results, suggest that by the 1840s they were the strongest club in the county.

Not that cricket in Holt was dead. Many years later, in 1926, a poem was written that eulogised the cricketers of that town in the early Victorian Age. It described one-armed Tom Ling with the words 'a harder hitter never lived' and continued

> 'Beyond belief his drives, his cuts, his sweeping hits to leg
> One feat deserves to live immortal, when the ball
> Soaring he sent above the distant houses
> Into the market place – tremendous hit
> Unrivalled quite almost beyond belief
> Large hearted Ling, giant in strength and skill
> Long will thy memory live! Unequalled Ling'.

The poem then described Tom Parke as 'not less in weight and massive frame' and 'famous as a batsman too, but famous more for his strength of lung and vocal powers', and his brother, Jim, as 'great in the cricket field, his strength of limb enabled him to throw a hundred yards and upwards' before finally extolling the skills of their professional Dick Pilch, Fuller's nephew.

It was also in the 1840s that the Colman family put out a side of their own. Almost 100 years before the Edriches fielded a family side, a team of 11 Colman brothers – the sons of Robert Colman of Rockland St Andrew – played matches against such as the Norwich Club and the Gentlemen of Holt and Letheringsett. Some of them were very capable cricketers and one of them, Jeremiah, would 30 years later make the Lakenham ground available to the Norfolk club.

Although some contemporary reports indicated that matches were played in meadows and fields made available for the occasion by a local landowner, a number of new cricket grounds began to emerge where the game was played more regularly and where the playing facilities were improved. Often, these grounds were associated with public houses, such as the Bell Inn in Watton whose pitch, according to William Andrews' *Bygone Norfolk* published in 1897, was said to have been the best in England. Andrews also referred to 'other fine grounds' at Elmham Park and Fakenham. In 1853, a ground opened adjoining the New Inn at Attleborough where a Mr Canham was the landlord.

The Lynn Club also had a new ground in readiness for the first visit to Norfolk, in 1852, of a professional travelling eleven. Twenty-two of the Town, including a few who usually played their cricket elsewhere in Norfolk, took on Clarke's All England Eleven over three days in early June. The hosts opened up with a score of 63 – with 14 wickets for Clarke – to which the visitors replied with 41, including eight ducks and six wickets for guest bowler Charles Arnold from Cambridge. Lynn made only 57 in their second innings, with a further 13 wickets for Clarke and his side then reached 66 for five leaving the match drawn. In those days of four-ball overs more than 330 of them were bowled for just 227 runs. It was, though, a creditable performance for the local side given that the opposition included players such as George Parr, Nicholas Felix and Alfred Mynn, some of the very best cricketers of the day. The Lynn Club themselves featured in another game in that same year to make the headlines, albeit for different reasons, when they entertained Litcham on their new ground which they occupied under an agreement with the owner. During the game, the area required for play was roped off and only players allowed within it. At one stage of the game, a member of the Lynn Club, but not of the selected eleven, by the name of Holmes was asked to substitute for a fielder who had been called away but almost immediately the Lynn captain, Richard Bagge, objected to his substitute's conduct on the field, in particular to his refusal to remove his coat. In the argument that followed the substitute was ordered off the field and, when he refused to leave, was forcibly removed. Holmes brought and won an action for assault against those who had removed him and was awarded £20 in damages on the basis that he had an equal right to be on the ground as the other members of the Club! This decision was upheld on appeal although the court indicated that had the defendants framed their defence differently they might have been successful.

As for William Clarke's Eleven, they returned to Norfolk in 1853 to play 18 of the Norwich Club at their ground in Newmarket Road in the city.

Admission was one shilling on the day but only sixpence if purchased more than two days beforehand from George Figg at the Cricketers Arms. Buses were also to run 'constantly' from the Norfolk Hotel to the ground. Thanks largely to Frank Tinley, a guest player, taking 13 wickets in the match for just 60 runs the home side won by 28 runs leading the *Norfolk Chronicle* to write that 'the result has fully maintained the reputation of the City and County'. There is no record of the gate receipts but one suspects that financially Clarke came out on top. Three years later, Clarke was back in Norfolk, this time to pit his Eleven against 22 of Downham Market at Crow Hall Park. On this occasion the 'given man' was Kent bowler Edward Hinkly, who in his first match at Lord's for his county against 'England' had taken all ten wickets in an innings, and on this occasion he duly obliged with 11 wickets for the local side. The match itself petered out into a draw after the local team, in their only innings, lost their first seven wickets for no runs! Clarke himself was dead by the end of that summer but others took up the reins and in 1859 a weaker All England Eleven played the Postwick Club and lost.

Team scores remained low, almost always under or just over 100. As an example, the scorecards of 6 two-innings matches that appeared in the *Norfolk Chronicle* on 12 August 1854 showed that only one side reached three figures. Increasingly, though, a match only reached a result on first innings with the team who went in first going in again and batting until the allotted time for drawing stumps or it was dusk. There was certainly no provision for games of limited overs, nor would there be for many years.

As the years moved on, teams were gradually prepared to journey further for games. For instance, compared with the 1820s when teams generally travelled no more than ten miles for a match, by the 1850s this had increased to 15 miles. However, sides rarely played more than ten games in a season.

At the same time, clubs often arranged matches amongst themselves, particularly at the start of the season as a form of practice game, but also many would organise 'Married versus Single' matches or, in the case of the bigger clubs the 'First Eleven' against the 'Next 22'.

There were also games such as those involving teams of tradesmen. For instance, in 1835, 11 shoemakers of Castle Acre defeated 11 players of the same parish, although the latter won the return game. In 1847, the farmers and tradesmen in Hingham played out a match, and in the 1850s there were annual fixtures between the farmers and tradesmen of Attleborough though these were not always 11-a-side.

Whilst some clubs were stable during the first half of the 19th century, albeit with limited fixture lists, others, as in earlier times, would form and dissolve and then re-form, often very quickly afterwards. The Lynn Club were one such example being described in 1834 as having been established for three years when there is evidence of them having had a side prior to 1831. Thetford were another, playing until at least 1839 and then reforming in 1844. In some cases, at least, re-forming may have been an annual event.

By the late 1840s some Norfolk schools had introduced the game. In 1847, the North Walsham and Aylsham Grammar Schools played one another at Blickling Park by permission of Lady Suffield on a day when 'uninterrupted harmony persisted between the schools'. During the 1850s, there were a number of reported matches played by the Norwich Grammar School and St Michael's Collegiate School in Aylsham often against adult opposition. Reports of 'youth' games, however, were all but non-existent.

In 1852, 44 boys from the Gressenhall Union – that is, the workhouse for the Mitford and Launditch area – were invited to play a cricket match at the home of one of the Union's Guardians, a Mr Brown of Dillington. At the close of the game 'they were regaled with cake and ale, and after giving three cheers for their worthy host and hostess, sang the National Anthem, and returned home much gratified with their afternoon's amusement'!


The overall impression of cricket in Norfolk in 1860, as elsewhere, is therefore of a game that was embedded into county life, not just as entertainment for 'Gentlemen' but amongst all classes. Although clearly there were significant differences, it was nonetheless played in a form we would recognise today.

# CHAPTER 3

# Competitions, Country Houses and The Church

By 1860, Queen Victoria had been on the throne for 23 years and the country was in a period of unparalleled prosperity resulting from a range of circumstances including the effects of the Industrial and Agricultural Revolutions, political stability, a long period of peace (the Crimean War excepting) and the expansion of the Empire. Britain was the workshop of the world and in a dominant trading position. There were also social trends relevant to this Chapter: the growth of the professional and middle classes, developments in education and with it an increase in literacy, better transportation systems and the improvement in working conditions, particularly in terms of wages and working hours. For the first time, the working classes had meaningful leisure opportunities.

Increasingly in Norfolk, and although agriculture was still strong, manufacturing industries were a major source of employment, particularly in Norwich. These included boot and shoe making, tanning and brewing. The railway network continued to expand, and during the second half of the century there were major improvements to people's living conditions particularly in the urban areas such that they would become much cleaner places to live. The gradual migration from the countryside to urban areas continued so that by 1861, of the county's population of 435,000, 74,400 lived in Norwich, 20,300 in Great Yarmouth and 16,700 in King's Lynn; and by 1901, the total population had risen to 477,000 of which 111,700 lived in Norwich, 51,300 in Great Yarmouth and 20,200 in King's Lynn. The educational reforms also meant a substantial increase in the availability of, and requirement for, schooling in Norfolk during the last three decades of the century. Church attendance was very much the norm; in 1851 almost two-thirds of people in Norfolk went to church at least once on Sunday.

Nationally, cricket developed in a number of ways. The first overseas tours took place in 1859 (to North America) and 1861 (to Australia); over-arm bowling was legalised in 1864; John Wisden's *Cricketers Almanack* appeared for the first time in the same year; and also in 1864 W.G. Grace made his first appearance in 'big' cricket.

In Norfolk, the trends established in the 1850s continued with cricket locally also responding to the wider social changes referred to above. The professional travelling sides still visited the county from time to time. In 1862, 22 of the Norfolk and Norwich Club took on the United England Eleven in a three-day game, losing by seven wickets. James Grundy, who had played for Norfolk in the late 1840s (see Chapter 6) took 24 wickets for 83 runs! Subsequently, the Norfolk and Norwich Club reported a surplus on the game of nearly £10 and, notwithstanding their defeat, also agreed that in future 'odds' matches should involve no more than 16 in a side. Four years later, a large crowd, including 'nearly all the principal families for many miles around', turned up to see George Parr's All England Eleven overcome 22 of King's Lynn by 76 runs in a game also played over three days. In 1869, the United South of England Eleven came to Norfolk to play the Norfolk and Norwich Club. On this occasion, the local side were victorious, dismissing their illustrious opponents for 33 and 161 and scoring 172 and 24 for eight in reply. Notwithstanding their previous decision, though, the local club, who played their fixtures on a ground in Newmarket Road in Norwich, still played 22. Whether it was a financial success is another matter for less than £15 was taken at the gate – the admission price was sixpence on the first day only – and expenses in the rain-interrupted match totalled £100.

Perhaps the most prominent game played in Norfolk around this time, though, involved not a professional touring side but the all-amateur I Zingari who in July 1866 played the Gentlemen of Norfolk at Sandringham. The report in the *Lynn Advertiser* began

'Great interest was occasioned by the playing of this match on the Royal Estate at Sandringham. So early as April last the present visit was determined upon, and H.R.H. gave directions for a suitable ground to be made, which directions were fully carried out under the superintendence of Mr Carmichael. The site selected was a piece of table land in front of Park House, on almost the highest ground on the estate, and this ground and its surroundings are extremely pretty. The area set apart for the match was encircled with flags, amongst which the I Zingari red, black and orange were conspicuous. There was a nicely arranged tent for the Princess of Wales, and other tents for luncheon, for the Zingari and Norfolk clubs, and for the scorers. A complete arrangement was made for telegraphing the total number of runs obtained, the wickets down, and runs for the last wicket, so that the whole of the persons present were kept regularly posted up as to the proceedings'.

The report continued with information on the royalty and others present as well as a full description of the luncheon menu.

As to the result, I Zingari's score of 277, with 101 from R.A. Fitzgerald and an unbeaten 52 from Lord Skelmersdale, was sufficient to beat the Gentlemen of Norfolk by an innings and 98 runs. The H.R.H. referred to in the report was the then Prince of Wales and future King Edward the Seventh but what it does not mention is that he opened the I Zingari innings and was bowled by Charles Wright for nought. The report in the *Norfolk Chronicle* also chose not to draw attention to this but did mention his fielding at short leg. However, as the game ended early, it was decided to arrange a match between I Zingari and 22 of the Royal Household and on this occasion the Prince of Wales scored three as a result of a 'fine leg hit'.

The report of the Sandringham game serves to illustrate cricket's continuing popularity within the aristocracy and upper classes generally, this being reinforced by the make-up of some of the leading sides in the county. One example was the Gunton Club, described in 1869 as 'perhaps the strongest in the county' albeit with the rider that perhaps they had the pick of Norfolk's players. The Norfolk and Norwich Club may have had cause to question their supremacy, but certainly Gunton Park, the seat of Lord Suffield, was a major venue for 'senior' cricket in the county as, increasingly, was Catton Park, the home of Samuel Buxton Esquire.

Other venues were less exalted and their wickets less predictable. For instance, the low-scoring in a match in 1863 between South Lopham and North Lopham was attributed to the ground being very rough and hard and dangerous for the batsmen. But often the *Norfolk Chronicle* was keen to stress the beautiful lawns, as at Thursford Hall, or the picturesque qualities of the grounds such as those at Oxborough, Great Snoring and Barford and Mr Canham's ground at Attleborough.

Team scores remained low, generally under 100 and often under 50. In an 1862 game between Tivetshall and Long Stratton only 115 runs were scored in the four innings, and these included 18 ducks; and there were 19 ducks in the 1865 return match between Guist and Ryburgh when the former's totals of 18 and 24 were sufficient to beat the latter who managed only 11 and 14. The low scores in the game between Alburgh and Bungay Printers in 1867 were specifically attributed to the length of the grass, but other reasons would include the state of the wicket and poor technique. That said, the scores of the better sides were tending to increase and occasionally even passing 200, and for the first time since the 1830s it was possible to identify individual centuries such as George Figg's 119 not out for the Norfolk and Norwich Club versus Croxton in 1863, John Dolphin's 121 for Gunton versus North Walsham in the same year and George Tuck's 115 in 1864, also for the Norfolk and Norwich Club, versus Dereham. Invariably, centurions would be presented with something to mark their achievement, often a cricket bat.

In those days of purely 'friendly' cricket, clubs did not have long fixture lists, usually no more that eight to ten games in a season and often including games between two sides drawn from within the club such as "Married v Single" matches. Indeed, the report of the Swaffham versus Dereham game at the beginning of July 1861 stated that it was the first match played in the district that season; and Thetford's game with Brandon in September of the same year was described as the second match on the Thetford Abbey ground that season. On the other hand, Attleborough played 18 games in 1866, winning 13 of them and at the end of the season were the first local club to publish their batting averages in the papers, following the precedent set by the County Club three weeks earlier. Some clubs now also ran second teams.

Mention of the Attleborough Club leads to the report of a celebration dinner for them in 1920 when a certain R. Sayer, who had just completed 50 years as secretary of the Rockland and District Club but had started his playing career at Attleborough, said that he could not understand why games were now only played over half a day rather than one or two days as in his youth. He also referred to the times when there were no restrictions and limitations on a player's qualifications with the result that a team might include players from 11 different parishes.

The Victorian Age is associated with the concept of Muscular Christianity – exemplified by Thomas Hughes in *Tom Brown's Schooldays* – and, in the cricketing context, the belief that the game expressed Christian values; that is, that cricket, and other team games, developed character and instilled courage, teamwork, selflessness and toughness in people. The level of clerical involvement with cricket generally around this time was high with nearly a third of all Victorian Oxbridge cricket blues entering the Church. This influence clearly extended to Norfolk. Not only were many of the county's leading cricketers around this time ordained ministers but also they often took a close interest in promoting the game within their community. For instance, Revd Richard Tillard selected the Gentlemen of Blakeney side to play Cley in 1860; the re-formation of the Croxton Club in 1862 was partly due to the efforts of Revd Henry Williams; and the 'beautiful private ground' at Barford previously referred to belonged to Revd John Turner who himself also organised teams in the village. In Norwich, the YMCA ran a side from the early 1860s and there is even a record of the Cathedral Choristers fielding a team later in the decade. A high proportion of schools at this time were church-based, sometimes – at least in the 'public' schools – with an ordained minister as their Head Master, and this, too, helped cricket's cause. This crucial role of the Church of England in the game's development, both nationally and in Norfolk, was to continue for many years to come.

The clerical influence was also evident in more informal games of cricket. In 1861, the annual Harvest Home at Gooderstone involved a 'goodly game of cricket' and in the following year, as part of the Harvest celebration at Morningthorpe, 'men and lads adjourned to play cricket and football on the lawn'. The report of the 1864 North Lopham versus South Lopham game recorded that 'rector, curate, schoolmaster and several principal farmers joined heartily in the game, and it was evident that much good arises from all classes joining together occasionally in an afternoon's friendly recreation and rivalry'. But only 'occasionally'!! The influence of the Church is also seen in the comments of Revd Samuel Hooke at Wimbotsham's end of season dinner in 1870 when he was pleased to report that it had been a pleasant and successful season and that he had not heard anyone use unseemly language nor had he witnessed any unbecoming conduct.

The more established schools had a full programme sometimes extending into September. Norwich Grammar School, Greshams in Holt, Great Yarmouth Grammar School and Aylsham Commercial School had regular fixtures not only against other schools but also some of the top adult sides. For example, by the early 1880s King's Lynn Grammar School had a fixture list that included games against North Runcton, Terrington, Dersingham, Sandringham and the King's Lynn Police Force. And an indication of the importance attributed to the game in schools is perhaps that sometimes even the scores of their second eleven matches would be published; and the strength of these schools is illustrated by the fact that those second elevens would often play against adult teams.

There were also 'youth' games such as those played in the 1870s by Dickleburgh Boys against Scole Boys and Diss Boys. Later, in 1880, a game played by the recently formed Boys' Club at Walpole St Andrew drew the comment in the *Lynn Advertiser* that to judge from their performance after only two or three months' training it 'evidently contains material out of which a good club will eventually be made'.

New clubs were also being formed, in the case of North Walsham in the closing weeks of the 1862 season. In particular, there was a growth within urban areas. In Norwich, this period saw the formation of Norwich Association, Lakenham Amateurs, Norwich Albion, Norwich Victoria and

Norwich United; in Great Yarmouth, the White Star, Travers House, St John's and St Nicholas' Clubs; in Diss, the Denmark Club; and in Dereham, the Excelsior Club.

The army regiments based in Norwich continued to field sides with a fixture list that included games with some of the top local clubs. Also, some of the Volunteer Rifle Corps ran teams, although in 1861 the local Corps prize shooting day was given as the reason why the Yarmouth Club were unable to honour a fixture with East Harling.

Significantly, works teams began to appear, most notably the Carrow side in Norwich who, as described in Chapter 13, were sufficiently strong to take on the touring Australian Aboriginal side in 1868.

Disputes occurred from time to time, sometimes, as had been the case in the past, over team strengthening or at least because a club had not paid their opponents the courtesy of notifying them beforehand of their proposal to include players from outside of their club. In the East Harling versus Yarmouth fixture referred to above the dispute was because Yarmouth had allegedly called off a game without giving proper notice to their opponents. The disagreement in a game between Long Stratton and Harleston arose because one of the latter's players did not leave the wicket when given out.

Games were no longer played for stakes although the 1861 match between Saxlingham and Tharston was played for a ball which, following a nine wicket win, Tharston 'triumphantly carried off'. Also, unusually, in 1863 East Harling organised two games between the 'Old Style' and the 'New Style', a reference to the alternative bowling styles. Reflecting Cromer's status as a holiday resort for the rich there were annual games with 'The Visitors'. Similar fixtures with 'The Visitors' games, in fact, continued for the rest of the century and beyond in Great Yarmouth, Caister, Overstrand, Sheringham, Cley and Blakeney; again, a reflection of the holiday seaside status of those settlements. (In 1880, Yarmouth played their 'Visitors' five times, attracting crowds of five to six hundred).

The bigger clubs, at least, often had their own professional, generally to bowl both in matches and at practice. In 1862, the Lakenham Club in Norwich engaged Charles Barker who was described as reputed to be 'the best professional bowler in England'. Another example around this time was James Hurr at Caister but the best known was George Figg who had previously played one game for Middlesex and was later to represent Sussex before being engaged by the Norfolk and Norwich Club in 1850. He served as that club's professional until 1872 during which period he also played for his adopted county and in other representative matches. In addition, he ran the Boar's Head Tavern and then the Rampant Horse Hotel in the centre of Norwich as well as managing two cricket grounds – the first being associated with the Tavern and the second being the Norfolk and Norwich Club ground in Newmarket Road and known for a while as 'George Figg's ground'. He was sufficiently well thought of by his club to be given a number of benefit matches, and on his retirement a testimonial game for him against the MCC and Ground raised £80 (approximately £6,000 in today's money). *Wisden's Cricketers' Almanack's* account of the match referred to Figg as being in his time 'one of the straightest bowlers that ever hit a middle stump, and who, throughout a long professional career, merited and obtained the good wishes and respect of all classes of cricketers'. Later, benefit matches were arranged for County Club professionals although the 1894 Senior Cup Final set aside as a benefit for George Rye was not a financial success because of the poor attendance.

It was not just the professionals who might be awarded benefit matches. John Goldsmith was the Norfolk and Norwich Club umpire from the early 1850s and a beneficiary in 1874 in recognition of his performing 'faithfully and diligently and with the greatest integrity'. He received a further benefit in 1878 to mark 25 years' service. Not that all umpires at this time were held in such high esteem. Long Stratton's 1874 victory over Forncett was attributed to 'one or two more than doubtful decisions of the umpire'.

It was in the 1870s that there was a significant growth in the amount of Saturday cricket. Hitherto, the playing of cricket was generally restricted to midweek but the reduction in working hours and the introduction of half day working on Saturdays, particularly for industrial workers, led to more weekend matches. This was especially, but not exclusively, the case in and around Norwich where a number of works teams were established. For example, the G.E.R., Norwich Police, Curl and Bunting, Chamberlins, Jarrolds and Norwich Printers all ran sides. Sometimes, like some other clubs in the area, they ran two sides. Further away from the city the report of the 1875 game between Tottington and Thompson drew the comment that both sides were only recently formed and consisted 'chiefly of working men'. And in a particularly low scoring game in 1872 between Wimbotsham and Stow the latter were also referred to as '11 of the mechanics of the new Hall'.

Cricket in the Great Yarmouth area seems to have developed in a different way, with most of the more newly formed clubs being named after parishes within the Borough such as St John's, St Nicholas' (as has been noted), St Paul's and St Andrew's as well the more established Yarmouth Club. Often these clubs also ran second elevens and many of the settlements outside great Yarmouth, such as Acle, Caister, Martham, and Winterton were now running teams.

Generally, too, the game continued to grow elsewhere in Norfolk. For a short period in the 1870s Fakenham published their fixture list in the local newspapers with between 11 and 15 games annually. It would seem, though, that this was generally about the limit; most clubs played fewer over the course of a season. For example, Swaffham had only eight fixtures in 1870. This may not seem many compared with the number of games played today but it was an increase on the past and, importantly, the number of clubs across the county – in Norwich, the towns and the villages – was expanding.

Although many clubs were by now long established, in other cases they formed and re-formed. Examples of the latter included Dereham (1875), Loddon (1876), Melton (Constable) (1877), Shipdham (1884) and Rockland (1885). In 1884, there was a public meeting in Swaffham for the purpose of electing officers and arranging fixtures for the forthcoming season, and taken together these meetings suggest that in many cases, and unlike today, clubs operated from year to year and in effect disbanded during the winter months.

Team scores continued generally to be low and extremely so in some cases. Watton's total innings of 7 against Rockland in 1876 was made up entirely of extras, this notwithstanding that they included a professional. Other single figure scores included Wortwell's 7 (versus Alburgh in 1879), Wroxham's 8 (versus Sprowston United in the same year) and Loddon's 9 (versus Harleston in 1876); and in 1881 Banham Grammar School bowled out Banham Town for just 3 and 7 in their two innings. The report of the Wroxham innings is instructive even if scarcely credible; it stated that the innings lasted 15 minutes and 6 overs. This, though, was not as frenetic as Norwich Teachers' first innings of 9 against Perambulators in 1878 which the *Norfolk Chronicle* indicated took a mere ten minutes!

Low scoring could not necessarily be attributed to the recently legalised over-arm bowling. Norfolk and Norwich's dismissal by Mulbarton in 1878 for 57 and 13 was due to the fast under-arm bowling of one G.F. Smith, which was described as 'too effective' for the opposition. That said, one can imagine that poor wickets, uncut outfields and poor technique continued to be the major reasons. Indeed, team scores below 20 were not uncommon for many years to come, at least until the First World War. Furthermore, as the amount of cricket played in the county significantly increased towards the end of the 19th century, and with no limit on the number of overs a bowler could deliver, bowlers would occasionally take nine or even ten wickets in an innings. Having said that, the general standard of fielding was not as nowadays, and as an extreme example one unfortunate Dereham bowler in 1891 had seven catches dropped off his first 11 deliveries!

On the other hand, there were increasingly occasions when particularly high scores were posted. Norfolk and Norwich totalled 326 versus Lowestoft in 1871; Scott Chad's Eleven scored 386, including two individual hundreds, against Holt in 1877; and in 1879 Middleton Tower totalled 309 versus I Zingari and 365 versus a Mr Seppings Eleven. Later, in 1882, Middleton Tower ran up 580 in one of their Cricket Week matches and Carrow scored 310 for one wicket against Holkham with S.H. Evershed and S. Colman hitting unbeaten centuries of 173 and 112 respectively and adding 286 for the second wicket. Into the 1890s, and Thorpe County Asylum's total of 340 against Belle Vue (from Norwich) in 1894 drew the comment from the *Eastern Daily Press* that it was a record likely to stand for some time. Quite what the newspaper had in mind was unclear, and certainly that score was surpassed three years later when Gunton scored 438 for seven at Fakenham, refusing to declare because they only had eight players! A week later, in the Houghton Cricket Week, J.H.J. Hornsby's Eleven totalled 642 against their hosts.

The Middleton Tower games were part of their Cricket Week organised at their home by Sir Lewis and Lady Jarvis, two of whose sons were prominent in the County sides of the 1880s. Other Cricket Weeks also started up in the late 1870s including those at Melton Constable Hall and Wattlefield Hall. These venues were very much examples of country-house cricket played in parks that did not necessarily host much cricket at other times in the season. They were, however, an opportunity for club players, at least those from a particular social class, to rub shoulders with first-class cricketers. Other such grounds were more frequently used, for example Gunton Park, Ellingham Hall – the home ground for the Waveney Valley Club – and Garboldisham Manor. This last-named venue was described in *Wisden*'s obituary of its owner, Cecil Montgomerie, as an 'excellent ground'. Later, in May 1894, the *Eastern Daily Press* referred to three landowners – at Dunston, Houghton and Raynham – arranging for cricket pitches to be laid out on their estates.

It is probably country-house matches, and other all-day fixtures between the stronger and more socially elite clubs, that the *Norfolk Chronicle* had in mind when in 1889 it commented that

> 'it's quite time to do away with the absurd fashion of having a big feast in the middle of the day in cricket matches. How can a man properly play cricket after 'putting away' salmon and cucumber, lamb and salad, gooseberry tart, cheesecakes, and biscuits and cheese! – cold beef and bread and cheese should be enough'.

According to the newspaper, it would save money and time and thereby enable more people to play. Cricket teas were, though, popular at other levels of the game with the *Diss Express* reporting in 1876 that the players of Diss and Dickleburgh did 'ample justice' to the fayre provided.

The 1870s saw the first visits by 'touring' sides to Norfolk. Leading the way were the Westminster Wanderers who played at Fakenham in August 1877 with the Norfolk club making the return trip a fortnight later. They returned in the following years with the 1881 fixture against Holt being described as the biggest game in that town for 60 years. And in 1880 the Middlesex Ramblers came to Norfolk to play Yarmouth.

Around this time, the county was visited by teams of Clown Cricketers who combined a game against local opposition with clownish and acrobatic performances, sometimes simultaneously. The first recorded visit was in 1870 when the Norfolk and Norwich Club played against 14 clowns in full costume; their antics 'afforded full amusement' but the game was not a financial success. In 1872, the Diss Club hosted a fixture with 12 East of England Clown Cricketers and a year later England's Clown Cricketers visited Norfolk to play matches at Great Yarmouth and Diss, in the latter case against 'Eleven Gentlemen of England'. Then, in 1875, the London Imperial Clown Cricketers played the Norfolk and Norwich Club in a two-day match and 'excited much merriment throughout the play by their drolleries'. The local report of that game states that they included Dick-a-Dick, one of the 1868 Aboriginal tourists, although more recent research suggests he had died five years earlier! Another Clowns' side played against Hingham later in that 1875 season, and there is a record of such a team competing against the Lynn Club in 1880 and Wymondham, Burnham and Holt in 1883. Lest one doubts the popularity of these fixtures, a game at Thetford in 1875 against The Royal Original Clown Cricketers attracted 2000 spectators and the 1876 match between Diss and a travelling Clowns' team drew in between 1000 and 2000 spectators as well as the comment in the *Diss Express* that there were 'not a few cricket lovers present who were able to witness some really good play'.

Much as today, clubs around this time relied heavily on members' subscriptions for their income. However, a fundraising event for the Old Buckenham club in 1876 was more unusual involving, as it did, a music and spelling competition! Other fundraising activities in the 1880s and even into the next century included bazaars, variety entertainment evenings and smoking concerts, the latter generally involving live entertainment, usually of music, before a male-only audience.

In a time when players did not generally have their own equipment funds were needed for clubs to buy an assortment of bats, pads and gloves as well as balls and stumps. In this respect, and as an example, in 1879 H.P. Colman and Company in Norwich were selling cricket balls for seven shillings and sixpence each or three for 18 shillings; and in 1880 they advertised practice bats for six shillings and sixpence and 'best spring handled' bats at up to

18 shillings and sixpence. And notwithstanding the general absence of personal equipment, occasionally a bat might be presented to a player for a fine innings or for topping his club's batting averages,

Funds were also required for general ground development such as the new pavilion provided at North Walsham in 1881, the works at the Harleston ground in 1884 (although the *Norfolk Chronicle* indicated there was still room for improvement) and a new pavilion at Wymondham in 1889. In 1897, Fakenham were able to build a 'spacious' pavilion at Baron's Court with the proceeds from a successful bazaar. But if there was no pavilion or other built structure to occupy, teams would make do with tents.

By the 1880s, the number of clubs had grown quite significantly, particularly in the urban areas, although the fixture details of individual clubs did not necessarily suggest that they were playing much more cricket. For instance, Brooke had seven fixtures in 1885, Diss ten in 1887, Loddon and Langley Park 16 in 1888 and North Elmham 11 in 1889. However, in the next decade there was greater club activity with many teams playing about 20 matches and some even a few more. In 1896, for instance, Carrow First and Second Teams each played 19 games; King's Lynn's equivalent sides played 18 and 11; and Dereham 15.

Mostly, organised games were now played on Saturdays (although still not on Sundays) but not always with an early or mid-afternoon start. Even Saturday games might begin at teatime; an 1880 report of a game involving the Yarmouth Club refers to it being played between 3.30 pm and 6.30 pm. At Lakenham, at least, morning starts, with earlier finishes, were not unknown. Bearing in mind that the ground accommodated more than one square – in 1900 it was reported that four games were in progress simultaneously – it is not so surprising to read in 1889 that the improvements to the pavilion then being carried were long overdue given that perhaps 100 cricketers had only two small rooms at their disposal; or that in 1892 the Lakenham groundsman was reckoned to have prepared more than 200 playing strips. Indeed, A.J. Forrest recalled an incident at Lakenham before the First World War when two cricket balls from adjoining matches collided with one another. Similarly, the Recreation Ground at Wellesley Road in Great Yarmouth, opened in 1889, had three squares which, it appears, were occasionally all in use at the same time.

Nor, and despite improved communications, is it apparent that sides were generally travelling greater distances to play their games around this time although the better clubs, such as Gunton and the Norfolk and Norwich Club, might go further afield in search of suitable opposition particularly if the rail network facilitated it. However, Diss's trip to Holt in 1885 and North Walsham's to Garboldisham in 1890 were extreme examples of the distances clubs were prepared to travel. Not that travelling by train was without its problems, particularly if, as happened to Yarmouth in 1898, they missed their train to a game in Ipswich. Or, as Fincham encountered with their 1896 Junior Cup game in Norwich, they had to concede because the tie was due to begin at 2.30 pm and their last train back to Downham was at 3.20 pm. Otherwise, the means of transport to away games was by horse and cart, bicycle or by foot.

The Laws of Cricket at this time provided that, in the absence of agreement between the two sides, even one-day games should be played over two innings per side; indeed, that was the 'default' position until well into the 20th century. As a result, matches very often ended at a point in their third or fourth innings with the result determined by whoever led after the first innings. Also, until 1889, there was no provision for declarations; a law change in that year introducing that possibility therefore allowed games to come to a conclusion. This change was in practice most relevant for the better sides; less skilful teams very often continued to have little difficulty fitting four innings into the allotted time.

Cricket Weeks continued to flourish amongst the country-house set and by the late 1880s included the Ryburgh Invincibles. Their invincibility is not surprising if their 1889 Week is a measure for they included in their side Sammy Woods, already an Australian Test player and in due course also to represent England as well as captaining Somerset. In that Week he collected 33 wickets at an average of under four as well as posting top scores of 125 and 94. In addition, Charles Kortright, reckoned to be the fastest bowler of his day, appeared in the Garboldisham Cricket Week in the 1890s playing at different times for both the host's eleven and the opposition. As a different slant on the Cricket Week concept, the interestingly named Billingford Incapables went on tours of Norfolk. By the 1890s Houghton Hall was also the venue for a Cricket Week – indeed in at least one year they held two – when a number of well-known amateurs appeared as well as, in 1897, the legendary Australian fast bowler Fred Spofforth and Middlesex bowler 'Jack' Hearne. Nor were Cricket Weeks restricted to country houses: Wymondham held one in 1891 drawing the comment in the press that there was a 'veritable epidemic of cricket weeks right now'. Three years earlier, Dereham were described as following the example of others in organising one.

Not that Cricket Weeks were the only circumstances when more famous players appeared locally. Arthur Jones, the future Nottinghamshire captain who led the 1907–8 MCC tour to Australia, was for a while on the staff of Paston Grammar School and regularly turned out for them and the North Walsham club in 1894. Gillbert Jessop, the England all-rounder and legendary hitter, was in 1895 similarly on the staff of Beccles College whose fixture list included sides from Norfolk. Both turned in performances that overwhelmed their opponents. In this context, it was not unusual for schoolmasters to appear for their school team around this time, at least against their stronger opponents. For instance, Norfolk player James Worman, who dismissed W.G. Grace twice in 1903, regularly played for King's Lynn Grammar School in the 1890s. Indeed, William Pollock, who taught briefly at Paston Grammar School in the 1890s, referred in his book *The Cream of Cricket* to the custom of school teams including two masters in their chief matches.

Major Robert Poore, at the start of his prolific first-class 1899 season with Hampshire, played for the Norfolk Club and Ground side whilst based in Norwich with his Army regiment. A hope that he might turn out for Norfolk did not materialise although he did reappear on the county's cricket fields in 1906. In addition, Yarmouth entertained a Nottinghamshire Eleven in each of the three years from 1898 and although not at full strength they included in one or other of these matches William, George and John Gunn, William Attewell and the aforementioned Arthur Jones. Also, in 1899, Richard Nicholls, who only a few weeks previously had shared in a world record stand for the tenth wicket when playing for Middlesex, set a new best score in Norfolk cricket by hitting 296 for Gunton against Peripatetics. It is a record that to the best of one's knowledge still stands.

From the 1880s, more is written of women's cricket in Norfolk. In 1888, 11 Ladies of Thorpe beat 11 Gentlemen of Thorpe (who batted with bludgeons and could only use their left hand throughout the game) by one run. In the same year the Gentlemen of Thetford defeated the Ladies of the same town by three runs notwithstanding having to bat with broomstick-shaped bats and field left-handed. And in the following year, the similarly handicapped Gentlemen of Long Stratton lost by 31 runs to the town's Ladies. There were other examples of similar contests in the 1890s when also, in 1898, a 13-a-side match took place between the Ladies of Holt and Sheringham with each team including two 'gentlemen'.

At a more organised level, Yarmouth hosted, at the newly opened Wellesley Road ground, an exhibition match in late August 1890 between two women's touring sides drawn almost exclusively from the London area and known as the Red and Blue Elevens. Appearing under assumed names, they had apparently played their first game in Liverpool on 2 May and apart from two days rest had played 'without intermission'. The participants received sixpence a day expenses and until recently were the only recorded professional women cricketers. They were accompanied by a chaperone and a manager and played in front of large crowds but by the end of the following season they had disbanded.

Across at Narborough Hall, Constance Critchley-Martin organised ladies' cricket matches in the late 1880s and early 1890s when the sides were drawn from the country houses of the district and included the names of many well-known East Anglian families.


The most long lasting development in Norfolk cricket around this time came about as a result of an initiative from the County Club. Traditionally, sport had been non-competitive in the sense that there were no organised competitions. This began to change in the 1870s with the introduction of national knock-out competitions such as the FA Cup and the Wimbledon Lawn Tennis Championships and even an abortive attempt at a knock-out cup for the major cricket counties. Whilst the concept of 'leagues' did not really emerge until the end of the 1880s the examples set by the national competitions prompted the County Club in Norfolk to initiate a Challenge Cup competition in 1884 following a failed attempt by others three years earlier. In that first year, the competing clubs comprised five Norwich-based sides – Carrow, Norwich Teachers, Norfolk and Norwich, Norwich Grammar School and Prince's Street – and Fakenham, Gunton and Wymondham. Initially, the competition was played over two innings with games occasionally running over to a second day, and in that first year Fakenham and Prince's Street contested the final at Lakenham. Fakenham opened up with 114 to which the Norwich side replied with 100. Fakenham matched that in their second innings leaving Prince's Street with 115 to win, a target they reached for the loss of five wickets. They duly filled the cup with champagne! Fakenham went one better in 1885 when, again at Lakenham, they overcame Norfolk and Norwich by eight wickets in a match that doubled up as a benefit for the Lakenham groundsman, Robert Chadwick. (Not that this success was any guarantee of a long club life; by 1889, the Fakenham club ceased to exist albeit to re-form three years later). Increasingly in those early years, clubs away from Norwich entered the competition so that it could soon properly be described as countywide, and it was two of these teams that contested the third final in which North Walsham defeated Melton Constable by 107 runs. Holt, Dereham, King's Lynn (sometimes under the name of the Conservative Club, St James' House), Reepham and Yarmouth all participated in one or more of the first few years as did CEYMS and the Norwich YMCA. By 1889, the competition had 14 entries.

The competition was not without controversy, with a particular issue being highlighted by a complaint in 1888 that Carrow had included a player who had already promised to play for the Norwich-based Kingsley Club. The County Committee agreed that the player, a Mr Shaw, was disqualified from representing Carrow and awarded the game to CEYMS. However, it did CEYMS little good for in the next round they came up against North Walsham who scored 395 and then bowled out CEYMS for 51. Fairfax Davies hit 246 not out for the victors, the highest recorded score in Norfolk cricket to that time. Occasionally in the following years disputes also arose where clubs could not agree a date, with the organising Committee being called upon to resolve the matter. By 1889, there was pressure to review the registration requirements so as to allow only players qualified for Norfolk to participate; and in 1890, there were also concerns that Carrow were able to play a professional but that other clubs could not afford them. The outcome was that for the following season a rule change prohibited the selection of professional players, although by 1901 their selection was merely regarded as against the spirit of the competition.

Notwithstanding these problems, the concept of a cup competition was popular amongst clubs and for the 1891 season the County Club introduced a Junior Cup competition and a Challenge Shield to be competed for by schools with both soon organised on a District basis. In particular, the Junior Cup proved popular with 31 entries in 1893, including some schools and Second Elevens of clubs in the Senior Cup; and 1899 saw the expansion of the Junior Cup so as to involve both Saturday and Thursday Divisions (Thursday being the day in Norwich when shops closed early at 5 pm). By 1891 there was also a Yarmouth Cup competition and the Sandringham and District League established at the very end of the century was in fact a knock-out competition in its first few seasons. However, there was a downside to cup cricket: Acle complained in 1894 that Carrow's calling off a friendly showed again what cup-ties were doing for cricket and suggested a league instead. Also, a consequence of the Junior Cup's popularity was that entries into the Senior Cup dwindled with only six entrants in 1895.

League cricket arrived in Norfolk in the 1890s. The first reference was in 1891 when the Langham and District Cricket Association was formed with 11 clubs and a silver shield to be presented to the one with most points at the end of the season. However, the competition was poorly reported and it turned out to be short-lived. Similarly, a five-team league established in Great Yarmouth in 1894 lasted for only two years. In 1896, a Thursday League (with five teams) and a Saturday League (with eight participants) were introduced in the Norwich area with teams playing each other on a home and away basis; two points were awarded for a win and one for a draw. These competitions were also not long-lasting, folding as they did after only two seasons although a Norwich Cricket League was re-introduced in 1900.

The game's popularity was evidenced, and fuelled, by its reporting. Nationally, in addition to the daily newspapers, there were a number of cricket annuals and the weekly publication *Cricket*. In Norfolk, newspapers, and in particular by the 1890s, the *Eastern Daily Press*, devoted considerable space to reporting both first-class and local cricket and often also to adding a twice-weekly commentary on both, not least in its preview and review of Senior Cup matches. There was also the *Norfolk Cricket Annual* published between 1889 and 1898, and again in 1909/10 and 1910/11 and in 1926 and 1927, and a detailed source of information about cricket in the county. Such, indeed, was the popularity of cricket that the 1898 *Annual*, without being completely comprehensive, listed 83 clubs, some with second teams, playing in the county as well as 12 Grammar Schools.

Local clubs at the end of the 19th century experienced a range of problems. Wymondham, for instance, were faced with boys trespassing onto their ground and breaking fences. In 1896, Holt were unable to arrange any matches because they were unable to secure a ground. And more generally the *Eastern Daily Press* in 1895 expressed concern at the apparently not uncommon practice, even in matches beginning at around 3 pm, of players leaving at about 5 pm and before the match had finished for the simple reason that they did not like fielding! By way of contrast, county player Fairfax Davies was quoted around this time as saying that 'next to scoring a century there is nothing more enjoyable than a day's leather hunting'.

Finally, the old practice of some of the best players turning out for different clubs over a short period of time had not completely disappeared at the end of the century. Furthermore, it seems that village clubs would often include players from outside their parish; for instance, in 1890 Scoulton decided to concentrate on village versus village matches rather than 'club' matches because for the latter it was necessary to recruit outside players. Indeed, the import of cricketers may well have been the norm at this time given Billingford's claim at the end of the century that they were the only *bona fide* village club in the county; that is, that they were the only club in Norfolk not to play outside members except in the rare case of a visitor staying in the village.

Cricket grounds at the turn of the century took a number of different forms. At one end of the spectrum, there were the grounds associated with country houses and Halls with their own groundskeepers. There were also the urban facilities such as Lakenham in Norwich and Wellesley Road in Yarmouth and other grounds set aside for cricket. On the other hand, there were the grounds recognised in the reports of club annual meetings as meadows 'kindly lent' by an obliging landowner. As an extreme example of this last category, an article on the Bradfield Club that appeared in the *Eastern Daily Press* in 1964 looked back to the end of the 19th century when they moved from meadow to meadow in order to fit in with crop rotation. And lest it seems only a current issue, there were concerns in the early 1890s about the loss to building development of playing fields and open spaces in Norwich.

Changing and related facilities for most clubs were generally very basic assuming they existed at all. However, the more affluent clubs, particularly those based on country estates, might have a pavilion. In this respect, by the end of the 19th century Boulton and Paul were manufacturing at their Norwich works a range of mostly wooden pavilions with their models at the more expensive end of the market including not only dressing rooms, a club room, toilets and a verandah but also a luncheon room, kitchen and rest room.

1901 marked the end of the Victorian Age. Also, around this time, the social changes that had already begun towards the end of the previous century continued. The political influence of the professional classes was increasing and the power of the landed gentry reducing. The extension of male suffrage and the growth of trade unionism were also evidence of a move towards a new social order as were the restrictions on the powers of the House of Lords introduced by the Liberal Government in 1911. Education was now compulsory to the age of 12 and school attendance had tripled in the previous 30 years. In 1902, state education passed into the hands of local authorities. Bicycles became more common in the 1890s and cars also started to appear on the nation's roads, although transport over any distance was still usually by means of the railway network or horse and cart or on foot. All these social changes impacted on Norfolk. In addition, the tourism industry continued to expand and the developments in public health noted earlier meant that by the turn of the century the urban areas, and in particular Norwich, were much more pleasant places to live than 50 years previously.

As for cricket, the years between 1890 and 1914 have been described as its 'Golden Age' with high quality amateur batsmanship, led by Charles

Fry, Ranjitsinjhi and Archie MacLaren supplemented by a rich seam of professional batsmen and bowlers.

In Norfolk, the most noticeable development in the years leading up to 1914 was the expansion of league cricket, this being seen as a means of invigorating the game locally. A small league operated in Norwich and from 1900 there was, albeit not continuously, the Soames Bowl, donated by the local MP and comprising a mini-league of four teams based in and around Diss. However, the first major initiative of the new century came from Revd Francis Ffolkes who had played one game for Norfolk in 1886 and would in due course become the Baron of Hillington. He was concerned about 'the deplorable state' of cricket in Norfolk – the County Club's fortunes were at a particularly low ebb at this time – and his vision to put this right was the establishment of District Clubs for West Norfolk, Mid Norfolk and Norwich. From this, there emerged the 'West Norfolk Scheme', based around the newly formed West Norfolk Club, which he believed would 'revolutionise' cricket in the west of the county. The Scheme was intended to put the best players in touch with one another; to provide a subsidy for a professional for the larger clubs; to provide a supply of efficient coaches for smaller clubs; and for a central body to be set up which would send someone to advise on grounds maintenance and ultimately supply materials at wholesale prices. The hope was that from all this the smallest clubs would have an equal opportunity of sending members to represent West Norfolk and that ultimately the County Club would benefit. As an example of this initiative winter indoor coaching was organised in King's Lynn and a few years later the press were able to refer to an improvement in cricket in the west of the county attributable to the efforts of the West Norfolk Club and Revd Ffolkes.

Then, in 1904, came the Mid Norfolk Village Challenge competition, initiated by Revd Francis Marshall of Mileham who had been concerned that teams tended not to play the game in a way that fostered its development. In particular, he disapproved of the way in which clubs recruited players simply to win games. He was also keen to encourage the labouring men of the villages to play the game and to make their lives 'a little more interesting'. He therefore helped to establish a league based on geographical lines, with the competing sides made up exclusively of bona fide residents of the village although smaller villages were allowed to amalgamate. The divisional winners then competed on a knock-out basis for a shield paid for by local subscriptions and held by the County Club as its trustees. In that first year, 11 teams took part and were divided into four divisions although in the years that immediately followed both numbers dropped. It was also agreed that the competing clubs should provide umpires to stand in matches in which their club was not competing.

Other leagues sprung up around the same time: the St Faiths League, the Yarmouth and District League and the Tas Valley Village League and, as an expanded successor to the Norwich Cricket League, the East Norfolk League. Whereas the first three leagues comprised only one division with perhaps half a dozen entrants in any season, the last-named for a short while ran to three divisions with up to eight teams in each – but with no automatic promotion – and included teams from as far afield as Overstrand, Thetford and Lowestoft as well as many Norwich sides, including the leading ones of CEYMS and Carrow. (The Carrow Works, incidentally, had their own league comprising their various works divisions). The Sandringham League also assumed a format that more correctly reflected its name. However, just because a club competed in a league did not necessarily mean that it did not also play friendlies.

The County Club continued to run their three Cup competitions although the number of competing sides began to decline in the early 1900s. In total, it had peaked at 39 in 1901 but by 1909 it had fallen to 24. In particular, the Senior Cup attracted few entrants. This decline was no doubt due to the growth of league cricket particularly in the east of the county with the consequent problem of arranging cup games. Elsewhere, there is evidence of very localised knock-out competitions, such as the Cromer Hospital Cup run for the benefit of the Cottage Hospital in the town and the Alfred Hall Challenge Cup based around Sedgeford.

The County Club's competitions for Norwich and King's Lynn schools also continued with the former operating on a league basis from 1906. In addition, in 1904 the local Member of Parliament, Frederick Wilson, donated a Shield to the Mid Norfolk Village competition, to be competed for by elementary schools – that is, in broad terms, schools for children of compulsory school age (then 13) – in the East Dereham area. Public and Grammar Schools had their own fixture lists and although organised representative schools cricket was still a long way in the future 1907 saw a match between Norfolk and Suffolk boys Under 15 sides.

The move towards competitive club cricket was not, however, proceeding quickly enough for many in the county, and in September 1909 the County Club called a meeting at which most of the key figures associated with the game in Norfolk were present. Some of the concerns related to the County Club itself, but the chief purpose of the meeting was to decide what could be done to extend the interest of cricket in the county and unearth local talent. The conclusion was to divide up the county into Districts based on the Parliamentary Divisions with each District to be represented on the Central County Committee. Individual clubs would affiliate to their District organisation – in some cases, itself a club – which would then affiliate to the County Club. Districts would also set up Leagues to operate in their area. It was also proposed that Districts play one another, albeit not on a systematic basis.

The result was that for 1910 new leagues were formed: the North Norfolk Village League, the Cromer and District League and the Gayton and District League (in that case, with North and South Divisions). In addition, the Mid Norfolk Village Shield converted fully into a league, the East Norfolk League set up a third Division specifically for teams playing on Mousehold Heath and other parks in Norwich, and the Norwich clubs formed the Norwich Cricket Association.

This is not to say that these moves were universally popular. Lord Battersea, the owner of the Overstrand ground, is reputed to have said that if ever the club dropped out of senior cricket he would shut up the ground on the basis that if the club was going back to village cricket it should have a village ground. Nor did this initiative necessarily have the desired effect as there was insufficient interest to run the Senior Cup and Saturday Junior Cup between 1910 and 1913 with only the latter restarting in the following year. In addition, and despite the initial enthusiasm, the number of leagues, and teams competing in them, reduced significantly by 1914.

Country-house cricket still had its place in Norfolk with the *Eastern Daily Press* reporting in late June 1901 that it was 'in full swing'. The related feature of Cricket Weeks remained part of the summer calendar, notably at Garboldisham Manor, Narford and Hunstanton, though not to the same degree as previously. It was at this time that there moved to Norfolk an Australian stockbroker by the name of Lionel Robinson. Seeking a country seat, he settled on Old Buckenham Hall which he promptly rebuilt. Apparently a difficult man, his sporting interests led to him laying out a cricket pitch in the grounds of the Hall from where he ran his own side. His wealth enabled him to recruit Archie MacLaren, the former England captain, as his personal cricket manager and also to bring in, even for one-off games against local opposition, other famous cricketers such as Albert Trott, Bernard Bosanquet, Sydney Barnes and Jack Mason. His biggest coups, though, were the 1912 and 1921 fixtures against the touring sides detailed in Chapter 13.

These were not the only famous cricketers to appear on the county's cricket fields in the years before the First World War. In May 1903, the Liverpool firm of Kinnears organised a series of matches across the country with three aims in mind: for charity, their own publicity and to allow the public to see Gilbert Jessop and other noted cricketers. Their first game was against CEYMS in Norwich but this proved to be a disappointment in that only six or so players turned up for Kinnears with the side being completed by local players. Jessop himself did not disappoint, scoring 73 before rain brought an early finish. Then, later that year and in 1904, W.G. Grace himself brought his London County side to Lakenham (see Chapter 7).

Back at local club level, fixture lists were tending to get longer with some teams playing between 20 and 30 games in a season and many more in the high teens. There are also instances of Second Elevens playing up to 20 games. Average team scores were gradually increasing with the senior clubs in the county regularly posting totals well over 100. Indeed, in the 1906 Senior Cup Final CEYMS scored 401 for six, although for junior sides to reach three figures was still relatively unusual. Individually, the end of season club averages revealed few batsmen with an average over 20 but perhaps two or three regular bowlers averaging under 10. Furthermore, it remained the practice for teams batting second to bat on after passing their opponents score.

Generally, and compared with today, clubs still did not travel great distances to play, although a conveniently located railway station – and there were many dozen stations across the county – was an attraction to offer potential opponents as the newly formed club at Northrepps recognised in 1904 when, in seeking home fixtures, they advertised that their ground was about a mile from the station. Occasionally, too, press notices for a game would indicate the departure time for the train. Transport by road had its challenges as the Quidenham Park team discovered in 1905 when, returning from a match at Roydon, a wheel fell off their horse-drawn wagonette throwing it into a ditch. Fortunately, no-one was hurt but the journey continued on foot until other vehicles arrived to collect the players. Mostly, either clubs relied on a limited number of people with vehicular transport (such as horse and cart) to convey them to away games and, for shorter journeys, players still often travelled by bicycle or on foot.

Clubs themselves were becoming more organised with most of the main officers' posts one sees 100 years later together with large committees to oversee the running of the club. Perhaps it was a reflection of the increasingly democratic times but it was not unknown for committees to comprise officers and ten or more others; in 1914, Hunstanton's committee totalled 17 and Long Stratton's 11 plus officers. Even a small club such as Necton had 11 committee members. Their business was not entirely unfamiliar to readers a century later. The minute books of Ingoldisthorpe Cricket Club before the Great War, and also the press reports of clubs' AGMs, reveal decisions on subscriptions, fixture cards, annual dinners, fundraising, player awards and payments to the groundsman. The purchase of club kit was also a prominent agenda item. In this connection, sports goods suppliers continued to see the potential, with George Pilch in 1908 offering a guinea bat to anyone scoring a century with a bat purchased from his premises.

There may have been no female representation on these committees but women's cricket still featured intermittently in Norfolk with Ladies Elevens from Ryburgh, Billingford, New Buckenham, Sidestrand, Alysham and Saxlingham. On an apparently more organised basis Hempnall are recorded as having their own Ladies' Club.

Nor was cricket reserved for the young and fit. For a time in the 1900s there was an annual veterans match in Great Yarmouth between 'ye olde cricketers' of Norfolk and Suffolk for the benefit of local charities and in front of crowds of up to 1500. Also, in 1907, an eleven a side match took

Terrington St Clement's cricket team, pre-1914. *Typical of village sides from this period, this photograph highlights that not all players appeared in "whites"..*

place at the rear of the Great Hospital in Norwich between two teams representing the Cottages and the Wards. The combined ages of the two sides were 839 and 827 respectively and to save running every hit counted as one run with two scored for a hit past a post. The umpires were both aged 86 and a tennis ball was used!

However, as the country moved towards war, there were signs that cricket's popularity was beginning to wane. The reduced enthusiasm for league and cup cricket illustrated this as did the debates within clubs before the start of the 1914 season. Fakenham, who had played 23 games in 1913, were now faced with a significant financial deficit but eventually agreed to continue. On the other hand, Dereham decided to suspend playing for a year, attributing their difficulties to the movement of 17 and 18 year olds away from the town. As another example, East Bilney decided to amalgamate with Beetley. Indeed, it is very possible that but for the war the decline in interest would have continued. As we shall see in the next Chapter, this was not to be the case.

# CHAPTER 4

# Marking Time

There was little cricket activity in Norfolk during the years of the First World War, reflecting the call of W.G. Grace within a few weeks of hostilities breaking out that 'all first-class cricketers of suitable age set a good example, and come to the aid of their country without delay in its hour of need'. League and cup cricket in the county was suspended and there were few friendly games. Such cricket as was reported generally occurred in the schools or involved army sides drawn from regiments based locally or teams of convalescents from the Norfolk War Hospital. In this respect, George Pilch (known in due course as 'Old George' to distinguish him from his son) was often involved in putting together scratch sides to provide the opposition. Occasionally, too, games were played to raise funds for charities such as the Red Cross or the Police Orphanage.

This is not to say that Norfolk's cricketers had no opportunity to play. In the Spring of 1916 Michael and Harry Falcon, Gervase Birkbeck and Ralph Thurgar took part in the opening match of the season in northern Egypt; Michael Falcon top-scored. Later that year, at a venue described in the *Eastern Daily Press* as 'somewhere abroad', the Norfolk Engineers took on and defeated the Australian Army Service Corps following which they were entertained in 'true colonial style'. In 1917 Second Lieutenant W.J. Daplyn from Mulbarton scored 121 out of a total of 306 for his Company against another Unit of the Royal Engineers 'somewhere in France'.

The 'war to end all wars' ended in November 1918. Britain alone had suffered two and a half million casualties including 750,000 dead. In addition, the economic cost of the war was substantial as, after an initial boom period, the country's trading position declined with the loss of overseas customers especially for traditional industries such as textiles and coalmining. Exports in the 1920s were usually only around 80 per cent of the pre-war level and this led to wage reductions, industrial unrest, higher unemployment and, in due course, the Depression of the early 1930s.

Nonetheless, the country moved forward. By the end of the1920s, the radio had developed as an effective means of communication and television sets began to appear in significant numbers in the following decade. Motorised transport was more common, although relatively few owned their own cars. The 'Railway Age' may have passed but there was still a heavy reliance on trains. Politically, the first Labour Government took office in 1924 and four years later, after decades of struggle, women achieved equal voting rights with men. Also, as the population continued to grow, the need to ensure properly controlled town and country development was recognised. And there was educational progress with the school leaving age raised to 14 in 1918 and a growth in both secondary and elementary schools.

In Norfolk, the war had a stimulating effect on agriculture. Farming became more mechanised and in much of the county over half of the labour force worked in agriculture. A more difficult period followed with redundant farm workers increasingly looking to the urban centres for employment in a range of industries taking root there and where wages were higher and housing conditions better. Improved road transport facilitated communication between the countryside and the larger centres of population and, with better services and utilities, the smaller market towns began to thrive. Norwich was of course still the major urban area, with a population in 1933 of 128,000 compared with just over half a million in the county as a whole. Food and drink production and the footwear and clothing industries were major employers in the city where the banking and insurance sectors remained prominent. On the other hand, the inter-war years were a period of stagnation for Great Yarmouth where the fishing industry began to decline and the growth of the holiday industry did not make up for the loss of port activity. King's Lynn, with its easier road communications out of the county, fared better and the seaside resorts on Norfolk's north coast continued to thrive.

To a degree, the face of cricket was also changing. The 'Golden Age' had passed and country-house cricket and the clerical influence were both much less prominent. The MCC continued to rule over the game conservatively but with a light touch with the result that structurally the game was less organised than football. League cricket for the stronger clubs was limited to the North and Midlands. Women's cricket at last began to be more organised with the formation of their own national Cricket Association in 1926. The game as a whole continued to be popular with participants and spectators alike and drew both from all classes of society.

Increasingly, players turned out in 'whites' although team photographs of the period are evidence that in many village sides in Norfolk the practice was often otherwise, as photographs from this period in Philip Yaxley's book *Looking back at Norfolk cricket* testify. There were improvements in players' equipment and kit although they would still seem quite rudimentary compared with those of today; bats were much lighter than now and helmets were still things of the distant future. There were also continuing improvements in techniques for maintaining cricket pitches (for example, the use of lawn sand to assist in weed-killing) although this did not necessarily manifest itself at every level of the game. Most matches were now played on Saturday afternoons with the tea interval increasingly a recognised part of the entertainment.

Club cricket in Norfolk picked up well after the war. Although it is reasonable to assume that most lost at least one playing member – indeed, five North Elmham players died or were killed in the conflict and the village of Heydon lost so many men that the local club disbanded and only reformed after 1945 – newspaper evidence suggests that a large number of clubs reformed for the 1919 season. As an example, the May 1919 meeting to revive the Weasenham club heard of a membership of 60 and arranged practice on three nights each week; indeed, boys at the local day school were reported as playing in the playground every evening. The Saturday and Thursday Junior Cups were revived and together attracted 17 entries including, as a reminder of the war, the newly formed Discharged Soldiers and Sailors team and the Comrades of the Great War Club, both based in Norwich.

Buckenham Tofts cricket team, 1930s. *Pictured are not just the team but also the umpire and the scorer.*

The following seasons demonstrated a renewed enthusiasm for cricket in Norfolk. The seeds for this can be traced initially to the creation of the Norfolk and Norwich Cricket Club Conference in the Spring of 1920. Under the chairmanship of George Pilch, its aims were to improve the links between the County Club and the junior clubs in Norfolk, to promote the better organisation of clubs and competitive cricket and, more generally, to awaken interest in cricket in the county. A number of competitions operated in that season, some for the first time – the South, North and East Norfolk Village Leagues, the Mid Norfolk Village League and Shield, the Gayton and District League, the Sandringham and District League, the Sedgford District League, the Marshland League, the Honingham and District League and the Soames Bowl; in addition, the Leicester Shield was re-established in 1921. All ran on a league basis but in some cases with Divisions, or Sections, and the winners playing-off for the overall title. Altogether, about 100 teams were involved with each Division generally containing no more than six or seven sides. This enabled the winners to be decided by early August, before Harvest-time.

In the decade that followed, other leagues were formed – the Wicklewood and District League, the Rudham and District League, the Weasenham and District League, the Freethorpe and District League, the Islington and District League (based in the King's Lynn area), the Upwell and District League, the Norfolk and Norwich League, the Keswick and District League and the Norwich Thursday League; and a few Norfolk villages competed in the Beccles and District League. There were also competitions called 'Cups' but, in reality, these were league-based just as, particularly before 1914, very occasionally a cup competition might be referred to as a league. Most notably, they included the two Boyle Cups (separately run by the Mid Norfolk Village and Honingham Leagues), the Calder Cup (in the south-west of the county and including clubs from the Brandon area) and the Falcon Cup, established in 1923 by the county captain and sitting Member of Parliament for East Norfolk. In establishing this competition, Michael Falcon was following the example set by the pre-war Parliamentarian in South Norfolk, Arthur Soames and also William Boyle, the MP for Mid Norfolk between 1910 and 1918. In addition, Lord Fermoy, the local MP, donated the trophy for the Rudham and District League. It is difficult to be precise but by the late 1920s almost 200 different teams were playing league cricket in Norfolk and in some cases clubs entered first and second teams in different leagues. However, the sections within Leagues remained small, very often with as few as five teams and never more than ten; and if harvest and a wet summer prevented finals from being played then they would be fitted in near the start of the following season. Given the extensive press coverage at the time, it is strange that local newspapers did not consistently publish tables with the result that, presumably, clubs often had to rely on word of mouth and communications from their league secretary to know how they stood.

The leagues, or at least some of them, appear generally to have operated reasonably tight registration rules. For instance, the decision of the North Norfolk League in 1922 to allow clubs to pick players within a three-mile radius was actually a relaxation of the existing rule; similarly, at the same time they reduced the registration period from 14 to seven days. If a club fielded an ineligible player they could expect a points' deduction. The same approach might also apply to cup competitions. The Hall Cup, perhaps the earliest example in Norfolk of an evening knockout competition and played for by the villages of Sedgford, Ringstead and

Heacham, had a strict rule limiting players to those born in the village or living or working there.

Leagues, though, were very much for junior sides in Norfolk. Roy Genders opened his 1952 book *League Cricket in England* with the sentence 'The mere mention of league cricket to thousands of ardent cricket followers of the summer game is sufficient for the subject to be quickly changed to the problem of Korea or the atom bomb; in fact to any other subject than league cricket'. It was very much a north-south issue with the senior Norfolk clubs aligned with their southern brethren and it certainly applied to cricket in the county in the period between the two World Wars and indeed for many years afterwards. The consequence was that a whole raft of clubs in Norfolk did not play league cricket. For instance, in 1928 the clubs that chose just to play friendlies included Attleborough, Carrow, CEYMS, Civil Service, Dereham, Diss, East Norfolk, Harleston, Hethersett, King's Lynn, Norwich Teachers, Norwich Union, Norwich Wanderers, Norfolk Ramblers, Overstrand, Reepham, St Andrews Hospital, South Norfolk, Thetford, West Norfolk, Wymondham, Yarmouth Town and Yarmouth Wanderers although in a few cases their second elevens might play in a league. Indeed, throughout this period, a substantial number of cricket matches in Norfolk were still 'friendlies' and would remain so for many years to come.

It was from players of a few of the clubs just listed that the county side was selected. In addition, and as an illustration of the division between those senior clubs and the ordinary village team, there was considerable discussion at the 1923 Annual General Meeting of the Sandringham and District League about the continuing benefit of affiliating to the West Norfolk Club given that the Club rarely gave trials to youngsters from teams in the leagues.

By 1921, the Norfolk and Norwich Cricket Club Conference had metamorphosed into the Norfolk Cricket Association (NCA) but still under George Pilch's chairmanship and with Ben Seaman as an energetic secretary. The NCA assumed responsibility for running the Senior and Saturday and Thursday Junior Cup competitions as well as the Norfolk and Norwich League. The Cups attracted as many as 50 entrants in 1923 including 34 in the Saturday Junior Cup the first-round draw for which tended to be geographically based. However, by the end of the 1920s their popularity had again declined to the extent that the Senior Cup, the numbers for which never reached double figures in this period, was suspended – further evidence that competitive cricket was not for the senior clubs.

The NCA itself continued to grow in the period up until the mid-1930s. indeed, the hope was expressed in 1921 that the number of its affiliated clubs would soon reach 200. This proved optimistic, although membership did climb steadily from 70 in that year to 90 in 1928, including all the senior and best junior clubs in the county, and, in 1934, to 95. Further, as it developed it did not just run competitions but also took on responsibility for managing the County Club and Ground games. And, in 1930, it engaged with clubs on the MCC proposal that they trial the use of higher and wider stumps and recommended that senior, but not junior, clubs consider using them that year, the reasoning being that the quality of pitches at that lower level already militated in favour of the bowler. However, from 1935 its membership began to fall and by 1937 stood at 63.

The NCA were not the only organisers of cup competitions. By 1930, the Chief Constable had given his name to the Van Neck Police Cup played for by Police Divisions in Norfolk; and there was also the Inter-Factory Beet Sugar Cup in which Norfolk sides were prominent.

Schools cricket retained a significant place in the game locally. Grammar and Independent Schools continued to play to a high standard with fixtures against one another and adult sides. For the less privileged the Mid Norfolk Schools Shield survived the war and a South Norfolk Schools League was also set up soon afterwards with a small number of participants. In the city, the Norwich Schools Athletic Association (Cricket Section) was established in 1926 providing league cricket for, in that first year, 16 council-run schools. The competition operated on the basis of two sections and a two-innings final between the section winners with a pitch 19 yards long and games not expected to last more than two hours including the interval. Elsewhere in the county, Boys teams in the Hunstanton area competed for the Thorne Shield, and a Lynn School Boys' League and a Whissonsett and District Schools' League were set up in the 1930s. That said, it has been estimated that nationally cricket was on the curriculum in only ten per cent of all elementary schools – that is, schools providing for children of compulsory school age -although the activity in Norfolk suggests a higher figure.

It was also clear that clubs were, in their way, willing to encourage young players, for example, by allowing their ground to be used by schoolboys for practice and through reduced subscriptions. Indeed, Walsingham's success in the 1928 North Norfolk Village League final was attributed to their having a second team which enabled a flow of promising cricketers to be introduced into their first eleven. On the other hand, the President of the Mid Norfolk Village Cricket League at the Shield final of the same year, in addition to commenting on the poor quality of village pitches and 'unwisdom' of winning the toss and asking the opposition to bat – similar, more general, comments were made in 1932 – went on to complain that young players did not put enough into their game; rather, they were too ready to go off on their motorcycle with 'of course' a girl behind them!

The need for organised coaching and practice, as much if not more so for adults as youngsters, was increasingly being recognised. Many clubs had designated practice nights, sometimes with different evenings for their first and second teams if they ran more than one side. Sometimes, also, clubs would engage their own coaches for a part of the summer or else make use of one of the County Club's coaches. In other cases, coaching was provided from within a club's membership. In addition to outdoor practice nets and matting wickets, indoor facilities became available for the first time at the Drill Hall in Norwich in 1923 with the County Club offering coaching as part of the affiliation package for member clubs although according to a report in 1925 the high bounce made them unsuitable for boys under the age of 14. In 1928, Jack Hobbs opened a new facility at the YMCA in Norwich although generally such facilities were very limited. Jack Nichols, the Norfolk professional, was also highly regarded as a coach. However, the coaching provided through the County Club did not come cheaply with the report to the 1935 AGM noting that the annual cost of employing three coaches, as they then did, was not far short of £400 when materials were taken into account.

The better youngsters from these coaching sessions might find their way into the annual Colts games with the very best being selected for the Club and Ground matches, but it is noticeable that those participating in

Jack Hobbs opening the YMCA nets in Norwich, April 1928. *Jack Hobbs had represented Cambridgeshire against Norfolk in 1904 but he now came to Norfolk as the greatest batsman of his time. Later, he became the first professional cricketer to be knighted.*

the former were almost exclusively from public and independent schools. In addition, a letter from the Colts match organiser to the press in 1934, whilst seeking nominations, went on to say that 'preference must of course be given to the sons of members of the County Club'.

It is clear that generally wickets still fell short of the quality one expects today. Whilst the more senior clubs often had the use of private grounds many others still played in 'meadows' made available by a generous farmer. There were, though, good intentions with Middleton, albeit a financially well-supported club, announcing in 1921 that no pains were being spared to produce a really good wicket, and no doubt other clubs would have said the same. However, even for senior clubs, team scores over 150 in the first part of this period were unusual although by the 1930s they were becoming more frequent and even totals over 200 were no longer rare for these senior elevens. For the run of the mill junior teams, scores between 20 and 50 remained very common. To illustrate the point, Happisburgh's averages for 1923 showed that although they played 18 games only one batsman scored more than 100 runs whilst seven bowlers averaged under 6.5 per wicket.

As a further example, the 1936 averages for the Eaton club, in a season when they won nine of their ten games, revealed a best batting average of 6.2 but three bowlers taking 123 wickets between them for a total of 312 runs. Sometimes, a club's published end of season averages also included the average number of runs per wicket throughout the season, both for and against, and in this respect the averages for even the top clubs in Norfolk, at least in the 1920s, would rarely exceed 15 and sometimes only be in single figures. Lastly, the total number of runs scored in the whole of the Diss and District League 1932 programme of 30 matches was 3653, or an average of 120 for each game. But the lowest team score in the inter-war period is reserved for Kings Lynn Corporation in a 1939 fixture with Giles and Bullen – all out in 2.5 overs for just 2, one of which was an extra.

Against this background, it is unsurprising that by today's standards it is individual bowling performances that stand out. The absence of a limitation on the number of overs one could bowl meant that taking all ten wickets was more likely but even so Albert Beales' performance of 10 for 1 for Garboldisham versus Botesdale in 1922 is remarkable in any circumstances, as are R. Cant's six wickets with his last eight balls to win the 1926 Senior Cup final for Carrow against Middleton by one run; Baldwin's five wickets in an over for Seething a year later; and W. Bartram's 9 wickets for 5 runs for Felthorpe versus Eaton in a 1937 Norwich and District League game. It is also unsurprising that batsmen fared less well by comparison. In particular, it was very rare for batsmen to score 1000 runs in a season, notwithstanding that many teams regularly played between 20 and 30 games. Individual centuries were almost unheard of in village cricket; H. Palmer's 165 not out for Poringland against Seething and Mundham in 1934 dwarfs all others in this period. Even amongst the senior clubs such scores were extremely rare although Raymond Perkins hit 204 not out for Yarmouth versus Carrow in 1938 and Ronnie Gladden 184 not out for East Norfolk versus West Norfolk four years earlier.

There was around this time a general concern about the lack of suitable playing fields in towns and villages across the country and this led in 1925 to the creation of the National Playing Fields Association. A county branch was set up in the following year, at a meeting described as 'influentially attended', with the aim of providing playing fields for young people. The Norwich Playing Fields and Open Spaces Society had existed since the mid-1890s but now there was a county-wide body to push for more public facilities.

At the inaugural Norfolk meeting it was recognised that cricket grounds were hard to find. Not least this was because their provision had until then usually depended on the generosity of local landowners, at least in rural areas. In this respect, the County Association estimated in 1927 that 30 per cent of villages had no cricket field; the figure for football pitches was 27 per cent. Three years later, they carried out a county-wide survey which showed that sports playing facilities were provided in 283 parishes (although generally due to the generosity of a local landowner), 202 parishes saw no need for, or could not secure, facilities and 72 asked for advice. Their 1930 AGM also noted that they had already helped 25 Norfolk villages to obtain a playing field. Whether in response to the Association's work or as a result of particular local initiatives, the years that followed began to see an increase in public recreational facilities, in particular with the village playing field sometimes being provided, together with a pavilion, by a local benefactor or the local council. However some may regard their quality today, they were an improvement on the 'meadow kindly lent'.

Nevertheless, for a great many village clubs the farmer's meadow continued for many years to come to be their home ground leading one village side in 1931 to express their concern about the quality of pitches in the Mid Norfolk Shield competition. The use of marl from about this time did, though, begin to lead to better playing surfaces for those clubs that could afford it. A consequence of the reliance on local farmers for a field meant that many clubs did not have a ground that they could call their own and that instead they would periodically have to relocate. Ingoldisthorpe, for instance, had as many as five grounds in the first half of the 20th century. Other village clubs were more fortunate, in particular those with a ground within the estate of one of the many country halls across Norfolk. Whilst country-house cricket in its original sense had died out by this time, many estate owners were happy to provide facilities for their parish. The local 'squire' might even have organised the team. Furthermore, such grounds usually had the advantage of a full-time groundsman employed by the estate, thereby ensuring that their quality was of a high standard.

By the late 1930s artificial wickets were being considered. Indeed, Ingoldisthorpe used a concrete strip covered with coconut matting from the start of the decade and in 1937 Docking were looking at the laying of a concrete pitch covered with grass. At the 1938 Fakenham Knock-out Cup Final Dr Fisher advocated the use of matting wickets by village clubs in order to improve batting, and some clubs introduced them.

Side by side with the provision of more suitable playing areas there was an improvement in grounds maintenance equipment with the very gradual introduction of motor rollers in place of horse or hand-drawn rollers, albeit that most clubs had still to make do with the latter. Also, by 1930 aeration was recognised as a necessary part of soil conditioning and within a few years equipment could be purchased to help with this. In addition, sightscreens, practice nets and pitch markers, although in limited use by the end of the 19th century, were now being marketed to clubs although the more expensive equipment would have been beyond the means of most.

Pavilions were by no means the norm and to the extent that they existed many, perhaps most, were wooden and generally without bars, showers or even separate changing rooms. Others, similarly basic, were made of brick or concrete or even corrugated metal. Some, though, were of higher quality, particularly at country estates such as Sennowe Park where one can still see today the remains of a wooden, two-storey pavilion complete with balcony. The new pavilion at Lakenham was also an example of a more sophisticated structure. Occasionally, the appearance was enhanced by a thatched roof. These developments notwithstanding, though, it was for many years to come not unusual, in the absence of any sort of pavilion, for players either to arrive ready to play or to change behind a hedge or in the village hall or local pub.

Club finances generally seem to have been reasonably stable although occasionally it might have been necessary for one or more members to pay off a club's debts. Subscriptions continued to be the major source of income, in the range of two to five shillings but reduced for youngsters.

Remains of the pavilion at Sennowe Park. *Sennowe Park, near Fakenham, has long since ceased to be a cricket venue but this is the shell of the pavilion in use in the 1930s*

The original pavilion at Pinebanks, Norwich. *This wooden structure was superseded as a cricket pavilion in the 1960s by a more functional building. Sadly, cricket is no longer played at Pinebanks and the ground is earmarked for residential development.*

As for fundraising, whist drives were particularly popular and were often followed by dances with music provided by such as jazz bands and dance orchestras. Sometimes, clubs held a fete or a jumble sale. More unusually, there would have been a cake competition or a ballot competition in which participants would be asked to fill in a coupon listing the leading cricketers of the day in order of popularity. And some clubs might send round a collection box on match days. Frugality was still needed, with, at least for village sides, a new cricket ball expected to last from match to match until it was damaged or lost.

Generally, and as before the War, only the more senior clubs journeyed far for away games. Village teams played most of their cricket in their local leagues and that naturally limited travelling although in 1925 the Langley Park and Loddon Club withdrew from the Falcon Cup because of the distances involved. In 1934 Walsingham withdrew from the Junior Cup for economic reasons, entering instead the North Norfolk League, and in the same year Tivetshall attributed their debit balance partly to the heavy transport costs incurred in long journeys. It might have been worse but for the successful lobbying to secure an amendment to the 1930 Road Traffic Act that exempted the use of motor lorries, useful for carrying teams, from a newly-introduced tax. Wagons and bicycles were a common means of transport for such sides although senior clubs, which tended to have wealthier members, might travel by car or charabanc. Motor transport brought its own challenges; in 1921, North Elmham's journey to Gissing for a Junior Cup tie took four and a half hours because of 'motor trouble'. However, the increased mobility which the motor car brought allowed clubs such as South Norfolk and Yarmouth Town to embark on week-long tours to the East Midlands and Yorkshire. Indeed, by the end of the inter-war period some senior clubs might occasionally have Saturday fixtures as far afield as Cambridge: in 1939 Norwich Wanderers travelled to play St Catherine's College leaving from Norwich by bus at noon for the by now usual start time of 2.30 pm.

At the same time, Norfolk continued to be a popular destination for touring sides and it was also not unusual for the fixture lists of the more senior clubs to include all-day games with similar sides from outside of the county.

Women's cricket in Norfolk rarely featured in the years immediately after the war and although there were ladies' teams in Ringstead and Stow and a team run by the Norwich Union Fire Office there is no evidence that fixtures were other than occasional. Indeed, in those less enlightened times, reports from annual meetings suggested, somewhat patronisingly, that the major role for ladies within clubs was to make and serve the teas. However, following on from the national initiative referred to earlier in this Chapter, the game became more organised for Norfolk ladies. The *Eastern Daily Press* in April 1929 carried a photograph of girls receiving coaching at the Drill Hall in Norwich and in the same year a Norfolk Ladies Eleven had fixtures against Denton Ladies and Norwich Union Ladies. Woodton (sometimes referred to as Bedingham and Woodton), Carrow and Howe also fielded women's sides that year. However, the major force in women's cricket in the county, Blofield, did not emerge until a year or so later. Such was their strength that in 1934 they were reported as having lost only one of their previous 39 games and that only because illness caused them to field a weakened side. Their leading players included Alice Edrich and Alice Key. Not that the development of the women's game in Norfolk was initially well publicised; in 1931 the *Eastern Daily Press* noted that it was developing slowly and that 'many were surprised to learn at a supper dance last winter that a Norfolk Women's cricket team had existed for two years'.

By the mid 1930s women's teams also existed in Aylsham and Sennowe Park and there was another side, the Argonauts, based in Norwich. That last-named team included, in 1935, pace bowler Mary Spear who during the previous winter had been part of the successful England touring side to Australia where she had opened the bowling capturing 14 wickets at an average of 5.78 and including five for 15 in the very first Women's Test Match. Over the 1935/36 winter the Norfolk Women's Cricket Association was formed with four member clubs and in June 1936 Norfolk played its first inter-county match, versus Kent at Aylsham. Unfortunately the match was ruined by rain although, against a side including several England players, Norfolk held their own and the Kent captain Marjorie Pollard wrote subsequently that she was 'very much struck with the keenness and ability displayed'. In addition, one of the county's players, Norah Gahan, was selected to play for the Midlands against the South of England in the same year, and in 1937 three Norfolk players represented a combined Hertfordshire, Essex and Norfolk Eleven that played the touring Australians at Stevenage. Also in 1937, the men's County Club reported an increase in lady membership. However, by 1938 the county side had disbanded because of a lack of clubs.

The men's leagues continued to flourish into the 1930s. The size of these leagues almost inevitably meant that some would not survive in the longer term but others were formed around this time, including the Beck League (also known as the Flegg League), the Stalham and District League, the Wymondham District League, the Diss and District League (including sides from north Suffolk), the Lynn Cricket League, the Raynham and District League, the Downham and District League, the Erpingham Village League and the Hunstanton District League. End of season finals, sometimes played on August Bank Holiday, continued to be popular events with 678 paying spectators recorded at the 1933 final of the Mid Norfolk Village Shield when Necton beat Bylaugh and Elsing at Holt. However, league cricket was still a long way from being to the taste of the senior clubs in the county with one club's secretary, in response to a question at their 1931 annual meeting about joining the South Norfolk League, offering the opinion that 'the spirit that prevailed in league cricket was not conducive to the best interests of the game'.

Apart from the occasional midweek match, these league games were played on Saturdays and still sometimes involved a second innings or the winners batting on. However, and although the Junior Cup was still popular, the major development in competitive cricket around this time was the introduction of the midweek knock-out cups. The Fakenham, or Dr Fisher, Cup started in 1936 and by the following year had 25 entrants. Similar competitions started up around the same time under the names of the Stanfield Cup, the Kimberley Cup and the Heacham Cup. In addition, some of the Leagues – the Beck League, the North Norfolk League and the Mid Norfolk League – ran their own knock-out competitions. They were also popular with the public: 800 people attended the 1937 Mid Norfolk League final at Dereham and 700 the 1938 Fakenham Cup Final at Baron's

Hall Lawn. Their popularity was such that cups might be donated by the most distinguished of 'sponsors': Viscount Rothermere gave the cup for the North Norfolk competition and likewise the Marquis of Cholmondeley presented the Houghton Cup. Team tactics were not necessarily so popular with the field settings employed by the Bircham captain in the 1939 Fisher Cup Final – five fielders on the boundary and no slips – drawing adverse comments.

Many clubs continued to have substantial fixture lists of up to 30 games, although others, even relatively senior ones, might have no more than 20. But only in the rarest of circumstances would cricket be played on a Sunday. Ingham, for instance, played their first Sunday game in 1938.

As may be gathered from the membership of the various district leagues that operated in the 1930s a high proportion of villages had their own teams. Indeed, some ran two Saturday sides and were still able to draw players only from within their own community. Cricket would often be a social centre of a village and undoubtedly contributed towards community life.

As already mentioned, scores in village matches in the 1930s were scarcely higher than in the past. This led the *Eastern Daily Press* in 1936 to write that it was by no means uncommon for two innings each to be completed by 6 pm and for the total aggregate of runs to be less than 100. The same article also referred to a game probably played many years previously in Norfolk that started at 1.30 pm and finished within two hours with the home side having lost by an innings. A second match was then played and by 6 pm the players were on their way home. According to the article, the home umpire was a great authority on the leg before wicket law so that if the ball hit the pads between the wickets the batsman was out! He gave 28 such decisions in the two games. As this illustrates, clubs generally provided their own umpires, who might expect to be paid, and inevitably this occasionally led to disputes. Nevertheless, a motion in one League in 1931 to appoint 'neutral' umpires was lost.

In 1931 the Chairman of the Norfolk Cricket Association used his address to the annual meeting to deplore the reluctance of many clubs to finish matches, leaving off when another half an hour's play would have led to a result. Five years later, this was still a live issue with the *Eastern Daily Press* referring to lots of unfinished matches with less than two innings completed notwithstanding that it was light until after 8 pm. The newspaper linked the enthusiasm for drawing stumps to unpunctual starts and commented that 'the bane of this kind of cricket is that not every player is given the opportunity of batting, and frequent repetition of it weakens a player's keenness'.

Cricket still occasionally came into contact with the law. In 1922, the Blofield Magistrates dealt with a case arising from a fixture between Moulton and Hassingham in which the father-in-law of the Moulton wicketkeeper came onto the field of play with an axe to attack him. The player defended himself with a bat taken from a Hassingham batsman, the incident taking place just as the batsman was 'taking centre'. In 1937, the Rector of Kirby Bedon, a Revd Sidney Merrifield, was fined one shilling for hitting a lad on the side of the face in order to stop him playing cricket on the village green outside the church; the lad had apparently been 'very cheeky' but may have assumed that the playing of games was exactly what village greens were intended for.

The outbreak of war brought many changes in Norfolk. Being geographically close to Germany, the county was in the front line for air attacks and Norwich and Great Yarmouth particularly suffered. For the same reason, several dozen airfields were laid out and, this, coupled with the need to maintain effective defences against invasion by sea, meant that throughout the war a high number of military personnel were based in the county. At the same time, the local economy, especially the engineering and textile industries and agriculture, prospered.

As in the First World War there was a major reduction in organised cricket played generally and in Norfolk but, in contrast to that earlier conflict, cricket was seen as good for morale and a means of raising money for war charities. Initially, some local leagues had hoped to continue and in March 1940 the Mid Norfolk League wrote to the 43 clubs that competed in 1939 asking if they wished to enter a league. The response led to the suspension of the Shield and Boyle Cup and in their place the establishment of a three-group regional competition for a new trophy. The Fakenham Knock-Out Cup continued for that year with a reduced entry of 12 teams and a final that attracted 350 spectators. On the other hand, the Norfolk Cricket Association suspended the competitions that they organised because many cricketers had been called up and because of transport difficulties. The Association did however look at forming a pool system for the county whereby lists would be maintained of players seeking a game and of clubs seeking players. A similar arrangement was proposed for fixtures. However, it is not apparent that these initiatives had any lasting impact although, at least to begin with, a number of clubs, both senior and junior, attempted to maintain fixture lists of sorts. Nor does it appear that the competitions just referred to continued after 1940 and more generally club cricket declined further after that year before picking up again in 1944. As the prospect of peace became more real, there was established in 1944 the Norwich Fitness League comprising 14, mainly work or Forces-related, teams. In addition, and as part of their Youth Service Scheme, Norfolk County Council's Education Committee in 1943 set up a competition for youth clubs and Army Training Corps with, as an example, 17 teams in the King's Lynn and Sheringham Districts entering the North Norfolk knock-out cup.

For much of the war, though, the reported cricket in Norfolk largely comprised matches either in schools or when local sides took on teams drawn from the armed forces based in the county. Servicemen might also appear for local sides. And the Forces Elevens would sometimes include well-known cricketers stationed in Norfolk such as Ian Peebles, the Test leg-spinner who skippered an Army side against Dereham in 1940. Dereham in fact had a fuller fixture list than most clubs with 11 in 1943.

Although British casualties were fewer than in the 1914–18 conflict still 300,000 servicemen, 60,000 civilians and 30,000 merchant seamen lost their lives. Politically, the post-war years were a time of change with the election, for the first time, of a Labour Government with an overall majority and a radical agenda. Furthermore, Britain was no longer the power it had been previously and was less strong economically, basically due to the effect of the war. Rationing of commodities such as food and petrol remained in force in some cases until the 1950s.

Cricket also took time to recover. Understandably, not all clubs in the county were able to resume playing in 1946 nor did all the competitions immediately re-start. Occasionally, grounds had been dug up either to prevent them being used by enemy planes for landing or to grow crops for the war effort. Mundesley's ground was one such example (and Brisley's was another) but happily they were soon able to report that their outfield had been re-seeded, and they would not have been alone. By the end of the decade league and cup cricket had participation levels similar to those before 1939 and the senior clubs, still avoiding such competition, had rebuilt full fixture lists, including an increasing number of Sunday games. A five, or five and a half, day working week was increasingly the norm which meant that people had more time for sport and recreation, including cricket.

Nationally, a number of initiatives began to emerge, aimed at developing key aspects of the game. The MCC took the lead with the formation of the Youth Cricket Association with responsibility for providing courses and qualifications for coaches; they also published the seminal *MCC Cricket Coaching Book* as well as other material designed to improve young players' technique. Following a meeting of league and club cricket representatives in 1945 the National Club Cricket Association was formed in 1946 with the overarching aim of looking after the welfare of league and club cricket. In 1948, the English Schools Cricket Association had its inaugural meeting with the remit of fostering and administering cricket in all types of schools and at all ages. The early 1950s saw the inaugural meeting of the national Association of Cricket Umpires, aimed at improving umpiring standards at all levels of the game.

Locally, the impact of these initiatives is not altogether clear. For instance, the coaching organised by the County Club was restricted both in the period it operated – the month of April – and the numbers of young players it reached. In addition, the response to a day course organised in March 1950 by the Club and the Central Council for Physical Recreation, to include talks, demonstrations and umpiring, and followed by mass coaching and net practices and ground care, was described as 'not as good as hoped for'. In 1952, clubs in and around Diss considered setting up their own District Association with the aim of developing coaching in their area although their plans did not materialise.

In addition, the commitment of clubs to the development of young players was much less than in more recent times. Although clubs often had practice evenings during the week there was no organised coaching for young players and no systematic attempt to foster youth cricket. The approach of the Norwich Wanderers in 1949, to field a third Saturday side as a way of encouraging schoolboys, was laudable in one way but this must be seen in the context of their stated hope to make the club a nursery for 'county cricket' by which one assumes they meant the county side.

Grammar and independent schools continued to promote cricket but otherwise opportunities to play at school were much more limited. However, following the Education Committee's initiative in 1943 a youth league was set up in the Great Yarmouth area in 1947 and two years later the North Norfolk League took a broader approach to this challenge by establishing a junior section for under 18's, initially with eight teams, with games to be played on a Thursday evening; the final (at Holt) in that first year attracted 300 spectators. It even had a sponsor! The county-wide Youth Centre competition also continued to run.

There now emerged at the highest level of the game a call for 'brighter cricket' and this was echoed locally during the 1950s particularly in the light of the frequency with which 'friendly' games amongst the county's senior clubs petered out as draws. A number of those senior clubs, particularly those in the wider Norwich area, did however participate in the Festival of Britain midweek 20 overs knock-out competitions held in the last two weeks of June 1951 in Norwich's Eaton Park. The Senior competition attracted 16 entries; the Junior Cup 24. These turned out to be the forerunners of two regular competitions that ran until the turn of the century. In addition, midweek cup competitions continued to flourish elsewhere in Norfolk, with some run by the relevant league and others freestanding.

Women's cricket, in Norfolk and elsewhere, was particularly slow in its post-war recovery. However, by 1952 there was a Fakenham Women's League comprising teams from Great Snoring (founded in 1947), Helhoughton, Fakenham and District (originally founded in 1931 under the name of Sennowe Park Ladies Cricket Club) and Houghton St Giles. There was also in the 1950s the Lady Townsend Cup for women's teams in the Fakenham area. Both the Great Snoring and Fakenham Clubs reported a membership in the mid 1950s of about 18, with the former, at least, playing 15 or so fixtures annually.

In 1954, the Norfolk Women's Cricket Association was formed. This was due largely to the work of a Miss Marjorie Bradley, a member of the executive of the national Women's Cricket Association, who had had similar success elsewhere in the region. This in turn led quickly to the re-establishment of a county team with a limited number of fixtures against others in the eastern region and also Middlesex Seconds. Unfortunately, by this time interest was again declining, with the national magazine *Women's Cricket* hinting at reasons in their 1960 *Winter Annual* when referring to the very basic facilities available in the area: long grass in the outfield and scorers carrying out their duties on hay wagons with a noisy tractor in the background. It also indicated that 'underarm bowling continues to flourish although an effort is being made with the rising generation to conform to the ways of the rest of the country'. It referred, as well, to the emergence of a Norwich club which, it was hoped, would lead to 'exploration of wider fields than the local village greens', and indeed 1960 and 1961 saw that club engaged in fixtures with Lincolnshire and Cambridge. (Uncut outfields were not restricted to women's games. It was a common feature of village cricket until well after the war, restricting scores and occasionally leading to shouts of 'lost ball').

The quality of cricket pitches surfaced periodically as an issue. Two clubs at least, Fakenham and Denton, benefited from grants from the Don Bradman Testimonial Fund which enabled them to lay concrete wickets but, although others experimented with artificial pitches (including the laying of coconut matting over hardened surfaces) in the years that followed, the idea did not take on other than for practice. Indeed, in 1953, Diss decided to play on a grass wicket rather than matting, a decision that was seen as very important in that it would allow better clubs to play there. 1953 also saw a more satisfactory solution to the concern about pitches with the formation of a county branch of the National Association of Groundsmen, itself established in 1934, to cover a range of sports including cricket and open to all interested in turf culture. At the same time, the number of publicly-owned playing fields, in the county greatly increased, particularly in urban areas, and by 1957 there were over twelve hundred acres of them in Norfolk with a large number incorporating cricket pitches. Many dozens of villages across the county were also in the process of establishing their own sports grounds and in addition a number of clubs, particularly from the early 1960s, began to invest in major practice facilities. But in terms of good fortune nothing could compete with St Barnabas who in the mid-1960s won £1000 on the Premium Bonds and used it to move from Eaton Park and develop a ground at Postwick.

Although improvements in technique and playing surfaces were resulting in higher team totals there were still the occasional low scores that would be regarded with incredulity today. Most notably, Gillingham were bowled out for 0 by Beccles Caxton Seconds in 1948, the innings lasting only 52 balls. Three years later, Houghton-in-the-Dale managed only 1 against Warham; and in 1964 Little Cressingham dismissed Cranworth in 20 minutes for just 3 and then hit the first ball of their innings for the winning runs. Good individual bowling returns stood out out but nothing compared with the performances of Scole bowler Harry Howlett in 1955 when, in the space of a few weeks, he took ten wickets for 11 and, in a 12-a-side match, eleven for 21, against Diss Foundry and Wortwell respectively.

By comparison, there were the occasional reports of batsmen reaching 1000 runs by the end of June; indeed, Rufus Leggett of the West Norfolk Club (and also a county player at the time) reached the target by 11 June in 1950. Very occasionally, too, players did the double of 1000 runs and 100 wickets, a reflection that the fixture lists of many clubs were now long enough to allow this.

As already mentioned, junior leagues continued to hold their own. Numerically, the strongest leagues in the 1950s remained the Mid Norfolk League (still with its two competitions and approximately 35 entrants), the North Norfolk League (with 27 participating teams in 1956), the Norwich and District League (19 teams in 1957) and the Rudham and Sandringham Leagues (each with more than one Division). A Lynn and District League, basically for works' sides, was re-established in 1950. Some leagues were less strong with the George Beck League in east Norfolk operating with only a handful of clubs. Fixtures were usually played on Saturdays although the small Yarmouth Weekend League often featured games on Sundays. It was also still not completely unknown for league games to run to more than two innings as in the 1957 Boyle Cup match when Necton (65) defeated Castle Acre (19 and 17) by an innings.

The midweek knock-out cups that emerged before the War continued with a large number of others also being established. To name only some, the list now included the John Smith Cup, the Ashill Cup, the East Harling Cup, the Dixon Cup, the B.A. Smart Cup, the Beck League Knock-out Cup, the Briston Cup, the Cragg Cup, the S.J. Massingham Cup and the Broke Cup (set up in 1951 and run under the auspices of the Mid Norfolk League). In addition, the 1953 Coronation was the catalyst for two Coronation Cups centred on Great Yarmouth and Necton. Some were invitation cups; others by application and in that latter case it was not unknown to have over 20 entrants. Indeed, by the 1960s, as Saturday league cricket amongst junior clubs declined, these cups were the major form of competitive cricket. For example, in one year in the 1970s Narborough entered 11 such competitions reaching finals in seven of them. Initially after the war, attendances at finals remained high – 1800 attended the 1950 Dr Fisher Cup final – but gradually they fell away. For instance, the 1963 final of the Senior 20 overs knock-out competition between Carrow and Norwich Union at Lakenham was watched by only a 'handful of spectators' with the occasion arousing 'little enthusiasm'.

There were also cups played for annually by just two sides, for example, Acle and Upton competed for the Fletcher Cup. And there were the Turner and Everitt Cups in the north-west of the county and open only to teams of farm workers.

However, throughout the 1950s and for most of the 1960s, senior clubs continued to play only friendly cricket at weekends. Increasingly, this would involve games on both Saturdays and Sundays, with Saturday fixtures tending to be the stronger. At the same time, there were a few such clubs who only played on one or the other day, thereby allowing their players to turn out for two different sides over a weekend. Generally, too, these senior clubs, and also many junior ones, ran a second team. And increasingly, as the motor car became more popular, senior clubs might have round trips of 100 miles, and sometimes even further, to compete against sides of similar strength and social background. The village cricketer, though, continued to travel much shorter distances to away games and in the period following the war would rely more usually on a bicycle or, occasionally, a hired bus that carried not only the team but also spectators.

Yet notwithstanding this continuing refusal to play league cricket the local press began in 1949 to publish from time to time an unofficial table known as 'The Little League'. Devised and complied by Norfolk player Peter Powell this was based on the performance of the leading sides playing in Norfolk against one another, with ten points for a win and initially five (but later reduced to three) for a draw and the overall 'winners' being determined on an average points basis. Initially, the teams listed in the table, and chosen by Powell, were Carrow, CEYMS, Dereham, Lowestoft, Norwich Union, Norwich Wanderers, West Norfolk and Yarmouth although by the end of the 1960s Cromer, Ingham and Mallards had replaced West Norfolk.

Into the 1960s and the development of young cricketers still left much to be desired. In 1958, the *Eastern Daily Press* published an article headed 'Norfolk search for Talent in Grammar Schools not very rewarding' that highlighted four young players all of whom were educated at public schools outside of the county. The article went on to note that for many years few players from local schools advanced further than the fringe of the Norfolk side. The County Club continued to run its Easter coaching classes in Norwich although they were still generally for the benefit of members' sons. It had also formed in 1952 a Norfolk Young Amateurs side that through its fixture list, albeit for several years very limited, provided opportunities for the best young cricketers in the county to broaden their experience.

Schools continued to provide the main opportunity for youngsters to play organised cricket and although this remained relatively limited there was introduced, in addition to the cricket played in grammar and independent schools, a knock-out competition for secondary modern schools. Coaching was generally in the hands of one or more of the teachers although the more exclusive schools might employ a cricket coach.

However, clubs themselves did relatively little to develop young cricketers. This led George (that is, 'Young George') Pilch, as Chairman of the Norfolk Cricket Association, to appeal in 1960 to clubs to encourage their younger members and thereby reverse a trend towards clubs closing through a lack of young players. Whether or not in response to this exhortation, a small Bircham Cricket League was formed in the early 1960s for boys' teams in that area and attracted entrants from both cricket clubs and youth clubs.

More generally, the Norfolk Cricket Association at this time continued to run its competitions and, in 1955, pointed to its 76 affiliated clubs and a surplus of £10, as a clear indication of the forward strides it was making. On the other hand, the Norwich Thursday League was discontinued after the 1957 season through a lack of interest and entrants for the Junior Cup began to fall away as well although, as with the two 20 overs knock-out competitions, it continued until the turn of the century. In 1957, the Association also extended the maximum time allowed for Norwich and District League games from four to four and a half hours. Competitions apart, it was concerned at its 1956 AGM about the difficulty of touring sides to Norfolk getting midweek fixtures; and in 1963 it was keen to ensure that the newly-established University of East Anglia would be offered fixtures. In the mid-1960s, it also organised cricket evenings showing films from recent Test series.

Nationally, though, the cricket landscape was about to change, and almost inevitably there were consequences for the game in Norfolk.

# CHAPTER 5

# Structure and Organisation

By the 1960s, the period of austerity that followed the end of the Second World War had passed and there was a new affluence manifesting itself in major increases in car and television ownership – indeed, the possession of household goods generally – and package holidays. These more prosperous times were to continue and, particularly as a result of the 1964–1970 Labour Government, were accompanied by a period of social reform, not least in public housing and race relations, and an expansion in higher education. Dubbed the 'Swinging Sixties', the decade was also notable for what became known as the Permissive Society with its increased personal freedoms.

In Norfolk, the traditional industries referred to in the last chapter were struggling and being replaced by new employers associated with such as the off-shore oil and gas industry and a range of miscellaneous enterprises. The service sector continued to flourish in Norwich where the University of East Anglia opened in 1963. Seaside resorts were beginning to lose their attraction in the face of competition from package holidays abroad although the Broads retained their appeal.

On the face of it, this may seem an arbitrary time to begin the final chapter of this part of the history of cricket in Norfolk. However, it concided with a series of changes in cricket nationally, spread over a few short years and aimed at revitalising the game, that would fundamentally affect cricket in this country. The abolition of the Gentlemen / Player distinction after the 1962 season; the introduction of one-day knock-out cricket (in 1963), Sunday first-class cricket (in 1966) and then, in 1969, a national Sunday League; national knock-out competitions for clubs; sponsorship; and, of significance to the development of recreational cricket, the establishment of the National Cricket Association – these all took place by the end of the decade. In broad terms, the organisation and appearance of cricket in 1960, particularly at a recreational level in counties such as Norfolk, was little different from 40 years previously and would not be easily recognisable today. But the developments that took place nationally in the 1960s led to changes in the game locally that helped to create, within a short space of time, a structure for cricket in Norfolk that continued into the 21st century.

One national initiative that did not last was the single-wicket competition. Norwich Wanderers, in September 1964, ran the first such tournament in the county, when 20 of their players competed against one other. The early rounds involved a maximum of three overs each that increased to six overs for the final. The first winner was county player Arthur Coomb and the event was described as 'a successful experiment'. Other clubs followed this example but by the late 1970s it had largely disappeared from a club's cricket calendar.

Six-a-side competitions, also run over one day, featured around this time. Such an event had been run successfully in the King's Lynn area since 1955 with 18 entries in 1958. By the mid-1960s there were a small number of similar one-day competitions run by other clubs and in 1965 the Norfolk Cricket Association organised a tournament for senior clubs. They had a sponsor, too, in the form of Rothmans, the cigarette manufacturers. Whilst the wider popularity of this particular form of competition was relatively short-lived, a very few clubs continued to organise these tournaments, particularly on Bank Holidays, well into the 1990s and beyond. Great Melton, for one, still do. As a variation, the North Runcton Club ran a six-a-side midweek competition throughout the summer attracting up to 28 sides.

Locally-based midweek knock-out cups continued to run, indeed even increased. A few were organised through the relevant league although the majority remained freestanding. But in 1965 there was nothing of significance at the weekend, apart from the Norfolk Junior Cup, still organised by the NCA as a Saturday competition, although in that year there were only 14 entries. 1966 saw innings limited to 45 six-ball overs but it was, by definition, a competition in which the stronger clubs in the county did not participate. However, the example set by the national Gillette Cup knock-out competition was eventually followed in Norfolk. Although initially there was reluctance from clubs loathe to break with traditional fixtures, support grew and for the 1969 season, and with Eric Bedwell the driving force, a Sunday, 60 overs per side, competition for senior clubs, was introduced under the auspices of the NCA. There were 16 entries in that first year and a sponsor found in RG Carter, the Norfolk building firm. And so the Carter Cup was established. Dereham were the winners in that first season, beating Hunstanton in the final. The NCA established a 45-over Sunday competition for junior clubs at the same time with Great Witchingham defeating Rollesby in the final. Initially without a sponsor, by 1971 the tyre company CTS Semperit had taken on this role. By that year, too, there were 24 teams competing in the Carter Cup and 16 in the junior competition.

The two midweek knock-out cups organised by the NCA continued to flourish and by 1971 there were 18 in the senior competition and 28 in the junior one. A rule change in 1966 saw innings limited (as with some other midweek competitions) to 15 eight-ball overs – to save time and thereby help to overcome the problem of failing light – but otherwise the rules remained unchanged. There was, however, for the 1968 season a sponsor: the brewery, Watney Mann, who provided trophies to replace the H.E.Theobald and G.E.Pilch Shields.

From 1969 there was also a national club knock-out competition played on a Sunday with innings limited to 45 overs per side. There were 256 entries in the first year with the early rounds organised on a geographical basis. Those first year entries included, from Norfolk, Barleycorns, Ingham and Norwich Wanderers with the last-named progressing to the last 16 before losing to Steetley Works from Nottinghamshire. Barleycorns went one better in 1971 and 1974, reaching the quarter-finals.

Three years later, the Haig Village Club Trophy was established, also played on Sundays but in this case with 40 overs for each innings and a maximum of nine overs per bowler. There were strict rules to ensure that only authentic village teams entered but such was its popularity that in that first year there were 795 participating teams divided into 32 sub-regional groups. They included a considerable representation from Norfolk: Bradfield, East Harling, Frettenham, Great Witchingham, Hales, Harleston, Holkham, Loddon, Martham, Mulbarton, Mundford, South Walsham, Swannington and Terrington St Clement all entered – with Bradfield winning their group only to be defeated at the next stage by Kimbolton. In 1974 they reached the quarter-finals.

The unofficial 'Little League' notwithstanding, there was still not sufficient enthusiasm amongst senior clubs for a more formal arrangement. However, by 1966, moves started to be made. The King's Lynn club, concerned about playing standards and the difficulty of attracting good players, sounded out other clubs on the possibility of setting up an Anglian Cricket League involving teams from Norfolk, Cambridgeshire and Lincolnshire. That initiative came to nothing as, in the immediate period that followed, did other calls for a proper league again with the intention of raising standards, encouraging young players and generally engendering more interest. Ted Childs, a leading advocate from King's Lynn, recognised that the support for the idea was countered by what he referred to at the time as 'veiled disinterest' from other clubs notwithstanding that they might be expected to have everything to gain from it. The NCA, without throwing itself behind the proposal, indicated in 1967, through its chairman George Pilch, that it would be willing to arrange a league if clubs wanted it.

Then, in time for the 1971 season, the Norfolk Cricket Alliance was formed, not by the NCA but by the clubs involved in the 'Little League' agreeing to formalise the previous arrangement. The teams in that first season were therefore Carrow, CEYMS, Cromer, Dereham, Ingham, Lowestoft, Mallards, Norwich Union, Norwich Wanderers, and Yarmouth. Ten points were awarded for a win, five for a winning draw and two for a losing draw, and, because clubs did not all play the same number of fixtures, league positions were determined on the basis of their average points per game. 'No decision' games were disregarded for this purpose. Matches were played over 92 overs (or less by agreement) with a maximum of 47 overs available for the team batting first; unused overs were carried over to the team batting second. However, as would remain the case in both the Alliance and other leagues in Norfolk until the early 1990s, there was no restriction on the number of overs allowed to an individual bowler. In that inaugural season the winners were Dereham. The League was established with the objective of providing the member clubs with a competition in which cricketers could play 'in the true spirit of the game' and it soon drew the comment, at the Ingham Club's 1972 Dinner that it 'had provided healthy competition in the right spirit'. Umpires were also praised for adapting to the new demands on their services. For 1972, the Alliance expanded to 12 clubs with Bradfield and Kirkley joining; Sprowston followed for the following season. By the end of the following season, there were concerns that the Alliance was little more than a friendly competition with points superimposed and also regarding the points system and the merits of the 'draw' – in this last case, the argument continues – but, notwithstanding this, the Alliance would soon grow and flourish.

At a time when otherwise league cricket for junior clubs had greatly declined in the county, this initiative proved to be the catalyst for the establishment of a second league competition initially operating under the auspices of the Norfolk Cricket Association. The Norfolk Cricket Federation was set up in 1972 with just one Division, comprising 14 teams, in that first season but with the intention of expanding. Twenty-one sides took part in 1973 and necessarily because they did not all play the same number of matches – in 1972 the number of fixtures varied between four and 15 – league positions were determined on an average points basis. For the 1974 season it operated independently of the NCA as the Norfolk Cricket League with 23 teams in three Divisions. Matches involved 45 overs per innings and fixtures were now on a home and away basis. There was even talk at this time of merging the Alliance and the Norfolk League but this came to nothing.

More is written later in this Chapter about the contribution of the leagues to the development of cricket in Norfolk suffice to note here the May 1972 comment of Bryan Stevens, son of Geoffrey and cricket correspondent for the *Eastern Daily Press,* that there was no doubt that most players and spectators alike were revelling in the fun of limited overs cricket. It is hard to imagine that reaction ten years previously.

(It should be noted here that the emerging leagues, and also the major Cup competitions, were not exclusively for Norfolk clubs, with teams from

Lowestoft, Beccles and Bungay being longstanding members of the Norfolk Cricket Alliance and Norfolk Cricket League. The West Norfolk Cricket League from time to time also has members from across the county border in Cambridgeshire and Lincolnshire.)

1972 also saw the setting up of the Norfolk Fixture Bureau. Initially run by Norman Neave and subsequently by Cecil Miller and Alex Evans, it operated as an emergency service for clubs suffering from late cancellations, particularly in the days when Sunday friendlies were very popular.

Side by side with these developments was the creation of the Norfolk Cricket Umpires Association. By the mid-1960s there was in place a King's Lynn and District Umpires Association affiliated to the national Association. With Ted Childs as the driving force it ran courses under the wing of the national body as well as holding monthly meetings. A separate Norfolk Cricket Umpires Association was set up soon afterwards under the chairmanship of Eric Bedwell and within a very few years the two had joined together in one countywide Association that provided training, organised cricket quizzes for clubs and met on a regular basis. The Association also provided officials for a number of cup competitions and in 1975 was able to report that in eight years since its founding membership had grown from eight to 50. By 1977, there was a call for a panel of umpires to stand in the Alliance and this came to fruition five years later when 'neutral' umpires were introduced in its top two Divisions.

For the rest of the 1960s youth cricket, at local level, continued to be centred around secondary schools (and particularly grammar and independent schools) where, to an extent dependent on the enthusiasm of staff, inter-school games took place and a degree of coaching provided. And often, in order to ensure an appropriate level of competition, those games would be with similar schools outside Norfolk. The English Schools Cricket Association remained the national governing body for schools cricket and inter-county matches for a limited number of age groups (specifically at Under 15 and Under 19 level) were organised through county associations. The Norfolk Schools Cricket Association (NSCA) was established in 1966 and entered an Under 15 side from shortly afterwards and an Under 19 team from the late 1970s. In addition, the NSCA organised knock-out competitions for schools – in the late 1960s, these were the Calder and

Scott Chad Cups – as well as coaching sessions at Wymondham College. In 1974, it also arranged an Under 15 Cricket Festival with three other county sides.

In 1968 the MCC Youth Cricket Association was disbanded with responsibility for youth cricket being transferred to the recently established National Cricket Association. The new body quickly went about developing their role, which importantly included the development of the National Coaching Scheme and necessarily involved working together with County Cricket Associations. The winter of 1969/70 therefore saw a series of meetings between the Norfolk Cricket Association and various youth officials in the county to see whether the Association could assist youth organisations with their work. To begin with, there were no significant changes in the delivery of youth cricket locally, the lack of an organised structure at club level being illustrated by the 1971 initiative whereby the NCA's Secretary would be informed of young players leaving school so that they could be put in touch with local clubs. Indeed, in that same year, applications to play in county colts matches were still being invited from the boys themselves.

The role of the National Cricket Association was to foster and coordinate all aspects of the game below first-class level with the intention that County Associations take on this role locally. The previous paragraph gives an early example of this; in addition, and as already noted, in 1972 the Norfolk Cricket Association set up the Norfolk Cricket Federation and a Fixture Bureau. Its membership grew to 122 affiliates by 1975 although this figure tailed off in the years that immediately followed. However, the relationship between the National and Norfolk Cricket Associations was not always smooth with the first major disagreement coming in 1974 when locally it was decided that it was not to its advantage to be a member of the national body. Their response was to tell the Norfolk Cricket Association that unless they affiliated member clubs of the Norfolk Cricket Association would be barred from entering any of the national competitions. As a consequence, the County Association agreed in 1975 to advise its member clubs to affiliate. This decision was re-affirmed in 1976 following the raising of the affiliation fee from 25 pence per club to 15 pence per player!

Relationships then improved, and the Chairman's report to the Norfolk Cricket Association's 1978 annual general meeting was able to refer to the growing influence of the national Association and to recommend Norfolk clubs to affiliate to it, not least because of the immediate and longer term benefits (in terms of advantageous insurance cover, grants towards the development of junior sides and general support and encouragement) that this would bring.

In the meantime, Saturday league cricket continued to grow. By the 1979 season the Norfolk Cricket Alliance had expanded to comprise two main Divisions of ten teams each together with two further Divisions made up of the 'A' teams of those 20 clubs; and in 1982 it grew again with the creation of third divisions for ten more clubs and their 'A' sides. The Norfolk Cricket League, who in 1979 decided to play all their fixtures on Saturdays in order to avoid clashes with the growing number of Sunday competitions, had also grown steadily such that by 1981 it had six Divisions of ten sides each, including a number who in due course would reach the very top rung in East Anglian cricket: Horsford, Great Witchingham and Fakenham. Also, for the 1980 season, the West Norfolk League was formed and in that first season there were 19 clubs in two Divisions. A total of 119 teams were now playing in these three Saturday leagues each with 16 to 18 fixtures.

There were a few small leagues operating on either Saturday or Sunday: the Market Cross League in the north-east of the county, a much-reduced Mid Norfolk League, the Burgess Shield (based in South Norfolk from 1982) and the Darby and Pymoor Leagues in the west. However, on Sundays, Cup competitions were now a key feature cricket in Norfolk. First and foremost was the Carter Cup, by now with 32 entries, as well as its junior competition, both with Plates. The Carter Cup final, held on the County ground at Lakenham, was regularly attended by over 1000 spectators and was regarded as the major club cricket event of the year in Norfolk. Also, for 1979 and in addition to the CTS Semperit Trophy and the Norfolk Junior Cup (which in that year became a Sunday competition), Stanley Biss, the owner of the Vauxhall Holiday Park in Great Yarmouth, set up a knock-out competition. Notwithstanding these competitions, though, the predominant form of Sunday cricket took the form of friendlies.

In midweek, the NCA-run cups, sponsored since 1977 by Norwich Brewery in succession to Watney Mann, remained popular with 16 and

35 teams respectively entering the senior and junior competitions in 1979. These drew teams mainly from the greater Norwich area, but elsewhere in Norfolk midweek cups continued to flourish; at a conservative estimate there were at least two dozen across the county at this time, almost all played on the basis of 20 overs per side or occasionally an equivalent in eight-ball overs. And in 1983 the successful Bernard Matthews Cup was initiated.

Both King's Lynn and Great Yarmouth were centres for midweek leagues in the 1970s and 1980s with the Business League in King's Lynn accommodating over 20 sides at its peak. Unsurprisingly, they were less popular in the rural areas.

Not that this greater emphasis on competitive cricket did not have its downside. The NCA President reminded the 1979 annual general meeting that it 'tended to bring over-enthusiastic responses sometimes leading to unsportsmanlike behaviour' and he was therefore glad to note the appeal of the Norfolk Cricket Alliance chairman to clubs not to tolerate any lowering of the accepted standards of behaviour. Concerns also began to emerge about the points system adopted by the Alliance, in particular that there was too great an incentive on the team batting second to play for a draw. To counter this, in 1980 the Alliance introduced the 90% losing draw.

Around this time, the strongest sides were probably Ingham, who won the Alliance Championship three years running between 1975 and 1977, and Cromer, winners of the Carter Cup five times and the Alliance twice in the 1970s. Dereham were also a force, winning the Carter Cup three times between 1969 and 1976.

Facilities in the 1960s were still generally fairly Spartan compared with today. At the most basic level, many junior clubs had no more than a shed or portakabin for a 'pavilion', not necessarily with electricity or even running water. As extreme examples, Deopham's changing facilities were an old double-decker bus, Morley's were a converted piggery and Whittington's a former stable jockeys' quarters! Others might change in a room behind the local pub or in the village hall. On the other hand, the more senior clubs were increasingly likely to have either a newer brick building or a wooden structure that had the appearance of a traditional pavilion. These facilities generally included separate changing rooms, showers and a kitchen but only from the late 1960s did bars start to feature. Particularly, from the 1970s, some clubs (for example, Acle and Mattishall) had the use of newly-built community sports facilities that provided a centre for recreational and social activities in the town or village. And occasionally, as at Swardeston, it was the cricket club who were the driving force behind the new facilities but with support from the local community.

Scoreboards were generally made of wood with tin numbers to hang on hooks; in Sharrington's case, the numbers were hung on the outside of the pavilion toilet door! Electronic scoreboards were very much for the future and even covered scoreboxes were uncommon; except at senior club level scorers could not expect to be accommodated in a covered area. Artificial wickets were, to quote the *Eastern Daily Press* in 1980, 'foreign to Norfolk' and where they had existed (for example, at Great Witchingham and Costessey) they were replaced by grass.

Most clubs now had a permanent home on an established cricket ground be it on council or parish-owned land or on land leased or rented from a local landowner. Rarely, a club might own its ground. The security that came from these more permanent arrangements led to an increasing willingness to invest in their improvement. In this respect, sports grants were becoming more available to clubs to help them improve their facilities but for general fundraising they tended to rely on raffles, jumble sales, scratch cards, cheese and wine evenings, race nights and quizzes. For a few, a bar and a fruit machine were a major income stream albeit with the challenges that went with providing them.

Hitherto, and as already noted, the related activities of coaching and youth cricket in Norfolk had been largely left to schools together with a limited input from the County Club. However, 1976 saw the introduction of the Andy Seeley Trophy organised by the Norfolk Cricket Alliance for Under 16 teams (with ten entries in that first season and within a few years to be for Under 15 sides), an early illustration of that League's commitment to developing young cricketers. This initiative was also a reflection of the fact that senior clubs in Norfolk now recognised their role in ensuring a more structured approach to this issue. Also in 1976, two small youth leagues, for Under 14 and Under 18 sides, were formed in Great Yarmouth as well as a youth league in West Norfolk, this supplementing a schools competition in the same area.

Gradually, too, the Norfolk Cricket Association began to be more involved, recognising that to take advantage of the grants that were increasingly available for youth tournaments, coaching and coach education closer liaison was required between itself, the County Club and the Norfolk Schools Cricket Association (who continued to organise a limited number of inter-county matches for its age groups as well as other local friendlies) and also that clubs needed to participate in the events open to them. The national initiatives introduced over the previous ten years were by the end of the 1970s starting to have an impact locally.

In 1978 the National Cricket Association appointed Peter Powell as its Development Officer for the Eastern Region with particular responsibility for developing youth cricket in clubs within the area. Norfolk Cricket Association President George Pilch told the 1979 Annual General Meeting that this was 'a magnificent idea that deserved full support'. The Association itself appointed Mike Spinks as its Youth Cricket Organiser and in 1979 Norfolk for the first time entered an Under 16 side in a small inter-county competition sponsored by Commercial Union. By 1981 they had four fixtures against other counties although initially they found the opposition to be of a higher standard. For the 1984 season the Norfolk Cricket Association also set up an eight-a-side Under 13s club knock-out competition comprising 14 teams in four 'zones' with the intention that the winners go forward to the national Ken Barrington Knock-out Cup. In addition, a coaching programme for this age group was put in place.

This increased activity associated with youth cricket led to the Norfolk Cricket Association setting up a Youth Committee and in February 1987 its Chairman, Graeme Wilton, was able to report on a county-wide coaching scheme that attracted some 400 boys between the ages of 12 and 15 – soon to be extended to 9 to 11 year olds – and irrespective of ability. Indoor six-a-side tournaments were arranged between teams representing the centres that hosted the courses and additional specialist coaching was organised for those of special ability. Particularly talented boys also had the opportunity of attending regional residential courses. The County Club, too, continued to run Easter coaching sessions for the sons of members.

Schools continued to play their part. The NSCA now ran knock-out competitions at Under 13 through to Under 15 level and there were leagues for Under 13, 14, 15 and 16 teams organised geographically in Norwich, Great Yarmouth and West Norfolk. In Norwich and Great Yarmouth, a Middle Schools League and Cup competition also flourished and there were countywide competitions for Primary and Middle Schools. In addition, many primary schools entered the national Wrigley and Esso competitions.

As the 1980s came to an end Norfolk clubs began to participate in the Harry Secombe Club competition for Under 15s. By that time, Norfolk also had representative sides at Under 13, 14, 15, 16 and 19 levels, now generally operating under the umbrella of the NSCA and with a fixture list that included games against other counties primarily in the Eastern region. Not surprisingly in the light of all this activity, the Chairman of the Norfolk Cricket Association reported to the 1989 annual general meeting that the previous year had been mainly taken up in dealing with youth cricket. It was a new era in the development of cricket in Norfolk. Not that it was all about youth cricket. Following earlier attempts to form an Over 50s county side (with one participating in an inter-county competition in 1984) a team was established in 1996 that has taken part in a nationally organised competition from that year with more than its fair share of success.

The coach education programme began to take off locally around the same time with 13 coaches successfully passing the Certificate of Cricket Coaching course led by National Cricket Association coach Graham Saville over the winter of 1979 /1980 at the University of East Anglia. But despite this initial success there was no great interest amongst aspiring coaches for courses in the early 1980s. However, in 1984 the Norfolk Cricket Coaches Association was established with the general aim of improving all aspects of cricket coaching in the county and at all levels and more specifically to increase the number of coaches such that there was one in every club and school.

The 1980s saw both the Sports Council and the National Cricket Association increasingly involved in encouraging County Associations to take the lead in cricket development. In particular, there was now an expectation that they should produce Development Plans covering County

Centres, Facilities, Junior Cricket, Coaching Courses, Coaching Programmes, Umpires, Indoor Cricket and Talented Cricketers. Whilst generally, and obviously, the Norfolk Cricket Association supported the development of these areas and also the national objectives of increasing liaison between schools and clubs, providing artificial wickets and making the better use of existing facilities, increasing indoor facilities, establishing high-level coaching courses and improving coaching opportunities, and increasing income and local sponsorship, they initially did not agree that they had an overall responsibility for all facets of cricket in the county. They also disagreed with (a) the concept of designating senior clubs as 'centres of excellence', by which schools would be grouped around those clubs and (b) the idea that priorities in terms of grant aid should be based on the influence that a club could be expected to have over a larger area rather than the urgency of the need or of local interest. In short, the County Association's view was that it existed for the benefit of all Norfolk clubs. Eventually, in 1985, the impasse was resolved through the Norfolk Cricket Association accepting a wider responsibility for cricket and preparing a Development Plan to cover all the required points except the provision of 'centres of excellence' (which was left for negotiation but which by 1988 had been accepted).

Other national objectives were more readily espoused. Sponsorship, in particular, was by now very much part of Norfolk cricket with adult leagues and cups and, to a lesser extent, junior competitions attracting companies happy to be support cricket in the county. Some were national companies; others were local, ranging from major commercial or professional businesses to small enterprises. Clubs also now began to attract sponsors with the grounds of the larger ones at least displaying advertising boards. In these days of escalating costs, the contribution of all sponsors has been necessary and gratefully received.

The promotion of winter indoor leagues for adult cricketers was initially more problematic. This had been on the local agenda since the early 1980s but even in 1987 sufficient suitable venues for indoor leagues had not been identified although independent competitions were run at North Walsham, Beccles and Attleborough. However, from 1989, the Norfolk Cricket Association launched an Indoor Cup (sponsored by the Eastern

Electricity Board) with leagues based at Attleborough, Beccles, North Walsham, Swaffham, Thetford and the University of East Anglia. The league winners played off in a county competition with the overall winners going forward to the regional and, potentially, national finals. That said, this particular initiative was not long-lived although locally-organised leagues continued to run for some years in Wymondham and North Walsham. The West Norfolk Indoor Cricket League was established in 2000 and now operates with 16 adult sides playing in two divisions. More recently, indoor leagues have been set up in Breckland and Taverham and a North Walsham league re-established, together providing competition for 25 teams over the 2013–14 winter.

The modern sports hall has also provided opportunities for indoor coaching. As a result, county age group players have been able to develop their skills in an environment and at a time of year not available to their predecessors. Similarly, clubs have been able to hire these facilities in the weeks leading up to the start of a season when outside practice is neither attractive nor practicable.

Meanwhile, the Saturday Leagues were going from strength to strength. The Norfolk Cricket Alliance was now settled at three Divisions for first teams and three more for their 'A' teams. For the 1991 season, the Norfolk Cricket League also included two 'A' Divisions and the West Norfolk League had grown to 49 teams and five Divisions. That is, 189 sides altogether and drawn from 130 clubs. Sunday league cricket was confined to the Mid Norfolk and Market Cross Leagues and the Burgess Shield with a total of 36 teams in that year, almost all drawn from the county's junior clubs.

During the 1980s the balance of power in club cricket in the county shifted to Ingham and North Runcton, each winners of the Alliance Premier Division for three years in a row in that decade with Swardeston, Vauxhall Mallards and Norwich Barleycorns emerging as their main challengers. The Carter Cup in this period had a wider range of winners although Lowestoft took the trophy three times between 1983 and 1991.

In the same period Ingham, Norwich Barleycorns and Swardeston were regular entrants in the national club knock-out cup without matching the success of Norfolk clubs in the first years of the competition. Similarly, sides from the county were making less of a mark in the national village trophy in which local interest had started to wane. On the other hand, Norfolk-based Sunday and midweek cup competitions continued to be popular.

It was in the 1980s that there emerged a development amongst senior clubs that would always be seen as a mixed blessing. An issue had arisen in 1980 over four Australasian cricketers, all with first-class experience and working in the Norwich area, playing for CEYMS and Norwich Barleycorns. Although none were paid to play there was sufficient concern for the Norfolk Cricket Alliance and Carter Cup competitions to consider introducing a rule limiting the number of visiting overseas players registered with any one club. Nothing came of that, but by the early 1980s concerns were also being expressed about the number of paid players in the game locally, be they overseas or home-based. Vauxhall Mallards, in particular, recruited a series of high-quality West Indian players and other clubs, not all of the highest level, followed suit. The arguments for their engagement were that it helped to raise local standards – many have been past or future international players – and that many also coached in clubs and schools, and it was the first of these, together with the difficulty of enforcing a ban, that led the Alliance to relax its initial stance.

An argument against the engagement of professionals was that it soaked up monies that might otherwise have been spent on developing a club's facilities both on and off the pitch. It is arguable whether this would have happened, but in any event this period saw the steady improvement in the quality of pavilions and related areas, at least where clubs had the necessary control over their ground. Less high-level cricket was now being played on pitches hired from local councils, in part at least due to increased hiring fees and deteriorating facilities – both a consequence of the public expenditure cutbacks that have been with us since the 1980s and the introduction of compulsory competitive tendering for local authority services.

Similarly, those clubs that were willing and able to do so gave greater attention to the improvement of their playing areas. The dedication of dozens of club groundskeepers, in most cases unpaid volunteers, across the county led to a perceptible improvement in the overall standards of pitches with clubs also increasingly willing to invest in the machinery and materials necessary for their proper care. Sightscreens were now the norm and not just at senior clubs. A few also had wheel-on covers; others relied on tarpaulin or similar sheets.

In addition to their on-field performances, an area where a club 'professional' played an important role was with regard to coaching. In this respect, and although even as late as 1993 Graeme Wilton expressed concern that only a handful of clubs were playing their part in the development of young cricketers, the number of youth sides run by clubs increased year on year. Although not a completely accurate guide the 1989 Norfolk Cricket Association Handbook listed 36 individual youth teams fielded by Norfolk clubs including nine at Under 13 level, fifteen Under 15 sides and sixteen Under 16 teams. By 1999 the total figure was recorded as 74 with the majority at either Under 13 or Under 15 level (21 and 19 respectively). By then, four clubs also had an Under 11 side. In terms of competitions, the Norfolk Cricket Alliance introduced the Allan Bridgewater Trophy for Under 13s in 1994; the Terry Moore Trophy for Under 11s followed six years later. Other, more localised, youth competitions were also in place including the well-established West Norfolk Under 13 and Under 15 Leagues and the Reuben Hales Under 18 League that operated briefly in the early 1990s. Increasingly into the 1990s, clubs provided regular youth coaching usually, at least to begin with, at weekends.

This growth in youth cricket within clubs was essential to counterbalance the reduction in the playing and coaching of cricket in schools to which there were a number of contributory factors: a broadening of school sports activities, the reduced availability of teaching staff on Saturdays, the drop in standards of wickets (also a consequence of competitive tendering), as much as the oft-given reason of the disposal of surplus school playing fields. Cricket in state secondary schools (though less so in the independent schools) was increasingly limited to shorter midweek games. That said, the NSCA continued to organise countywide competitions: the Calder Cup (for Under 13s), the Lord's Taverners Trophy (for Under 14s) and the Scott Chad Cup (for Under 15s) as well as a schools' league. In 1996, Richard Jefferson organised an inter-county cricket festival in Norfolk, an initiative that led to the formation of the Friends of Norfolk Youth Cricket.

At County level, also, there was an increasing emphasis on developing young cricketers. The Norfolk County Youth Committee was fully established by the end of the 1980s and the years that followed witnessed a steady increase in the youth development programme in Norfolk. By 1990, ten centres for winter coaching the 12 to 15 age groups were up and running throughout the county. They involved 12 weeks of coaching followed by an indoor six-a-side competition. Then, during the summer, there were 15 centres providing coaching for six weeks for 9 to 12 year-olds. Additional coaching and team practices were also available for Norfolk's representative sides and advanced coaching, led by top coaches from the Eastern Region, was organised at a Centre of Excellence for the better youngsters in the various age groups. The Committee also continued to oversee the running of the county representative sides.

By the early 1990s there were concerns elsewhere about the reduction in cricket played by youngsters, but the growth that was already taking place in Norfolk refuted this and was underlined by subsequent developments. By 1997 and with the Youth Committee now involved in running the older age groups, there were County teams at each level from Under 11 to Under 17 as well as the Norfolk Young Cricketers (for Under 19s). Furthermore, there was now a system in place whereby every young cricketer from the age of nine to fifteen had access to a structured course of coaching within 12 miles of their home. Also, winter coaching was provided for the county squads and the Norfolk Cricket Academy, established in 1993 with the aim of producing a Minor County side completely made up of Norfolk-based players, offered coaching to talented ten and eleven year-olds.

None of the progress being made would have been possible without a development of the coaching base in Norfolk. In this respect, Norfolk was fortunate in this period to be able to call on a large number of teacher-cricketers supplemented by regional officers such as Graham Saville and Mike Dunn, the Eastern Region Development Officer, but in addition courses were now organised for aspiring coaches. Norfolk also benefitted from the arrival in the county of Steve Goldsmith and Paul Newman bringing with them skills that not only assisted the County Club on the field but also, by building on the high standard of coaching already in place, contributing significantly to coaching development off it.

On 1 January 1997 the England and Wales Cricket Board (the ECB) came into being, replacing both the Test and County Cricket Board and National Cricket Association and so providing a single body responsible for the whole game, at both recreational and first-class level. Their expectation was also that Cricket Boards be set up for each county with the intention of bringing together the leading cricket bodies in their area. In Norfolk this meant the creation, in 1997, of a Board comprising representatives of the County Club and the Norfolk Cricket Association. The overriding objective of this new body was to promote and support cricket in Norfolk with particular reference to the stimulation and support of club cricket, the development of youth cricket, the selection and development of talented cricketers and the encouragement and development of cricket coaches. (The Norfolk Cricket Association continued for four more years until it became the Norfolk Club Cricket Forum although it now had no representative role and effectively ceased to function from the turn of the century).

County Boards were to be a vehicle whereby the ECB, in particular, could channel funds to develop cricket in their counties and for that first year this amounted to a grant of just over £51,000 for Norfolk. Also, and as part of these new arrangements, full-time Cricket Development Officers (CDOs) – employed and funded by the ECB – were appointed for each county with the remit of promoting the game in their county and helping to implement the Development Plan. Norfolk's first CDO was Godfrey Batley, a schoolmaster and member of Diss Cricket Club, who would make a clear and beneficial mark in his ten years in the role.

As to Saturday league cricket the number of Divisions in each of the three leagues was largely constant, although for the end of the 1994 season the Norfolk Cricket Alliance introduced promotion and relegation between themselves and the Norfolk League. In that first season, Mattishall exchanged places with CEYMS/Gothic, and for the 1996 season Great Witchingham were elevated to the Alliance. At the top end of the Alliance, Swardeston were champions three times in the eight years to 1998; Vauxhall Mallards and Norwich Barleycorns twice each.

The constitution of the Saturday leagues was about to change, though, as a result of another initiative from the England Cricket Board. The failures of the national side led to them introducing, amongst other things, a pyramid system in recreational cricket. At the top of the pyramid there would be a county premier league, although for this area it took the form of the East Anglian Premier League. Initially (in 1999) comprising ten sides, including Norwich, Swardeston and Vauxhall Mallards from Norfolk, it expanded to 12 teams in 2009 by which time it also included, Fakenham, Great Witchingham and Horsford. The objective was that the best sides and, by inference, the best young cricket talent in an area would play at the highest possible level so aiding their own individual development and generally raising playing standards. The games start at 11 am and are played over 120 overs and have undoubtedly had the intended effect of raising standards. For a number it has been a stepping-stone into the county side; for a few, a pathway to a first-class county. Perhaps inevitably, and at least in the early days, it led to concerns of 'player poaching' but in reality it is difficult to argue with the concept provided the decision to move is that of the player and any approach does not amount to an enticement. Whatever, Norfolk clubs have been particularly successful with Vauxhall Mallards and Swardeston each winning the League on five occasions and Norwich twice.

A further, more controversial, consequence of introducing the pyramid structure was, with pressure from the ECB, the establishment of both the Norfolk League and the West Norfolk Cricket League as feeders to the Alliance, with automatic promotion and relegation, subject to meeting specified facilities and youth development criteria. For the 2004 season, this meant a streamlined Alliance with just four Divisions and expanded feeder leagues comprising ten Divisions in the Norfolk League and five in the West Norfolk League. This new structure was not universally popular and for the 2009 season, in a move that aroused emotions, the Alliance increased their Divisions to seven by inviting applications from clubs in the feeder leagues who met their criteria for acceptance.

The Mid Norfolk Sunday League has developed more smoothly. In 1998 it still only comprised two Divisions – the Shield and the Boyle Cup, with seven teams in each – but by 2002 it had expanded to 40 teams and five Divisions with two more Divisions following in 2003. For 2014, and under the driving force of their President Colin King, the League comprised 61 teams and eight Divisions as well as running their own cup competitions and the Bernard Matthews Cup. There are now no other Sunday leagues in Norfolk although non-league cricket still features; in that respect, the Friendly Alliance (with a membership in the high teens) helps to organise matches for clubs who prefer a more traditional version of the game.

The position of overseas players continued to be an issue to the extent that in 2003 the Alliance was occasionally referred to as the 'League of Nations'. However, for the 2011 season they introduced a ban on such players in all but their Premier Division.

In more recent years the Carter Cup has had to face the challenge presented by the domination of East Anglian Premier League sides but it remains the showpiece knock-out competition in Norfolk cricket and indeed in 2014 was the only one in the country played over 120 overs. There is also now the popular Sunday NACO competition run by the Norfolk Association of Cricket Officials. Other cup competitions have proved less durable than the Carter Cup with the CTS and EDP (in succession to Norwich Brewery) competitions, as well as the Junior Cup, all falling by the wayside by the turn of the century. There are fewer local knock-out cups than in the heyday of the 1970s and 1980s, although many remain, for example, the Dr Fisher Cup, Bradley Cup, Suckling Cup, Mundford Cup and Wicklewood Shield. Similarly, Norfolk clubs have shown less interest in the national competitions with only four teams entering the National Village Cup in 2014, a substantial decline from the 1970s.

This is in part a consequence of the reduction in purely village sides that in turn is linked to senior clubs running more sides; in 2014 eight Norfolk clubs fielded four Saturday teams and 11 fielded three. The number of Norfolk teams playing league cricket on Saturdays stood at 166 in 2014 (plus 12 from Suffolk) but they came from only 86 clubs.

Most adult cricket in Norfolk is played by clubs. However, particularly in the Norwich area there are a number of midweek sides playing what one might describe as 'social' cricket with rules designed to maximise involvement in the game. Often these are work-based teams or perhaps centred around a local pub.

Many older cricketers are faintly amused by the 'innovation' of 20/20 cricket, pointing out that this was the basis for the plethora of midweek cup competitions over the previous 60 years. It has, though, taken on a new significance nationally, and in Norfolk the Horsford club has successfully run such a competition since 2005. Until recently, the winners went through to the national Cockspur Twenty20 Cup and it was in 2010 that Swardeston appeared in the televised finals at the Rose Bowl ground in Hampshire. In the semi-finals they beat Wimbledon by 9 runs. Batting first in the final, they reached 129 for eight with Peter Lambert scoring 72 from 52 balls with 5 sixes. Their opponents, South Northumberland, could only manage 118 for six wickets leaving Swardeston the winners by 11 runs.

Not that this has been the only national success for Norfolk clubs in recent years. The Horsford Under 13 side won the Ken Barrington Cup in 1997 and their Under 15 team won the Harry Secombe Cup two years later. Earlier, in 1989, Thorpe Hillside Avenue Junior School in Norwich won the Wrigley Softball competition. And in 2004 North Wootton Primary School were the national Kwik Cricket champions.

Throughout this most recent period there has continued to be a substantial investment, in both time and money, in developing Norfolk's young cricketers, all under the auspices of the Norfolk Cricket Board. For 2014, there were County Age Group boys' sides at every year from Under 10 to Under 15 as well as Under 17 and Under 19 sides. All have substantial fixture lists, mainly in competition with other county sides and in some cases involving festivals and tours elsewhere in the country; indeed, even the occasional overseas tour. Together they have in recent years been successful to a degree that belies the status of Norfolk as a non first-class county, with particularly notable performances from Under 15 and Under 17 teams in 2011 and 2012. All sides have their own manager, coach and sponsor and the system is organised and underpinned by a dynamic and efficient Youth Committee.

At club level, also, youth cricket has continued to flourish. The Norfolk Cricket Alliance now require all of their clubs to run at least one youth side and to provide youth development facilities, including nets. In addition to the long-running Under 15 Trophy they created a competition for Under 13s in 1994, for Under 11s in 2000 and for Under 9s in 2009. The Carter Cup, too, established a Junior Cup competition in 2005. All this supplemented the national Under 13 and Under 15 competitions for which the county entrants competed against one another to produce a Norfolk winner who then progressed to the national stages.

In addition, the South Norfolk Community League was formed in 2007 and by 2014 comprised 49 teams in five age groups. The long-running West Norfolk Youth Cricket League now provides cricket for 18 teams from 10 clubs at three different age groups: a record entry. The Broadland Youth Cricket League is now established for Under 12 and Under 14 sides in the north-east of the county. Also, a few clubs organise their own summer cricket festivals.

Indoors, there have been winter competitions for young cricketers including the opportunity for the winners of the county Under 12 and Under 14 events to progress to the regional stages of the Lord's Taverners' competitions. Lady Taverners indoor schools competitions for Under 13 and Under 15 girls' teams also run. The South Norfolk Community League run their own winter indoor league, although the West Norfolk competition is in a period of abeyance.

Schools continue to play their part. At secondary school level, there were in 2014 six competitions, covering the Under 12 to Under 15 Age Groups, with a total of 87 entrants. Leagues for secondary schools also run in Norwich and West Norfolk. For junior schools, the major events have been the national Kwik Cricket competitions for girls and boys teams with each competition involving a county finals day for those who qualified from their local area. There is also the Under 11 County Cup, attracting four entrants in 2014.

The promotion of cricket in schools has been greatly assisted since 2005 by the Chance to Shine programme whereby the Cricket Foundation fund clubs to organise over, normally, a five-year period coaching in clusters of local primary and secondary schools, perhaps five or six of the former and one of the latter. The clubs at North Runcton, Topcroft, Hales, Bradfield, Vauxhall Mallards, Old Buckenham, Swaffham, Brooke, Norwich, Garboldisham and Dersingham have participated in this scheme to date and the Norfolk Cricket Board also run disability and girls' projects. The latest application of the scheme in Norfolk involves the establishment of 'clubs' within selected secondary schools. In 2014, there were altogether nine Chance to Shine projects in Norfolk involving over 90 schools and reaching over four thousand pupils.

Club/school links were also a key element in the Focus Club concept. Introduced by the ECB at the turn of the century, these are clubs strategically placed in each county to work in partnership with four schools and one community group. Chosen for their capacity to develop as well as their geographical location, they received priority from the ECB in terms of capital investment and general revenue support as well as more general assistance from the Norfolk Cricket Board through their Cricket Development Manager. In 2012 there were 22 Focus Clubs in the county but by then the initiative was felt locally to have run its course and the Norfolk Board decided to discontinue it.

Particularly at County Age Group and club level, it became essential to build up the pool of qualified coaches. There were only five in 1996 but following its formation the Norfolk Cricket Board set out on an intensive programme of coach education facilitated by the grants now available for this work. In 1999, the Norfolk Association of Cricket Coaches was re-established and the result was that by 2003 over 200 coaches were qualified to some level of competence, ranging from the basic Level 1 standard to Level 3. The Association itself now has approximately 180 members and has been headed since 2008 by Norfolk's first Level 4 coach, Chris Brown (who, in 2010, was also appointed as the Board's Performance Manager). Shorter courses are also organised for schoolteachers.

The Norfolk Association of Cricket Umpires and scorers, more recently re-named the Norfolk Association of Cricket Officials, continue to meet regularly and to recruit and train new members, most notably in 2010 and 2011 when over the two winters 78 umpires qualified for the first time. Many officiate in the higher Divisions of the Norfolk Cricket Alliance as well as the major cups in the county and representative matches; some stand in the East Anglian Premier League and Minor Counties Championship.

The drive to improve standards applied equally to facilities. Locally, a Grounds Association was set up in 2004 and exists to train groundskeepers and advise clubs. The Norfolk Cricket Board also appointed a pitch adviser. This has all helped to produce better wickets and outfields, as have the Norfolk Cricket Alliance's requirements and marking system. Those requirements extend to sightscreens and, for higher Division clubs, good practice facilities and also cover the provision of showers and separate changing facilities. Indeed, many clubs outside of the Alliance also now have facilities that are much improved and unrecognisable compared with those found in Norfolk half a century ago. 'Pavilions', usually brick-built, are often multi-use serving other sports and in some cases wider community activities and occasionally far removed from the traditional wooden structures, or basic shed, of the past.

Whilst clubs themselves have striven to improve their facilities, the overall situation has not been helped by the loss or deterioration in council-run facilities in Norwich, King's Lynn and Great Yarmouth, made almost inevitable by a combination of competitive tendering and financial cuts. For those who do not remember it is difficult to think that in the past they hosted the highest level of club cricket in the county.

Few of the major improvements that have taken place over the last 30 years would have happened without the support of a range of local and national grant-aiding bodies such as local authorities, the Sports Council, Sport England, the Lottery Fund, the Lord's Taverners and the England and Wales Cricket Board. Their funding has contributed to a whole range of cricket-related developments, from artificial wickets, practice nets, sightscreens, motor rollers and mowers to subsidised kit for schools and clubs and other items associated with youth development. The nationally-run Nat West Cricket Force initiative has also been a catalyst for clubs to carry out some capital works themselves, as well as the more routine maintenance jobs around a ground that are always required before the start of a season.

To meet their more routine expenditure clubs have continued to supplement match fees and annual subscriptions with a range of fundraising activities and, though not always easy to attract, sponsorship. To run a medium to large cricket club in Norfolk much greater efforts are required given they may well have an annual turnover exceeding £25,000.

Reference has already been made to the County Age Group sides run in Norfolk. At the other end of the spectrum there is now an Over 60s team that, as with the Over 50s, has an 'A' team. And for 2014, Norfolk fielded an Over 70s team.

As already indicated the Norfolk Cricket Board was by the turn of the century, and to a very substantial extent, funded through the ECB. The piper calls the tune and, as a result, and as with all County Cricket Boards, the Norfolk Board were increasingly expected to deliver national initiatives. At times, the ECB may have been a little over-zealous although in the main it is difficult to disagree with their objectives. An obvious example has been in the development of women's and girls' cricket. Organisationally and in terms of club activity, little had happened between the 1960s and the early 1990s when clubs were formed in Norwich, Great Yarmouth and King's Lynn with fixture lists of friendlies that included games against other clubs in East Anglia. There was a further initiative in the late 1990s, and in 2000 a ladies' league was established with teams from Great Hockham, Great Yarmouth, Cawston (but shortly to be re-named Horsford where they became based), Norwich (who won it) and three from Suffolk. The following year saw the formation of Ladies County side that, after playing three games, qualified for the 'emerging counties championship' in 2002. A Development Squad was also formed and, later, Under 15 and Under 13 sides, both with inter-county fixtures, and then a Development/Under 17 team. Although ladies' club sides have tended to be transitory, 2011 saw a new ladies league of five clubs: Fakenham, Garboldisham, Lowestoft, Norwich and Winterton, and now expanded to eight teams. A winter indoor competition was also introduced in early 2014 with six competing sides. And at club level, girls are now an integral part of many youth sections.

Another area that has received increased attention in recent years is disability cricket largely due to the Norfolk Cricket Board's Chance to Shine project and involving a range of indoor and outdoor activities. Efforts were initially concentrated on Special Schools where cricket coaching has been welcomed and activities such as Kwik Cricket, adapted cricket and table cricket are enthusiastically received. Inter-school competitions for each of these activities are also organised. In addition, cricket opportunities are provided to special needs children in secondary schools. The Board's coaches are also now providing an extensive programme of Kwik Cricket and table cricket at Adult Community Day Centres as well as opportunities for adapted and table cricket in charity-run centres. Many hundreds of children with special needs and adults with learning difficulties benefit from

Great Melton. *Formed only 40 years ago Great Melton moved to their parkland ground in 1993. The attractiveness of the ground is matched by their reputation as a progressive club.*

Swardeston. *Cricket on Swardeston Common, home to the county's most successful club side in recent years.*

Great Witchingham. *Great Witchingham are another example of a club that has progressed quickly over a relatively short period from playing 'village' cricket to the higher echelons of the East Anglian Premier League.*

Fakenham. *Fakenham are one of Norfolk's older clubs. They moved to their present ground in Field Lane in the late 1990's when their previous home at Baron's Hall Lawn was redeveloped.*

this work, and the longer term aim is to establish a county representative side to compete with neighbouring counties.

It will be apparent from the immediately preceding pages that much falls on the shoulders of cricket clubs, particularly the senior ones, to ensure the development of the game. In this context, more and more clubs in the county have in recent years achieved the ECB Clubmark accreditation, a quality mark for clubs that helps to demonstrate that they have in place the people, plans and procedures necessary to ensure that they have a vibrant and healthy infrastructure. Altogether, 36 clubs in the county are now accredited in this way with those clubs providing over half of the Norfolk teams playing Saturday league cricket.

In addition, and in order to comply with the national Safe Hands Policy, it has been a requirement since 2007 for all clubs affiliated to the Norfolk Cricket Board (and therefore all league clubs playing in the county) to have a trained Child Welfare Officer. It has also helped, together with other national initiatives such as requiring young batsmen to wear helmets and regulating the overs to be bowled by young bowlers, to show that cricket is a sport that cares about the welfare of its junior players.

The last part of this Chapter helps to indicate the extent to which cricket in Norfolk has in recent years become more structured and regulated. It does not cover the challenges now facing recreational cricket nor how they might be addressed. That is covered in Chapter 14.

PART TWO

# The Norfolk County
# Cricket Club

# CHAPTER 6

# An Uncertain Start
# (1826–1894)

Although matches had been played in the name of counties since the middle of the 18th century the first recorded reference to a county club as such was to Oxfordshire in 1787. Soon afterwards, the Essex County Club was formed although the next, Cornwall, was not established until 1813. Others followed, although to begin with, and for whatever reason, they tended not to be counties that in due course would be designated as first-class. However, it should not be assumed that teams playing under a county name around this time were necessarily a constituted county club. For example, the Bury Club might assume the name of Suffolk, Louth the name of Lincolnshire and Sheffield the name of Yorkshire. Locally, it is very doubtful that the 'Norfolk' side that was defeated heavily at Lord's in 1820 was a county club. Rather, the first reference to a county club appeared in the *Norfolk Chronicle* on 13 May 1826 when Lord Suffield (of Gunton Hall) and others placed a notice stating that the original members of the Norfolk County Club intended to hold a meeting at the Rampant Horse (that is, the inn of that name in Norwich) on Saturday, 15 July 1826. The object of the meeting was the formation of a cricket club in the county to play in the course of the summer at Gunton Park (the country seat of Lord Suffield), Norwich, Yarmouth and Swaffham. The notice concluded with a request that gentlemen wishing to become members apply to the original members listed at the foot of the notice.

At least one of those matches took place when, on 25 August 1826, ten members of the Norfolk Cricket Club plus a given bowler – Heyhoe of Shipdham – played Eleven Gentlemen of the Swaffham Club at Swaffham Heath. The result of this contest was a six-wicket win for Swaffham 'after an interesting game and a fine display of scientific and hard hitting'. However, it appears that the other intended matches did not materialise.

In the months that followed further meetings were held for the purpose of electing new members and making the necessary arrangements for preparing grounds at Norwich, Yarmouth and Swaffham. Lord Suffield was elected as the Club's President, Henry Hobart as secretary and Revd Philip Gurdon as treasurer. Rules were also agreed, although it may not have been until a little later that it became a requirement for all members, except clergymen, to wear at annual meetings a dark blue coat with buttons lettered NCCC and the club's motto. The rules even stipulated the jeweller in Norwich – a Mr Etheridge – from whom they were to be procured! It was also agreed to have two practice days each week and to play four matches in the 1827 season on suitable grounds near to Norwich, Yarmouth, Swaffham and Gunton, these venues being considered to be the centres of cricket in Norfolk.

In April 1827, the Norwich Cricket Club took a lease of a field at Lakenham opposite Lakenham Terrace and within the area of land that in due course became part of the larger Lakenham Cricket Ground. Henry Bentley, who had played as a batsman in matches at Lord's and was himself a fine cricketer as well as a prominent umpire and recorder of match scores, was engaged by the Norwich Club not only to coach and play but also to lay out the new ground. The pitch itself was described at the time as 'one of the best in the Kingdom'. Although it would be many years before Lakenham became the regular county ground it was here that the newly-formed County Club played its second fixture, overcoming the Norwich Club by nine wickets in Assize Week (6–10 August). Evening entertainment involved a dinner and a public ball at which 'the waltz was introduced for the first time [in Norwich] in the course of the evening but a very select few appeared inclined to join that rotating movement'. A return game with the Norwich Club took place at the end of August (when the wickets were pitched at 9 am) but was left drawn because many of the Norfolk side had 'engagements which compelled them to leave town'. It was originally intended to play this fixture at Great Yarmouth but it was moved to Norwich because theirs was a more suitable ground. A match with the Bury Club was also proposed but the only other games played in 1827 were *between* members of the County Club.

(As an aside, it is relevant to this history to mention here that there remain in existence and held at the Norfolk Record Office three scorebooks covering much of the County Club's first 40 years. The second of these records scores in the years 1833–36 and 1854–56 and appears to be the earliest surviving pre-printed scorebook in the country in contrast to a book of blank pages in which scores could be written. There are two further scorebooks at the Record Office covering the period from 1931 to 1956.)

For the following season, a ground at Hoe Road in Dereham, described as 'one of the best in the provinces', was laid out and this was the venue of the County Club's first game against another county. Lincolnshire were the visitors and also the victors by an innings and 6 runs with Norfolk totalling only 74 and 30 in their two innings.

In the same year, J. Sparkes (a 'star' bowler in his younger days but now aged 50) was engaged at £3 per week to bowl in club games and also stand as umpire. Practice matches were played at the Dereham ground and Norwich, and the County Club also had fixtures with the 'Players of Norfolk' which the 'Players' won by an innings and with the Norwich Club who also inflicted a heavy defeat on the Norfolk Club (223 and 173 to 19 and 46) in a game in which Bentley had not-out scores of 74 and 88. This was believed to be the highest individual match aggregate to that date without being dismissed although *Scores and Biographies* comments that he had 'to contend against very inferior bowling and fielding'. This comment and the two results indicate that at least in this season the County Club was far from representative and was no more than a gentlemen's club.

1829 saw a growth both in the number of county matches and the quality of the opposition. There was a trip to Lord's where Norfolk won a low-scoring game – Norfolk scored 56 and 51 to MCC's 48 and 44 – and the outstanding performances for Norfolk were Fuller Pilch's 38 not out in the first innings and Herbert Jenner's 11 dismissals (both as a bowler <u>and</u> wicketkeeper) and 20 runs in the second innings. Ten days later, Norfolk entertained Suffolk in Norwich in a game advertised as being played for £50 per side. Admission was one shilling but only sixpence for 'servants and working people'; there was also a booth and seating for ladies. In another low-scoring game won by Norfolk there were more wickets for Jenner and also for William Pilch although on this occasion the latter's more famous brother appeared for Suffolk as a result of his engagement with the Bury Club. Suffolk won the return game in the following week but when the MCC came to Dereham in August Norfolk completed the double over their famous opponents. That same year also saw the Norfolk side, which at that time drew its players mostly from the Norwich Club, take on Lincolnshire (that is, the Gentlemen of the Louth Club) and those of its own members who were Old Etonians.

Herbert Jenner was an interesting character. Born in 1806, he was educated at Eton and Trinity College in Cambridge where he played in the first Cambridge v Oxford University match in 1827. He then found his way to Norfolk at the time he was qualifying as a barrister. He was a right-handed bat good enough to score Norfolk's first individual century – 115 against Essex in 1831 – and semi-under arm bowler as well as an accomplished wicketkeeper. His all-round skills were such that he was known to bowl at one end and keep wicket at the other! He was President of the MCC in 1833 when still only 27 but very soon afterwards was effectively lost to cricket at this higher level. In 1864 he changed his surname to Jenner-Fust and lived on until 1904, dying in his 99th year.

Jenner was a member of the Norfolk Club that defeated the MCC in the home and away fixtures in 1830, again playing a major part with Fuller and William Pilch. In that same year, a side going under the name of the Norfolk Club (in one report, but Swaffham in another) but without these three (notwithstanding that the advertisement for the game indicated that William Pilch would play) easily overcame the Cambridge Town Club at Swaffham. 1830 also saw success against the Essex Club at Dereham with the published scorecard referring to this as a game between the Gentlemen of the two counties.

In 1831, again with the three Pilch brothers and Jenner, Norfolk returned to Lord's and lost by seven wickets to a particularly strong MCC side. A contemporary report says that at the start of the match the betting was 6 to 4 on a MCC win. The return fixture, at Dereham, again saw the MCC victorious, bowling the County out for 11 (Norfolk's lowest-ever score) and 38, but notwithstanding this it was in 1831 that the Norfolk County Club was described in the *New Sporting Magazine* as in effect the next best side in England after the MCC. On the face of it, this was an indication of the progress made by Norfolk cricket after its unsteady start although the reality is probably that county clubs elsewhere in the country were generally not so developed.

The comment in the *New Sporting Magazine* also masks the fact that the County Club was then essentially an amateur side that frequently did not contain any paid players. However, in 1833 and 1834 three matches were played by a side under the name of Norfolk against the newly-formed Yorkshire County Cricket Club. These sides included professionals, most notably Fuller Pilch, and were not put together by the official County Club. 1833 saw the first of these matches, at Sheffield. Indeed, it was the first time that Yorkshire had taken the field under that name although then and for some time afterwards they were not organised in any way and most of their players came from Sheffield. In the 1833 fixture Fuller Pilch, his two brothers and eight others were unable to prevent a home victory by a margin of 120 runs. A return fixture was arranged for the following year when the venue was described as 'the New Ground at Norwich' – presumably the ground laid out by Bentley in 1827 – and on this occasion Norfolk triumphed by the wide margin of 272 runs – 215 and 191 to 37 and 97. Fuller Pilch took the batting honours with scores of 87 not out and 73, both unusually high individual scores for the period. The last of the three games took place later in 1834, back in Sheffield. Yorkshire batted first and scored 191 to which Norfolk replied with 75. In their second innings the home side reached 296 leaving the visitors to score 413 to win. By the time the rain came, with Norfolk on 289 for 7, the match had already lasted for five days, an exceptional length for a game at that time. Equally exceptional were Fuller Pilch's second innings score of 153 not out and the total of 128 extras in the game! One report of the game suggested that Norfolk 'gave up the match'; another indicated that it was awarded to Yorkshire and, as the report continued, 'the stake money was paid over'.

Also, in 1833, there were fixtures against Swaffham and Norwich. Although again some reports indicated that the first of these games involved a Gentlemen of Norfolk eleven this in fact was perhaps no more than a recognition that the County Club was simply a club for gentlemen cricketers. In the same year, a Gentlemen of Norfolk side went to Lord's to play the MCC although, embarrassingly, three of the Norfolk side failed to appear and the match was consequently reduced to eight-a-side. Similarly in 1835 (for which season William Pilch was engaged as a player and umpire), there were two fixtures with Hingham, both won by the County Club although again there is evidence in the match reports and scorecards that the names of the County Club and the Gentlemen of Norfolk were sometimes used interchangeably. In the second, there is an early reference to a player being dismissed as a result of handling the ball, Norfolk's Henry Knatchbull being the unfortunate batsman. (Also round this time, the Norfolk Club/ Gentlemen of Norfolk played matches against the 'Players of the County'; presumably, the respective team names reflected the conventions of the day with "Players of the County" being professionals and unpaid players not of sufficient social standing to be regarded as "Gentlemen").

By 1836, Fuller Pilch had moved to Kent to be the coach and groundsman at the Town Malling club as well as the landlord of a local tavern. Nevertheless, he appeared in a further fixture with Yorkshire, again played in Norwich. The visitors won a low scoring game by 24 runs despite William Pilch's 12 wickets. A return match, the last in this series of fixtures with the White Rose county, took place at Sheffield later that summer with Norfolk – although this again was not the official County Club – winning a low scoring game by one wicket. This was Fuller Pilch's last game for Norfolk for some years and this chapter in his career unfortunately ended with two ducks. By this time, though, he was playing regularly for Kent, MCC and England and establishing a reputation as the best batsman in the country.

Together with Lord Suffield's premature death in 1835, Pilch's departure appears to have been the catalyst for a decline in the County's fortunes. Between 1835 and 1843 there are records of games, played in the name of Norfolk, against Hingham, the Players of Norfolk, Litcham (won by the village side), Cambridge Town, and Swaffham. Generally, Norfolk were second best and in 1840 Knatchbull, now Treasurer, referred to the Club 'having to all intents and purposes ceased to exist'. Fuller Pilch reappeared for the county in 1844, in a game at Lord's against the MCC and made a major contribution to Norfolk's 30-run victory. The scorecard for that game recorded the odd dismissal of the MCC tailender, H. Raymond Barker, as 'left his wicket thinking he was bowled by Rippingall 0'. The return fixture at Swaffham, in which Fuller Pilch also played, brought a ten-wicket win for Norfolk, bowling MCC out for 19 and 32. *Scores and Biographies* recorded that 'the MCC had a great "tail" to their Eleven, several good ones not coming'. It seems that this was not an uncommon feature of their return matches played away from Lord's.

However, there is a further complication in that there is a suggestion that from the late 1830s two sides went by the name of Norfolk. Firstly, there was one based in Norwich but in addition it seems that the Swaffham Club may occasionally have used that name. For instance, the *Norfolk Chronicle* headed their report of the 1847 game versus the MCC on a 'new ground' in Swaffham as being against that town but the body of the report and the details reported in the following week's edition of the paper indicated that the game was with the county side. Certainly, the Swaffham club appear to have been the stronger in this period.

The Norfolk Club resumed their poor run in 1845 when Cambridge Town bowled them out for scores of 22 and 24 and not even Fuller Pilch could prevent two innings defeats inflicted by the MCC.

The best of Norfolk's regular players at this time was Charles Wright. Born in Rougham in 1812, he was described as a 'very fine fast round arm bowler' with a high delivery. So high, in fact, that in 1845, before the legalising of overarm bowling, he was no-balled several times in the MCC match at Lord's. He was also a reasonable batsman occasionally batting as high as first-wicket down. By profession he was a solicitor as well acting as a coroner. Unfortunately, though, his performances could not prevent the decline in the county's fortunes in the 1840s that came to a head at Swaffham in 1848 when they lost to a team from Essex by the name of the Auberies. The visitors played with only nine men, albeit that this number included John Wisden, in due course to become famous for producing the annual cricketers' almanack and at that stage an outstanding bowler. Norfolk scored 79 and 29 for 8 to the Auberies' 101 and then 'gave up the match' with two wickets to fall.

Generally, Norfolk now played their home games – such as there were – at Swaffham although Holkham Hall was the venue for the 1847 fixture with the MCC. The county side in that game included the Earl of Leicester, who himself was a good cricketer, and also James Grundy who had been engaged by the Earl at Holkham and was embarking on a successful all-round career with Nottinghamshire and the travelling Elevens. It was written of Grundy that he always acted as his own statistician, keeping a mental note of his analysis throughout the innings. He was also said to be 'very fond of mutton chops, particularly the fatty bits which he cut off and devoured with gusto'! Grundy also appeared for Norfolk in their 1848 game against the MCC at Swaffham and on this occasion John Wisden played for the county as a 'given player', taking 14 wickets.

Apart from games with the MCC and Cambridge, there was little cricket played in the name of the County Club in the 1840s. Indeed, some authorities state that the Club went out of existence in 1848. This may well have been the case although in the immediately following years the occasional match was played in Norfolk's name. In 1849, the MCC were entertained at Swaffham by a side of nine Gentlemen of Norfolk and strengthened not only by Grundy but also Daniel Day, a professional who played his representative cricket with Surrey, Hampshire and Dorset. However, their inclusion could not prevent an MCC win by 86 runs with their own bowlers, William Lillywhite and James Dean, bowling unchanged in both innings. Similarly, in the following year, there was just one game, also at Swaffham against the MCC. The Norfolk side triumphed, with assistance from not only Grundy but also William Buttress, a professional bowler from Cambridge. Buttress, a right-arm slow to medium pace leg-spin bowler was recognised as one of the best bowlers of his day and, like others in the days before player registration and qualification rules, turned out for a number of different counties, in his case as far apart as Devon and Durham.

In 1851 the only match played in Norfolk's name was also versus the MCC but this time at Holkham Hall. The Earl of Leicester again appeared for the home side but for this fixture Grundy represented the visitors and, with 13 wickets, was instrumental in securing a four-wicket win for his side. This game marked the county debuts of Nottinghamshire-born brothers Robert and John Gibson who accounted for 11 of the 16 MCC wickets taken. This turned out to be last match played in the name of the County Club for 11 years although in that period games were played by the Gentlemen of Norfolk against such as I Zingari and the Gentlemen of Suffolk. In one of these fixtures, against the Gentlemen of Suffolk at Stowmarket in 1855, Wright took 15 wickets but his side still lost heavily.

None of this is to say that Norfolk were alone in their decline. For instance, the Cambridgeshire Club also appears to have folded around the same time. Indeed, the loose nature of county organisations, which often fell short of what ordinarily might be recognised as a 'county club', meant that many ceased to operate. The competition from the wandering professional elevens compounded this.

However, in May 1862 a meeting was held at which it was agreed to re-form the County Club with Thomas Bagge elected as captain and secretary. Lord Suffield told the meeting that he did not believe a county club had existed for 30 years, although the evidence points to this being an exaggeration. The *Norfolk Chronicle* reported the first game of the resurrected club as taking place in July 1862 against Cambridgeshire when Norfolk overcame their neighbours by an innings and 331 runs with Herbert Salter scoring 113 (out of a total of 442) and taking seven first-innings wickets. (One should note that *Scores and Biographies* recorded both this match and a return fixture four weeks later as being played between Gentlemen of the two counties, and Haygarth also stated that the County Club was not re-established until the winter of 1863–64. If that is correct, then the re-formed club did not play its first game until April 1864 when they travelled to Fenner's to take on the 'Undergraduates of Cambridge', or Cambridge University as they would be known today. In a two-day match, the county had much the worse of a draw. However, it is difficult to accept Haygarth's comment in the light of the clear decision in May 1862 to re-form the Club).

There followed Norfolk's first game at Lord's since 1846, which the *Norfolk Chronicle* stated was the first time that Norfolk had met MCC and

Ground (as they were now called for such games) as a county club. The home side won easily, dismissing Norfolk for 20 in their second innings. Wright, at the age of 52, appeared for Norfolk and captured seven wickets. Top scorer for the county, with 36 in the first innings, was Henry Gale, another amateur who also played a few games for Hampshire. The return game at Dereham was much closer with the visitors winning by only three wickets, although their eleven was not their strongest. The two Norfolk players who came out of that game with most credit were opening bowlers George Figg and Thomas Curteis. Curteis, from Shelton (near Long Stratton), was still at Cambridge University where he obtained his cricket blue in 1864 and 1865. Later, he entered the Church of England and played for Suffolk and Cheshire in addition to the county of his birth.

These bowlers' success continued in 1865. In their first match of that season, Norfolk defeated the Cambridge Undergraduates by 26 runs with Figg and Curteis capturing all the wickets that fell to bowlers. It will be noted that Curteis chose to play for his county against his university, as did three others in the county side. Later that summer, Norfolk returned to London but were heavily beaten by MCC and Ground. The return match, at Dereham, also went the way of the visitors. The same year also saw a game against Lincolnshire although the *Norfolk Chronicle* and *Scores and Biographies* again differ on whether this was a county club or 'Gentlemen's' match as they were to do in some of the fixtures referred to in the next paragraphs.

The following season, for which the captaincy had passed from Bagge to Robert Gurdon, opened with a seven-wicket reverse against Cambridge University despite seven first innings wickets for Figg, and was followed by the now regular home and away fixtures with MCC and Ground and matches with Lincolnshire and Suffolk. Around this time, too, the County Club also organised games between the East and West of Norfolk and even 'Old' versus 'Young'.

Increasingly, clerics appeared in the county side. Altogether, five different Anglican ministers appeared in their three 1866 matches, this in addition to Curteis and another future cleric, Edward Fellowes from Lingwood. Born in 1845, Fellowes was also an Oxford Blue and an accomplished allrounder. On the occasion of his debut, in the second MCC game, he top-scored with 57 not out and took six wickets. Two of the 1866 games deserve comment. The victory against Suffolk, by 12 runs, was the first win by a 'Gentlemen's' side over the county neighbours; and the defeat of Lincolnshire by an innings and 310 runs, helped by their opponents batting two short in their first innings and four short in their second innings, included outstanding individual performances from William Collyer (160), Revd Charles Cooke (94) and Fellowes (73 and eight wickets).

1867 and 1868 brought two more sets of fixtures with MCC and Ground. Only the 1867 home game was won, and individually there were few Norfolk performances to cheer although Fellowes captured 12 wickets for 75 runs in that victory. In addition, in the 1868 game at Lord's, Thomas Mack, in his first game for Norfolk, finished off the MCC's second innings with four wickets in four balls – all bowled – although this was not enough to prevent a heavy defeat. These two years also saw 'Gentlemen's' fixtures with Cambridgeshire, Essex, Lincolnshire and Suffolk with mixed results. Noteworthy individual Norfolk performances in 1867 included those 12 wickets for Fellowes and a century for him against Lincolnshire; and in 1868, 99 by Revd Charles Brereton against Essex, 13 wickets (including nine first-innings wickets for 36) for Fellowes in the return fixture and a further 12 wickets for him versus Suffolk. Home games were played at Dereham.

By 1868 the Club was struggling and in the close season it was reported that its officers held out no hope that it could carry on and that 'the persistent apathy of those who call themselves members, many of whom have failed to pay their subscriptions, has left the Treasurer with a large amount of debt and no hope of being able to meet them'. It was therefore decided that the Club should fold and that subscriptions already collected for the 1869 season would be applied to meet the debt of £40 owing to the Secretary and Treasurer. The hope was expressed that the club would be revived, although the *Norfolk Chronicle* in June 1869 referred to the dis-establishment of the County Club and indicated that it was the Gentlemen of Norfolk who played matches that season against Essex, Suffolk and MCC and Ground.

In August 1869, 22 of the county played host to the United South of England Eleven. The visitors were another of the touring elevens, brimful with the leading professionals of the day, who travelled the length and breadth of the country against 'odds' and on this occasion, the United South Eleven included Henry Jupp, Edward Pooley, George Griffith, James Lillywhite, Heathfield Stephenson and James Southerton all of whom had very substantial first-class experience. Notwithstanding the undoubted quality of the visitors, the Norfolk side prevailed by 13 wickets after bowling out their illustrious opponents in their first innings for a mere 33, with nine wickets for Revd Curteis. Norfolk replied with 172, Curteis top-scoring with 32, and although the United South Eleven fared better the second time around the damage had been done.

As an indication that the County Club no longer existed the Dereham Club took over the county ground in the town in 1869. Furthermore, the advertisement for the 1871 game against MCC and Ground, as well as naming the home side as the 'County of Norfolk', also stated that only Dereham members would be admitted for free. If there were still a properly constituted County Club, with its members paying a subscription, they might also have expected free admission. Rather, this and other 'Norfolk' games at this time appear to have been played by a group of gentlemen cricketers coming together from time to time.

As already mentioned, the Norfolk Club was not the only one to hit troubled times in this period. However, and by way of contrast, the 1860s and 1870s marked the emergence of what are known today as the first-class counties. By the early 1870s, nine counties regularly competed against one another and the concept of a 'champion county' was recognised. The counties concerned were Derbyshire, Gloucestershire, Kent, Lancashire, Middlesex, Nottinghamshire, Surrey, Sussex and Yorkshire. But, sadly, no Norfolk.

Between 1871 and 1875 there were no games played by a Norfolk County Club; instead, such 'Norfolk' games as took place were in the name of the Gentlemen of Norfolk. The next reference to a Norfolk county game is in July 1876 when they took on the Essex Club at Brentwood, the game ending in a draw but with Norfolk, without clerical assistance, holding the upper hand. Within a week, the county side were entertaining Suffolk at Dereham and triumphing by ten wickets. This was notwithstanding that their number ten batsman in the first innings was recorded as 'absent when play was called'. Later in August, Dereham was again the venue for a match with MCC and Ground, with *Wisden's Almanack* for the year commenting that 'it is pleasant to find this good old annual not yet pushed from position in MCC's programme by more modern or pretentious fixtures; and equally pleasant is it to record the old County settling MCC and G in one innings with 18 runs to spare'. The only reverse that season followed at the end of August when Suffolk avenged their earlier defeat.

However, whilst the records suggest that these were county games, it appears from a development in October 1876 that they did not involve a formally constituted county club. This is because there was then a meeting at the Royal Hotel in Norwich when 'a number of gentlemen interested in cricket' convened to 'consider the advisability of reviving the Norfolk County Club'. Robert Gurdon was elected as chairman and the then Lord Suffield as president. The meeting was also informed that Lord Suffield would be willing to make available his ground at Gunton and that Mr Gurney Buxton also agreed to lend his ground at Catton Park although the latter was of the view that the Club should have a ground where they could have a good professional. The chairman advised the club to have no regular ground for the first year but to play matches at Dereham, Gunton, Norwich and elsewhere in order to see which they liked the best and which was likely to attract most members. He was also of the view that they would not find a professional who was worth the expenditure that having one would involve. The report of the meeting closed with the comment that a committee was formed and a number of gentlemen enrolled as members of the Club.

In that first season of the reconstituted club, 1877, there were games against Suffolk, Essex, MCC and Ground and I Zingari. Another fixture, with a Cambridge University side, was unfortunately called off because Norfolk could not raise a team. Two new venues were used in this season – Garboldisham and the Norwich Club's ground in Newmarket Road. The best individual performance came from Charles Tillard when he captured 15 wickets for 60 in the home game with Essex. Henry Birkbeck was also forcing his way into the side. Described in one source as a 'capital batsman' he had, in 1875, scored a century for Gunton against I Zingari. He went on to captain Norfolk and, for a short while in the early 1880s, to act as Secretary.

At the end of the 1877 season, a meeting was called to consider the establishment of a county ground. The preference was for somewhere in Norwich although the sum of £20 was paid for the right to continue using the ground at Dereham for county games, and this was the venue for the 1878 fixtures against MCC and Ground and Suffolk. At this point, the County Club benefitted from the generosity of Jeremiah Colman. Without being an outstanding cricketer himself, although he was a member of the Colman family eleven of the 1840s, Jeremiah Colman was better known as the Member of Parliament for Norwich from 1871 to 1895, a philanthropist and, of course, a member of the famous mustard family. Indeed, it was Jeremiah Colman who oversaw the major growth in the family business in the second half of the 19th century. But he was also a supporter of cricket and he provided the answer to the search for a new county ground by setting aside a part of his estate in the city for recreation, this being land that the Colman family took over when they moved from Stoke Holy Cross in the 1850s and which included the original Lakenham ground. In addition to foregoing the rent for the land, he enclosed it and kept the ground in good order at his own expense. By 1879, the ground was being described in the *Norfolk Chronicle* as 'the beautiful cricket ground at Lakenham' with a splendid new pavilion for which much credit was due to the builder, a Mr Rogers of Chapelfield Road in Norwich, and the groundsman, Robert Chadwick.

The Norwich Cricket Festival was held for the first time in 1881. Following the trend set by some of the country houses in the county and indeed county clubs elsewhere in the country – for example, Canterbury and Cheltenham – the County Club set aside a week in early August when a number of county fixtures would be played at the Lakenham ground. In that first year, there were games, all won, with the South East Circuit, Lincolnshire and MCC and Ground and the whole week was reported as a success. The *Eastern Daily Press's* report of the first day of the first match was that it was all that 'could be desired', over 1000 spectators were present, the ground was in 'splendid condition' and the Carrow Band played some 'splendid selections'. It was, no doubt, the Cricket Week, together with the Club's on-field success, which encouraged the *Norfolk Chronicle* at the end of the season to express the hope that Norfolk would soon take their place 'against the leading cricket counties in England'. Indeed, at the AGM in the following Spring it was reported that a number of the major counties such Hampshire, Surrey and Sussex had been challenged although these names did not appear in the fixture list when it was subsequently published.

To assist the County Club in picking the best available side matches were arranged between sides representing the east and west of the county; the First Eleven against the Next Sixteen; and the Colts of the City (that is, Norwich) and the Colts of the Country. Later, in 1890, the County Club began to run a Club and Ground side, in effect a Second Eleven strengthened by one or more of their professionals. And it was in the 1880s that the County Club decided to organise a Challenge Cup competition for Norfolk teams, to be followed by a Junior Cup and Shield competitions for schools (see also Chapter 3).

Results began to improve. In this respect, Norfolk were able to call on the services of a number of very capable amateurs, not least two of the

The Norfolk County side that played Leicestershire, 1883. *Norfolk won by an innings and 48 runs. Included in the team group are the captain H Birkbeck (cap and blazer in the back row), Revd AP Wickham (in front of him) and the brothers CJE and LK Jarvis.*

four Jarvis brothers who represented Norfolk, the most accomplished of whom was Lewis (but known as 'Kerry') Jarvis. Hailing from Middleton, he was a triple Blue at Cambridge University and on returning to Norfolk he played an important role in the County Club's renaissance. Stand-out performances, all against MCC and Ground, were 78 not out (out of a total of 147) in 1881; 103 and 131 in the two 1883 fixtures, in a season when he also topped 500 runs for Norfolk; and 181 in the famous 1885 contest detailed later in this Chapter. The first of the two 1883 centuries also deserves special mention. Norfolk had followed on 116 behind but, led by Jarvis, totalled 366 in their second innings and then bowled out their hosts for 98 to win by 152 runs. He clearly had a liking for the MCC attack, scoring exactly 100 against them for Middleton Tower in 1884.

Charles, his brother, was no mean cricketer either, good enough to score 130 in the 1885 game at Lords. He was also a handy bowler and served as both captain and Honorary Secretary of the County Club, in the latter case jointly with Sir Kenneth Kemp in the 1880s.

Kemp was born in Erpingham and went to school in Canterbury where Fuller Pilch coached him and gave him a bat inscribed with the words 'with Fuller Pilch's love'. He played a little for Cambridge University but, unlike some other Norfolk players of the period, did not win his Blue. He represented the county from 1877 to 1885 and was Secretary until 1889. He also played for Suffolk. For many years around this time he ran an amateur theatrical company which performed at the Theatre Royal in Norwich during the annual Cricket Week. He later practised as a barrister and was also a banker.

Other notable amateurs of this period included Ernest Raikes, born in Carleton Forehoe in 1863. Also a barrister by profession, he was described as a 'good average batsman' as well as being a successful slow bowler who later played with some success in India. In the 1888 game with Hertfordshire at Lakenham he took 17 wickets – eight for 47 and 9 for 44 – the best match figures ever returned for the county side. In seven matches in that season he captured 58 wickets altogether. Later, in 1897, he took 6 for six against Cambridgeshire. Previously, against MCC and Ground in 1886, he returned figures of four for 11 and six for 33. There was also Philip Morton, right-arm fast bowler and lower-order batsman from Tatterford, who was a Cambridge cricket Blue in 1878, 1879 and 1880. (In the first of those years he and Kerry Jarvis were members of a very strong Cambridge University side that included amongst its 100% record in first-class matches an innings victory over the touring Australians in which Morton returned match figures of 12 for 90). His career in school teaching limited his cricket after graduating but he stayed long enough in Norfolk to take seven for 15 and seven for 43 against MCC and Ground in 1881 and altogether 29 wickets in three matches that season at the phenomenally low average of 4.45.

There were also, as one might expect for the times, some impressive cricketing clerics including Revd Arthur Davies, an allrounder good enough to score 70 and take five for 18 against MCC and Ground in 1884, as well as 120 versus the same opposition in 1887, 143 versus Hertfordshire in 1888 and 126 versus Bedfordshire in 1891. More famous was Archdale Palmer Wickham. Born in Surrey in 1855, on leaving Oxford University he became a priest in Norwich and stayed – and represented the county side – until moving to the South West where, as well as carrying out his religious duties, he played 82 games for Somerset. He was recognised as an outstanding wicketkeeper both for Norfolk and Somerset.

There were professionals, too. Fred Rudd, from Briston, was a fast medium left-arm bowler who represented Norfolk between 1883 and 1890 and whose best match performance was seven for 38 and six for 14 against Staffordshire in 1886. In the second innings of that match he and Tillard bowled out the opposition in half an hour for just 18, the lowest score ever recorded against Norfolk. Jack Hansell, from North Elmham, was a left-handed batsman and fast-medium right-arm bowler, who played for Norfolk between 1884 and 1890. His best performances were 136 against MCC and Ground in 1885 and seven for 25 versus Suffolk a year earlier.

George Rye was born in Norwich and engaged as a professional firstly by the Norwich club in 1877, then for eight years by the County Club and after that by Norwich Grammar School where he coached Geoffrey Stevens. He was also for some while the landlord of the Freemasons Arms in Hall Road, Norwich. He, too, was a medium-paced bowler with a best county performance of eight for 34 against Lincolnshire in 1891. Altogether, he represented Norfolk from 1878 to 1895, taking 272 wickets in all games, and received a benefit of £50 (roughly £4,500 in today's money) in 1894. He also umpired in the Minor Counties Championship from 1895 to 1932.

The County's growing fixture list in the early 1880s also demonstrated that the Club was moving forward. Fixtures against MCC and Ground, usually still home and away, continued to feature as well as games against other counties in this part of the country. Lakenham was also now firmly established as the County Club's home ground .

1882 saw a fixture as part of the Norwich Cricket Week against an 'Eleven of England'. Their title rather overstated their strength but they did include, amongst a number of reasonably well-known players, Arthur Shrewsbury who was considered in the 1880s and early 1890s to be the best professional batman in England, indeed the next best batsman, professional or amateur, after W.G. Grace. He did not disappoint with a second innings score of 63 (out of 222) but this was not sufficient to prevent a Norfolk victory by ten wickets after Morton and Tillard had bowled out the visitors for 37 in their first innings and the hosts had replied with 211. The *Eastern Daily Press* at the time described Norfolk's performance as the 'most creditable victory the county has ever obtained'.

For the games in the 1882 Cricket Week, admission to the ground was sixpence and to the seated enclosure, one shilling. There was an extra charge for carriages and a separate enclosure provided for members. The Carrow Band also played on three days, by kind permission of Jeremiah Colman. For the 'Eleven of England' game over 1000 spectators attended on the first day, and for other games that week several hundred were present on any day. The consequence of this support was a financial report to the AGM in the Autumn which showed income for the county that season exceeding £420 compared with £230 in the previous year. There was still a deficit of £23 but this was due to a considerable amount of one-off expenditure. The AGM also noted that the Lakenham wicket had played well.

Three years later, the first day of the game at Lakenham against MCC and Ground attracted 2000 spectators even though the weather was dull and cold. This was put down to the reduced admission charges which were half of those just quoted although it now cost one shilling to sit in the members' enclosure, two shillings and sixpence to bring a four-wheeled carriage into the ground and one shilling for a two-wheeled carriage. It was also suggested that the record score at Lord's detailed in the next paragraph helped.

As the decade progressed, fixtures were also obtained with a number of counties that in due course became first-class. Essex have already been mentioned, but they were joined by Leicestershire (1882), Northamptonshire (1883), Hampshire (1887) and Derbyshire (1890). These games had their highs and their lows but the 1885 visit to Lord's to play MCC and Ground was one of Norfolk's finest hours. Batting first, Kerry and Charles Jarvis opened up with 241 for the first wicket. Hansell then added 113 with Kerry. Henry Birkbeck contributed 89 not out and Norfolk finished with 695. It was only a two-day game, and this ensured that the MCC saved it. The hosts' bowling attack was not particularly strong but nonetheless this was a fine achievement and indeed was to that point the highest score recorded in a match at cricket's headquarters. The full Norfolk scorecard reads

| | | | |
|---|---|---|---|
| L.K. Jarvis, Esq | c Hearn | b Price | 181 |
| C.J.E. Jarvis, Esq | c Hearn | b Smith | 130 |
| Hansell | c Hay | b Wilson | 136 |
| Revd C. Kennaway | c Wheeler | b Mycroft | 39 |
| C.H. Morton, Esq | c Wheeler | b Mycroft | 16 |
| H. Birkbeck, Esq | not out | | 89 |
| Revd A.P. Wickham | c Mycroft | b Fothergill | 0 |
| J 'Blunt', Esq | b Fothergill | | 2 |
| F.E. Patteson, Esq | st Wheeler | b C. Wilson | 31 |
| A.M. Jee, Esq | c Smith | b Mycroft | 14 |
| Rudd | b C. Wilson | | 19 |
| Extras (26 byes, 12 leg byes) | | | 38 |
| Total | | | 695 |

(This scorecard reproduces the style of the day in referring to the two professionals simply by their surnames with the names of the amateurs more politely recorded. The reference to J 'Blunt' also requires clarification. He was in fact Charles Gurdon. One can only speculate as to why an alias was used although this was not unheard of in Victorian times. Indeed, one of the MCC team also appeared under an assumed name!).

The boot was on the other foot two years later when Norfolk travelled to Southampton to play Hampshire. In this, their first game against their southern opposition, the hosts prevailed by an innings and 342 runs. Indeed, Norfolk's scores of 77 and 139 were easily surpassed by the Hampshire batsman F.E. (later Sir Frederick) Lacey who hit 323 not out – at that time, the highest individual score made in a match between two counties.

By the late 1880s, there were only eight first-class counties, Derbyshire having dropped out in 1887. There was increasing interest in their performances with the *Eastern Daily Press* carrying full reports even though the nearest competing county was 100 miles away. This general interest encouraged other counties to aim for elevation to the first-class family – a number of 'minor county' clubs were established around this time – and to foster this *Wisden's Almanack* decided from the 1888 season to rank these second-class counties who initially included not only Norfolk but also Derbyshire, Essex, Hampshire, Hertfordshire, Leicestershire, Northamptonshire, Somerset, Staffordshire and Warwickshire. In publishing the first such table – for the 1888 season – *Wisden's Almanack* commented that 'county cricket shows further considerable development and it is probable that in another year or so we shall have as close and almost as keen a competition among the counties of the second class as we have among the leading teams'. That first table, reflecting a decline in Norfolk's fortunes, showed the county as eighth out of ten and also as having played only four games – home and away fixtures with Hertfordshire and Hampshire – compared with up to ten fixtures for the others. Leicestershire, incidentally, topped that table.

Norfolk were ranked tenth out of 11 in 1889, again playing the same four 'qualifying' games but nine altogether including fixtures with the MCC (and Ground) and the Cambridge University Long Vacation Club. The Joint Secretaries' report for the season expressed the hope that more of the public should attend matches so that, with the extra income, another professional could be engaged. On a different tack, *Wisden's Almanack* reported that 'the county has introduced several young players, and we hope in the course of a year or so they will be more successful than in the past two seasons'. Sadly, this did not happen immediately for in 1890, and together with Hertfordshire, they dropped out of this unofficial second-tier championship. The county side did however retain a fixture list that included games against Hampshire, Hertfordshire, MCC and Ground and, for the first time, Derbyshire. The Eton Ramblers also made their first appearance at Lakenham in the Cricket Week. Generally, the county was second-best in its contests with other counties, but although only one of their seven fixtures was won *Wisden's Almanack* was able to write that 'a praiseworthy effort was made to discover some fresh talent', this comment being based on the county club's decision to arrange, for the first time, a small number of Club and Ground matches. These were effectively second team games, although the club's professionals tended to do most of the bowling. Moreover, it was also agreed that these be played away from Lakenham, at venues such as Yarmouth, Dereham and Billingford. Not only was this initiative seen as a way of finding 'new blood' but also, by going into other parts of the county, it might help to increase membership. However, interest in these games was not always great; in 1893, 35 players had to be asked to play in one such game versus Gunton Park. In the Club's search for good young players it was also usual for the County Secretary to ask in the local papers for club secretaries to put forward names to play in the County's Colts games although when, in 1892, the secretary sought applications from those who had scored three centuries in a week or taken ten wickets in an innings on half-a-dozen occasions in the season, it might be thought that expectations were too high.

As an aside, the annual membership subscription at this time was 21 shillings (over £90 today). This entitled county club members to free admission to home matches, the right to bring a friend for ten shillings and sixpence and the use of the professionals to bowl at them.

1891 brought better fortunes with four victories in seven matches, that included return fixtures with Bedfordshire, Lincolnshire and Hertfordshire,. The highlight was an overwhelming victory in the fixture with Bedfordshire when Norfolk piled up 522 in their only innings. Revd Arthur Davies (126) and Revd William Sandwith (123) both scored hundreds and together added 207 for the third wicket. The season also saw the emergence of Charles Shore as a leading bowler on the non-first class county scene with 69 wickets at an average of 8.51, including eight for 24 against Lincolnshire. The other bowlers took just 53 wickets between them. Importantly, there were also ten Club and Ground games, against Essex Club and Ground, London Ramblers, Ryburgh Invincibles, Billingford Incapables, Dereham, Gunton, Melton, Narford and Yarmouth.

The improvement did not continue in 1892 with just one win from eight games against Hertfordshire, Lincolnshire, Cambridgeshire, MCC and Ground and Eton Ramblers. The season was summarised as 'disastrous', with satisfaction to be taken only from Shore's 44 wickets and Vincent Hoare's batting, which included a round 100 against Eton Ramblers. There were just five Club and Ground games and one, the Gunton match, was abandoned due 'the unsettled state of the county during the period of the General Election'. The end-of-season accounts for 1892 are revealing. The expenditure included Daisy Picking on Pitch (£1); Talent Money to Shore, Rye and Thomas Morley (£1) each; Use of Lakenham Cricket Pavilion (£35) and had 'the usual rider' that 'through the generosity of Mr JJ Colman, MP no charge is made for the Club for the use of the Ground'. Shore's wages were £63 (equivalent to approximately £5,500 today), Thomas Morley received a gratuity of £5 and Rye a retainer for the same amount. Subscriptions showed a slight increase which was offset by a reduction in gate money, the total income for the year being £428 18s 3d.

The following summer was one of glorious weather that was not quite matched by the Club's results. There were six games against other counties as well as the regular MCC fixture. Three were won including, by one run, the home match with Cambridgeshire who on this occasion were captained by the incomparable Indian K.S. Ranjitsinhji who, within three years, would make a memorable debut for England and generally would be recognised as one of the great batsmen of his day. In this match, though, his contributions were negligible. Altogether in the seven games in 1893 Shore took another 58 wickets and George Raikes topped the batting averages, and together they bowled out Cambridgeshire in the first innings of the away match for a meagre 39. The end-of-season plea was for a couple of really good bowlers and, not for the first or last time, for improved attendances from the general public in the hope that this would enable the Club to afford them.

Prior to the start of the next season the *Eastern Daily Press* published correspondence expressing a variety of concerns about cricket in the county, including the staging of only two Club and Ground matches and the inability to attract good professional batsmen and bowlers to Norfolk to coach young players, and calling on the County Club to arrange more attractive fixtures and for the committee to be more energetic, and generally to be more forward thinking.

Nonetheless, 1894 brought an upturn in the county's fortunes, in large part due to the success of the two professionals Shore (55 wickets) and Morley (56 wickets). Of the nine games played by Norfolk, comprising home and away fixtures against Cambridgeshire (still with Ranjitsinhji), Hertfordshire and Lincolnshire and single games against MCC and Ground, I Zingari and the Quidnuncs, five were won and only two lost. Playing fortunes may have improved but it seems that attendances in the Norwich Cricket Week did not with less than £70 in gate money being taken over the six days, an amount considered to be 'absurdly small'. Assuming each paying spectator was charged sixpence that equates to no more than 450 for each day. The I Zingari game attracted less than 100 spectators on the first day and although gates were generally better than this the general lack of interest was attributed to 'the lamentable want of patriotic feeling innate in the Norfolk public'. 1894 saw the Wellesley Road ground in Great Yarmouth hosting the fixture with MCC and Ground when Morley bowled the county to victory.

By 1894, the County Championship still only had nine teams, Somerset having filled the gap left by Derbyshire's withdrawal four years earlier. However, in May 1894, the captains of the first-class counties agreed that Derbyshire, Essex, Leicestershire and Warwickshire should be admitted to the County Championship for 1895. Later that year, it was decided to add Hampshire to that list, bringing it to 14 in total. Indeed, for the 1894 season, the first four just named played matches against the existing first-class counties and one another. This decimated the list of clubs who until then had been playing competitive 'second class' county cricket. So, in the autumn of 1894, the Worcestershire County Club wrote to eligible counties who would not be participating in the expanded first-class competition in 1895. And in December 1894, representatives of 16 of those county clubs, including Norfolk, approved a resolution that 'a second-class county cricket competition for the second-class cricketing counties be instituted and be open to all cricket clubs arranging a programme of four home and away county matches. The method of scoring shall be the same as adopted in the first-class county championship competition'.

And so the Minor Counties Championship was established.

# CHAPTER 7

# Phoenix from The Ashes (1895–1914)

Such was the enthusiasm of the 'second-class' counties who met in December 1894 that it was agreed that the new competition should begin in 1895. A further meeting was held in March of that year (at which Norfolk was not represented) when the Minor Counties Cricket Association was formally established and a range of constitutional, management and administrative matters agreed. Norfolk were not listed as one of the 17 members of the new Association but joined in time to take their place in the competition's inaugural season.

The championship in that first year operated on the somewhat unusual basis that, in order to qualify, counties had to play eight fixtures – four at home and four away – and that games played by clubs qualifying for the competition against counties who did not should count as championship matches for the former provided the latter agreed. Against this background, seven teams (Bedfordshire, Durham, Hertfordshire, Norfolk, Oxfordshire, Staffordshire and Worcestershire) qualified for inclusion by arranging the required eight fixtures whilst another seven (Berkshire, Buckinghamshire, Cambridgeshire, Cheshire, Lincolnshire, Northamptonshire and Wiltshire) did not but were involved in matches against the first group that counted in the table as championship games for their opponents. As would be the case until the year 2000, games, apart from Championship finals, were played over two days.

For that first season Norfolk arranged the minimum of eight qualifying matches including four against non-qualifying counties. A slow start meant that Norfolk drew two and lost one of their first three games. However, the second half of August brought five games in quick succession, resulting in four wins and one draw. Firstly, Lincolnshire were beaten by an innings and 19 runs, Jack Skrimshire top-scoring with 54 in Norfolk's only innings and then Charlie Shore returning match figures of 11 for 67. Next, Hertfordshire were also beaten by an innings, Skrimshire again leading the way with 82 with support from George Raikes (65) and ten more wickets for Shore. Norfolk then got the better of a draw with Oxfordshire with Philip Fryer hitting their first championship hundred (129) and half-centuries from skipper Redmond Buxton and Thomas Morley. The return fixture followed a few days later and this time Norfolk made no mistake, triumphing by 69 runs. Fairfax Davies hit 94 in the second innings; Shore, Morley and Revd Edgar Mack shared the wickets. Shore, with 57 wickets at 9.05, was the outstanding performer.

Norfolk's last game of the 1895 season was away to Cambridgeshire on 28 and 29 August. At the same time, Worcestershire were playing host to Durham in the final games for both sides. The nature of the points scoring system was that a team's total points were calculated by subtracting the number of defeats from the number of wins with draws ignored. Going into these final matches, Durham had four points and Norfolk and Worcestershire two each. Worcestershire beat Durham and Norfolk easily overcame Cambridgeshire by nine wickets with Shore again capturing 11 wickets. So, all three counties finished with three points with Durham and Norfolk each having won four and lost one and Worcestershire having won five and lost two. Confusion now reigned. One chronicler gave the title to Worcestershire on the basis that they had won most games. *Wisden's Almanack* decided that Norfolk and Durham were the joint winners on the basis of the rule applying to first-class counties whereby in placing teams with the same number of points the one with the better proportion of wins to matches finished took the higher place. The magazine *Cricket*, in its table, showed all three teams as sharing the title and that was what was later decided.

So who were the county's key players in these first championship seasons? Of the amateurs, the most outstanding was George (in due course, Revd) Raikes. Born in Carleton Forehoe and the younger brother of Ernest Raikes, he was an allrounder who made his Norfolk debut in 1890 at the age of 17 and played for his home county until 1897 and then from 1904 to 1913. His Minor County appearances in his two spells with the county produced 2466 runs (at an average of 32.02) and 224 wickets (at 16.08). He also represented Oxford University and Hampshire at first-class level. He is, though, more famous as a goalkeeper for England's soccer team. Fryer, an opening batsman and lob bowler, came from Wymondham and played for Norfolk from 1890 to 1905 scoring 1006 Championship runs with an average of 25.79. In 1908, he had two games with Northamptonshire.

As continued to be the custom, there were professionals to assist with the donkey-work of bowling out the opposition. Mention has already been made of Charlie Shore. He came originally from Sutton-in-Ashfield in Nottinghamshire, a town that was a rich source of first-class cricketers. Shore himself had played for Nottinghamshire and Lancashire before coming to Norfolk in 1889. His debut match for the county in the following year included one five-ball over in which he conceded 19 runs but things got much better, to the point where Ranjitsinhji said that he knew of no harder bowler to face than Shore. A slow left-arm bowler, he played for Norfolk for 13 seasons, bowling more than 3,700 overs in county matches (including those played before the inception of the Minor Counties championship) and taking altogether 582 wickets. Of these, 251 wickets were obtained in Minor Counties' matches at an average of 14.73.

The professional duties were shared with Thomas Morley, also from Sutton-in-Ashfield. He was a right-arm fast bowler and stylish middle to low-order batsman. He first played for Norfolk in 1886 and continued to represent his adopted county until 1900. In his six years of Minor Counties Championship cricket he took 115 wickets at 14.35. As a goalkeeper, he also played soccer for Norfolk.

Returning to the 1895 season, the home game with Lincolnshire gives an indication of how the game was played around that time. Rain prevented a prompt start and when play eventually got under way Norfolk's batsmen scored very freely until, with an hour to go before the finishing time on the first day, the Lincolnshire captain complained to the Norfolk secretary that it was unfair for his bowlers to have to bowl with a greasy ball. At once, the Norfolk secretary ordered the umpires to end play for the day, and so they did!

After the success of that first competitive season the next few years proved to be difficult ones for the County Club. The problems began in 1896 when, for whatever reason, they did not put together sufficient fixtures to qualify for inclusion in the Championship table. Coincidentally, Durham (and two other counties) were in a similar position, so perhaps it was pique at the failure of those organising the Championship to resolve the title issue in 1895. For whatever reason, Norfolk had just six inter-county fixtures – home and away games with Cambridgeshire, Hertfordshire and Worcestershire. Only the pairs of matches against those last two-named counted as Championship games so enabling the results of those two counties to be included in the Championship table. The sole victory came in the Lakenham Festival Week when Cambridgeshire were defeated by five wickets. The low point came with the visit to Worcestershire when Norfolk were bowled out for 67 and 28, the latter being the county's lowest ever score in Minor Counties matches; 19 of the wickets were bowled suggesting a problem with technique. The only player to emerge from the season with credit was Shore who, including games against MCC and Ground and I Zingari, took 50 wickets for his employer. Moreover, it was not just performances on the field that caused concern: the county declined an offer from Durham to meet them on the grounds that 'they could not afford to go so far north'.

At least for the 1897 season, for which Revd William Sandwith was appointed captain, Norfolk played the eight fixtures sufficient to qualify for the Championship. They included, for the first time, competitive matches with Durham and Northumberland but they chose to avoid Worcestershire, the eventual winners in 1897 as indeed they were in 1896 and 1898. (It was this success for the Midlands county which led to their elevation to the first-class county championship for the 1899 season.) After losing their opening two games in 1897, Norfolk recovered to finish sixth out of ten competing sides. Again, they owed much of their success to Shore and a rejuvenated Morley – 50 and 45 wickets respectively – with the former returning outstanding figures in the home fixture with Durham. In the first innings he took all ten wickets for 50 runs and followed that up with six second-innings wickets for 22 runs when again he bowled unchanged. The full first innings scorecard reads

| | | | |
|---|---|---|---|
| R.H. Mallett | c Blake | b Shore | 0 |
| C.Y. Adamson | c E.B. Raikes | b Shore | 5 |
| E. W. Elliot | b Shore | | 15 |
| M.H. Horsley | b Shore | | 2 |
| F. Simpson | c E.B. Raikes | b Shore | 7 |
| A.B. Horsley | c G.B. Raikes | b Shore | 18 |
| T. Hutton | st Blake | b Shore | 7 |
| Middlemiss, G | c Cowles | b Shore | 4 |
| J. Lee | not out | | 16 |
| Gregory, J | c E.B. Raikes | b Shore | 12 |
| Lambert, T | lbw | b Shore | 5 |
| Extras (1 leg bye) | | | 1 |
| Total | | | 92 |

The batsmen performed less impressively although there were consistent performances from Sydney Page and Revd Sandwith. The latter was another of a number of all-round sportsmen who played for Norfolk at this time having been awarded a football Blue when at Oxford University. He also acted as joint secretary in the early 1890s.

1898 saw Norfolk rise to fourth equal out of nine. For the first time, they played a home Minor Counties fixture away from Lakenham – at the Wellesley Road Recreation Ground in Great Yarmouth against Northumberland. They returned in 1899 to play Durham but that was the end of Minor County cricket in the town although it did host fixtures against the MCC in 1910 and 1912.

On the field, the most notable event was the debut of Albert Relf. Born in Sussex, he was a middle order right-handed batsman and right-arm medium pace off-break bowler as well as a fine slip fielder. He had previously played two seasons with Berkshire and stayed only two years with Norfolk before returning to the county of his birth. Back in Sussex, his career took off to such an extent that he made 565 first class appearances, scoring over 22,000 runs and capturing 1897 wickets, plus 537 catches. His performances brought him 13 Test caps between 1903 and 1914, all but one on tours to Australia and South Africa. His solitary home Test was against Australia at Lord's in 1909 when he took five first-innings wickets for 85. Sadly, he committed suicide at the age of 62, in a fit of depression attributed to his wife's serious illness although, ironically, she recovered and inherited a substantial estate. On a happier note, his debut season with Norfolk was marked by a 100 not out against Hertfordshire at Lakenham.

For 1899, Norfolk were led by Lawrence Bathurst. Born in Gressenhall, he had followed the well-worn track of Norfolk's amateur cricketers to Cambridge University where he won his cricket Blue in 1893 and 1894. In the second of those years he also accompanied Lord Hawke, the Yorkshire 'supremo', on a short tour to North America. There, he turned in a number of creditable performances, including eight for 64 against Philadelphia, the leading American club. He also performed well as Norfolk's captain in a season when they finished fifth out of 11 competing teams. Relf's performances stood out, scoring 464 runs (at an average of 51.55) and taking 31 wickets (at 20.74). Included amongst his runs were two hundreds, 103 versus Northumberland and 102 against Durham. Other highlights were an opening partnership of 178 by Fryer (130) and Revd Sandwith (99) away to Northumberland and 131 not out by Eric Penn against Cambridgeshire, batting at number eight and made in a little over two hours out of a total of 166 scored whilst at the wicket. Shore, with 40, again took most wickets.

Unfortunately, the green shoots of recovery did not continue. Particularly in the context of the County Club, Sir Kenneth Kemp had, as part of a debate on the subject, expressed concern in 1898 about aspects of cricket in the county. He noted a number of reasons for the county's failures: a natural lack of interest on the part of the public at large in Norfolk; a consequent lack of openings or employment for professionals, without whom no county could prosper, improve or foster the love of the game; a lack of private grounds and the necessary means to keep up those that did exist for public benefit; and a decrease in the county of boys at public schools where, he asserted, the best cricket was taught. Others identified

Albert Relf. *Relf played for Norfolk in 1898 and 1899 after taking up a coaching engagement at Houghton Hall that in turn gave him a residential qualification to play for the county. He then returned to Sussex, the county of his birth, to pursue a successful first-class career that included 13 Test appearances.*

A. E. RELF

Copyright.
PHOTO BOWDEN BROS

additional causes: the decline in agriculture in the county; that cricket was not indigenous to Norfolk; the recreational opportunities offered by cycling, golf, bowls, lawn tennis and quoits; the proximity to the coast; and even that 'we are not an over-quick people in assimilating anything that is new to us'. Some, though, questioned Kemp's basic assumption.

The results of the 1900 and 1901 seasons justified this gloom. Now captained firstly by Fairfax Davies and then by Gerard Blake, not a match was won in either season and in both Norfolk finished equal last in the Minor Counties Championship, which by the second of these years had expanded to 17 teams including the Second Elevens of Surrey and Yorkshire. In that season, the batsmen in total averaged under 15 whilst the bowlers' wickets came at an average cost of over 30. The reasons for this dramatic decline are not just to be found in the concerns articulated by Kemp. In addition, Relf had left to join Sussex; and Morley had not been re-engaged after the 1900 season when his contribution had been negligible. Shore's performances also fell away steeply in 1901 and at the end of that year his services were also dispensed with. To these reasons can be added one given in *Wisden's Cricketers Almanack* for these two seasons: several members of the 1899 side were now in South Africa representing their country in the Boer War. Unlike the First World War, all returned alive.

The response of the County Club was decisive and prescient. They agreed to engage two new professionals, Edward Gibson (a slow left-arm bowler) and Billy Smith (fastish right-arm). In recognising the need for professional bowlers Norfolk were not alone. The tendency in first-class cricket was for the amateurs, and there were some very good ones, to bat and for the bowling to be largely undertaken by paid players although there were some first-rate professional batsmen as well. This approach more often than not also applied in the Minor Counties Championship where the bulk of the bowling around this time was done by contracted players.

However, because Gibson and Smith each had to serve a 24-month qualification period and also because of the extra costs involved, it was decided to withdraw from the Minor Counties competition for the 1902 and 1903 seasons and instead play a limited number of friendly matches. Altogether in those two seasons, Norfolk played 15 matches including fixtures with Suffolk, Cambridgeshire, Essex Seconds and MCC and Ground. In 1902 the batting performed moderately well with centuries for Albert Shingler and Edward Orams but in 1903 only two batsmen passed 50 in an innings in eight games. At least, though, the decision to employ Smith and Gibson was quickly justified, in particular in the second of those seasons when they shared 81 wickets. Also, against Suffolk in 1902, Penn took ten wickets in the match and a year later Maurice Ireland took eight first-innings wickets for 38 against the same opponents.

That 1903 season saw W.G. Grace bring his London County side to Lakenham for a two-day game against Norfolk. The hosts, for whom Gibson took 13 wickets, won a low scoring game by 62 runs with 'The Champion', now aged 55, scoring 0 and 31, each time bowled by James Worman, and taking four first innings wickets for 74. He was nevertheless sufficiently content to write to say how much he enjoyed the game although he is said to have blamed his second-innings dismissal on having taken the wrong guard. Indeed, he returned the following year, this time including the former Australian captain Billy Murdoch in his side. Norfolk again prevailed with Grace again performing to limited effect. The highlight of this match was Smith's second-innings return of nine for 28 in which he bowled both Grace and Murdoch.

By 1904, the list of competing Minor Counties had grown to 20 with Northamptonshire having emerged as the dominant force following Worcestershire's elevation to first-class status; indeed, they too would join the County Championship at the end of the season. Also, a new points system had been established, based on a percentage of points obtained as against the maximum number of points obtainable. The points themselves were three for a win and one for a first-innings lead in a drawn match.

Norfolk struggled in their return season finishing 16th out of 20 and winning only one of their eight games. *Wisden's Almanack* considered that 'though they had a fairly useful all-round eleven they did not meet with so much success as had been expected'. Revd Raikes topped the batting averages scoring 145 against Suffolk in the sole victory; there were solid contributions from two other clerics, Revd Arthur Hoare and Revd Gough McCormick. Billy Smith headed the bowling averages with 44 Championship wickets but Gibson's figures were not nearly so impressive. Hoare had the distinction of dismissing Cambridgeshire's Jack Hobbs for a duck in his last season before moving south to join Surrey and, in due course, represent England. The captaincy had by now passed from Blake to Legh Barratt.

Then, in 1905, with much the same squad of players, but with Raikes as the appointed captain, the county had an altogether better season. The opening match, away to Hertfordshire, was drawn with Norfolk securing two points for leading on first innings. A second-innings hundred and six wickets from Penn was the best individual performance with that century contributing to a sixth-wicket partnership of 200 with Len Leman, a county record which still stands. The next game was away to Suffolk and resulted in a disappointing defeat by 76 runs. Then followed an historic run starting with a six-wicket victory against Suffolk after conceding a 77 run lead after the first innings; nine wickets in the match for Worman and a second innings 79 not out from the new captain were the major performances. Next came an innings win over Oxfordshire at Lakenham, set up by a third-wicket stand of 152 between Barratt (92) and Raikes (112) and cemented by a ten-wicket haul from Raikes. That win was

WG Grace at Lakenham, 1903. *Grace played two matches at Lakenham (in 1903 and 1904) but with limited success.*

immediately followed by a nine-wicket success in the return fixture with Hertfordshire when fifties from Hoare, Arthur Watson and Worman were followed by nine wickets for Smith and eight for Worman. Cambridgeshire were then beaten by an innings with further half-centuries from Hoare and Watson and 11 wickets in the match for Worman. The return fixture with Oxfordshire resulted in a ten-wicket win with another 11 wickets (for 93) for Worman and 141 not out from Revd McCormick batting at number seven. The final match, against Cambridgeshire at Lakenham, began badly for the home side. Winning the toss and batting first, Norfolk were soon dismissed for 40. Gibson and George Starling restricted the visitors' lead to 68 but that seemed too many as the county slumped to 62 for 5 and then 108 for 7. At this point Watson and George Pilch came together and with scores of 83 and 88 respectively added 152 for the eighth wicket; this also remains a Norfolk record more than 100 years later. Set 193 to win, Cambridgeshire collapsed to 68 all out with Smith taking six for 28 and Gibson four for 24. The Championship was Norfolk's!

Altogether, ten batsmen averaged over 20 with the highest aggregates coming from Watson (319 runs), Barratt (315), Raikes (253) and Hoare (197), all of them averaging over 32. The bowling was dominated by four players with the averages being headed on this occasion by an amateur, Worman (42 wickets at 11.11 each). Smith took 31 wickets and the second professional, Gibson, captured 17, amply justifying the decision at the end of the 1901 season to engage them. The captain, with 25 wickets, was the other leading bowler.

Of this Championship winning side, Legh Barratt was a good enough batsman to be selected for two private tours of the West Indies in the 1890's albeit with limited success. Captain in 1904 and again in 1907 and 1908, he scored 1920 Championship runs at 23.41. Arthur Watson's Minor County contribution was 1045 runs at the higher average of 32.65. Worman, a schoolteacher from King's Lynn, captured altogether 127 Championship wickets at 15.68.

1906 saw a return to mid-table – equal eighth out of 20. The batting was consistent without being spectacular – Raikes, Barratt and Cyril Dunning leading the way; the wickets were almost all shared between the same four successful bowlers of 1905 with Worman's 13 wickets in the home game with Suffolk the leading individual performance. The season was very much one of two halves with Norfolk losing their first four games including the return fixture with Suffolk by one run when Leman carried his bat for 44 not out and Smith and Gibson shared equally the ten second-innings wickets. In contrast, Norfolk won their last four games, two by an innings and two by eight wickets, Revd McCormick hitting the only hundred of the summer in the home win over Oxfordshire.

Perhaps, though, in retrospect the season was most notable for the debuts, in non-Championship games, of two teenagers; Michael Falcon (aged 18) and Geoffrey Stevens (only 15). Each started their Norfolk career with a duck; both were to more than make up for this in the years that followed.

For the 1907 season, an entirely new system of deciding the Minor Counties Championship was adopted. With the intention of providing a more effective test of merit the (now) 21 teams were divided into four Divisions – North, Midlands, East and West – with the winners of each going forward into two semi-finals and ultimately a final. Norfolk, naturally,

A young Michael Falcon. *This photograph dates from about 1910, around the time he took on the County captaincy.*

were placed in the East Division where, with Barratt now at the helm, they finished second to Hertfordshire. *Wisden's Almanack's* summary of the season was that they played 'a little better than in the previous year' without approaching the success of 1905. Twelve batsmen averaged over 20 with the bat with the two youngsters just referred to already making their mark as the leading run makers. Falcon topped the averages with 285 runs at 57.00 including a maiden century versus Bedfordshire and another against Cambridgeshire. The other batting highlight was a sixth-wicket stand of 189 by Watson (105) and Barratt (115) against Hertfordshire. As to the bowlers, Smith (60) and Gibson (33) took most of the wickets and between them helped to compensate for the loss of Revd Raikes. Their best performance was against Cambridgeshire when, apart from three overs from Worman, the two bowled throughout both innings each taking five wickets in each innings. 1907 also saw the debut for the county of the professional Thomas Allsopp, a slow left-arm bowler and useful batsman who had been released by Leicestershire for whom he had played 36 games over three seasons from 1903 to 1905.

The same championship format was retained for 1908, with Norfolk in the East Division with Hertfordshire, Bedfordshire, Suffolk and Cambridgeshire. They dropped to fourth, recording only two wins from their eight games. There were nonetheless some good individual performances, none more so than that of Geoffrey Stevens. Still only 17 and in his last year at school, he scored 696 runs in the Minor Counties Championship at an average of 63.27. Particularly impressive were his three hundreds against Bedfordshire, Hertfordshire and Cambridgeshire, with his 170 not out against the last-named county the highest. Other centuries came from the bats of Barratt (166) and Basil Cozens-Hardy (102 not out), both against Bedfordshire. The bowling relied almost exclusively on the two professionals Gibson and Smith with a combined total of 79 wickets. The other bowlers collected a total of 29 wickets. Gibson also took a hat-trick in the away fixture with Hertfordshire. Off the field, the 1908 season marked the end of Edward Buxton's service as the County Club's honorary secretary. He had taken up the position in 1891, sharing the role for some of the time with others. He was a member of the well-known Norfolk family of the same name and served as Lord Mayor of Norwich in 1907–8.

1909 saw a continuation of the same divisional format but with Lincolnshire joining the other five members in the East Division. *Wisden's Almanack* records that the county, now led by Brereton Wilson, 'were unable to always place a representative side in the field and, although they possessed some useful bowlers, the batting lacked strength and consistency'. The records confirm this with four defeats and only two outright wins from ten games. The leading performers were again Stevens and Gibson with 466 runs and 58 wickets respectively. Stevens was in fact the only batsman in those ten games to post an individual score more than 66, and the only regular player to average over 17. The batting averages made dismal reading with the low points coming in two successive completed innings of 39 against Hertfordshire and Cambridgeshire and later when bowled out for 38 by Lincolnshire. The bowling was stronger with Smith's nine for 63 in the first innings against Lincolnshire being the pick of the individual performances, although Gibson took five wickets in an innings on seven of the 17 occasions that he bowled. The batsmen's most successful day came on the occasion of the county's first Minor Counties match (against Cambridgeshire) at the King Edward VII Grammar School ground in King's Lynn when Stevens' 104 was supported by Watson's 66 and Richard Beresford's 63. In all, Norfolk played seven more Championship games at the School over the following 40 years.

Revd McCormick played his last Championship game in 1909 finishing with 1239 runs at 25.28. In due course, he became the Dean of Manchester. Billy Smith also played his last game for Norfolk in that year – his 226 Championship wickets had come at a cost of 16.18 runs each – and the following season marked the end of wicketkeeper Page's Minor County career finishing with 1199 runs and 59 dismissals.

Also, in the Autumn of 1909, the County Club held the meeting referred to in Chapter 3 and before the start of the new season, Charles Prior took over as secretary serving in that capacity until 1923 in three separate spells.

So to 1910. For this season, the championship format was changed again. There were now two Divisions each comprising 11 teams – one, North and East and the other, South and West – with the winners of each playing off in a final called the Championship Match. Norfolk played ten divisional games although that included two against each of Suffolk, Durham, Cambridgeshire, Bedfordshire and Nottinghamshire Seconds but none against Yorkshire Seconds, Staffordshire, Cheshire, Northumberland or Lincolnshire: a slightly odd arrangement presumably designed to limit travelling and costs. The season began with an innings victory over Suffolk, with Revd Raikes – again captain – taking nine for 24 in the first innings. An innings defeat (with a depleted side) to Durham at King's Lynn followed but there were then successive wins away to Bedfordshire and Nottinghamshire Seconds with Raikes hitting a century in each game. The game in Durham was drawn with Norfolk finishing on 73 for 9 chasing 77 to win in what turned out to be 25 overs. In Durham's first innings, the first four batsmen all scored ducks in the face of the opening spell from Falcon and Allsopp. Without both Raikes and Falcon, the away game with Suffolk was lost, and at this point in the season, with four games to play, the county were little higher than mid-table. The first three of these remaining games were played in the Lakenham Cricket Festival. Firstly, Nottinghamshire Seconds were beaten by an innings and 9 runs, with another century for Raikes and main support from Falcon and Gervase Birkbeck; Falcon took ten wickets including seven for 53 in the first innings. Next up were Cambridgeshire who were beaten even more heavily, by an innings and 131 runs. It was this match, perhaps more than any other, which demonstrated the strength of the side. In their only innings of 414, Raikes, Falcon, Stevens and Birkbeck all made major contributions; with the ball, Raikes and Gibson each took six wickets in an innings. The last of the Festival games saw Bedfordshire soundly beaten, by 112 runs; on this occasion, Raikes, Gibson and Falcon each captured five wickets in an innings. The final championship fixture was away to Cambridgeshire with Norfolk again winning by an innings; this time Birkbeck, whose father Henry had also played for and captained Norfolk, hit 111.

The consequence of these four straight victories was that Norfolk topped their Division, just clear of Suffolk. They had therefore earned the right to meet the winners of the South and West Division – Berkshire – in the Final. This was played at Lakenham at the end of August with Berkshire the favourites, having very convincingly won nine successive divisional games. But as *Wisden's Almanack* reported 'the result upset all anticipations'. Berkshire batted first and were dismissed for 153 with Allsopp taking five for 42 and Raikes four for 50. Norfolk replied with 397 to which the major contribution was a magnificent innings of 201 by 19 year-old Stevens. His innings was scored in only 220 minutes, and he received lower-order support from his brother Norman with 57. Demoralised, Berkshire crumbled in their second innings to 94 all out, still 150 short of Norfolk's score. The wickets were shared amongst the four main bowlers. All in all, this was a remarkable performance.

The season's successes were very much the result of a team effort although the captain's performances clearly stood out. Raikes (679 runs) and Stevens (608) led the way with the bat but there was considerable support from Birkbeck, Falcon, Eric Fulcher and Ralph Thurgar. The bowling duties, and rewards, were shared by Raikes (57 wickets), Allsopp (50), Gibson (45) and Falcon (35), and it was very much the case that one, if not two, of these four would deliver the goods in any particular innings. The fielding was of a high standard with Thurgar performing well behind the stumps and Geoffrey Stevens taking 20 catches.

The 1910 Norfolk Championship-winning team. Standing (l to r): *BK Wilson (Hon Secretary), E Gibson, EJ Fulcher, G Williams, GW Birkbeck, RW Collinson, T Allsopp, CBL Prior (Hon Secretary). Seated (l to r): GA Stevens, M Falcon, Revd GB Raikes, RAA Beresford, RW Thurgar. Norfolk won their last four Divisional matches and then the play-off versus Berkshire to capture the Minor Counties Championship.*

The 1911 season was not nearly so successful with Norfolk dropping to ninth out of ten in the North and East Division. For the first time, they played as many as 12 championship games, and of the first nine, six were lost outright and three lost on the first innings. Some honour was restored and hopes revived for the future in the final three games of the season that brought two wins and a win on first innings. Although Raikes' batting fell away, there were still consistent performances from Stevens (908 runs at an average of over 40), Falcon and Birkbeck and, to a lesser extent, Fulcher. The last-named was earning a reputation as a fast-scoring big hitter and in this season, against Suffolk, he scored 76 in 39 minutes. However, the bowling lost much of its effectiveness with the professionals, Gibson and Allsopp, in particular returning poor figures. Fulcher, who was becoming a reliable allrounder, and Harold Watson, the latest paid player to join the county's books, were more impressive but without providing the required cutting edge.

Revd Raikes stood down as captain at the end of the 1911 campaign in which Gervase Birkbeck had also led the side on four occasions. In his place, the county chose Michael Falcon. Another change saw the Minor Counties Championship, now comprising 20 teams, reverting to one Division with the top two playing off in the event that they had not otherwise played one another during the season. Norfolk's professional ranks were swelled by the addition of Roderick Falconer, a right-arm medium-pace bowler who had played a handful of games for Northamptonshire. The county played only eight games in the competition, with King's Lynn dropped as a home venue. In their first fixture, away to Hertfordshire, Norfolk secured a one-run lead on first innings in a drawn game; Falconer marked his debut with 11 for 89. There then followed seven straight wins, including three by an innings. The strength was in the bowling, with Falconer fully justifying his engagement by taking 65 wickets in the eight games, including nine hauls of five or more wickets in an innings. His wickets cost less than eight each and to all intents and purposes he had bowled Norfolk to the top of the Championship. He was supported by his captain (29 wickets), Gibson (28, of which 18 came in the last two games) and Watson (22). The best bowling performance came when Falcon and Falconer bowled out Suffolk for 39 and 40, the first innings total being the lowest ever recorded against Norfolk in the Championship. The batting did not reach the heights of previous seasons but this is not surprising given the wet summer. Nevertheless, Falcon, Birkbeck and Stevens all made solid contributions with the first two named being the county's only centurions that summer.

Staffordshire finished second, and because the two counties had not met during the season they were expected to play one another to decide the championship. However, the match did not take place. *Wisden's Almanack* wrote that this was because Norfolk could not raise a representative eleven so late in the season as several of their best players had 'gone away'. Efforts to arrange the match failed so, according to *Wisden's Almanack,* the Minor Counties' Association decided that the championship should remain 'in abeyance'. This version is wrong. The real reason that the game was not played lay in the devastating floods that hit Norwich and the surrounding area on 26 August that year. These had already severely delayed the game at Lakenham between the touring Australians and an England Eleven, with the

The 1912 Norfolk table-topping Championship team. Standing (l to r): *E Gibson, H Watson, CBL Prior (Hon Secretary), RW Thurgar, RF Popham, GW Birkbeck, LF Wynne-Wilson, R Falconer.* Seated (l to r): *EJ Fulcher, GA Stevens, M Falcon, Revd GB Raikes, RG Pilch. Norfolk won seven games in a row to top the Minor County table although the serious floods in late August meant that the play-off match against Staffordshire could not be arranged..*

*Eastern Daily Press* reporting that the groundsman had likened the ground to Breydon Water. A few days later, on 5 September, the *Eastern Daily Press* indicated that Staffordshire had issued their challenge but that Norfolk had to refuse because the 'flood disaster and general distress in Norwich' made it impossible to arrange the fixture. Staffordshire and the Secretary of the Minor Counties' Association then suggested the game be played at Stoke-on-Trent. The Norfolk Committee met on 7 September and offered to play at Norwich on 18 and 19 September. Staffordshire's response was to say that in view of the 'undue delay' in Norfolk accepting the challenge they could not now play with the result that the title remained undecided.

As 1911 demonstrated, one year's success is not always followed by another. It is therefore an indication of the strength of the county side at this time that the 1913 season brought further glory to Norfolk. The campaign started with a win against Bedfordshire with Falconer taking six for 28 in the first innings and Watson seven for 62 in the second. The next two games were drawn and lost. However, the Lakenham Festival began with a first-innings win against Hertfordshire when 557 runs were scored in six hours on the first day; Reginald Popham (94) and Stevens (97 in 55 minutes) led the way. Watson then took six for 84 and Stevens hit 142 in the second innings. Cambridgeshire were the second Festival opponents and were beaten by an innings; Thurgar (155) and Popham (112) took the batting honours with Falcon and Watson each taking five wickets in the visitors' second innings. Then came a drawn game with Bedfordshire, Falcon top-scoring with 155 and more runs for Popham and Stevens before rain intervened. The next opponents were Staffordshire whose star performer was Sydney Barnes. He had eschewed the daily grind of first-class cricket for an easier and more lucrative career in league cricket, but was nonetheless good enough to be a first choice for England, provided he was prepared to play, and indeed to be considered by many as one of the truly great bowlers of all time. Eighteen months previously he had helped England regain the Ashes in Australia but now he was taking nine first-innings wickets for 31 against Norfolk. Staffordshire then secured a lead of one run but, set 137 to win, were bowled out for 101. Altogether in this match, Falcon took ten for 69, Falconer nine for 63. Cambridgeshire were beaten in the final match, which meant that Norfolk shared top place with Glamorgan. At the beginning of September, the two counties played off at Lakenham. Batting first, Norfolk (without their captain) reached 244, with Popham top-scoring with 74 and Stevens, Fulcher and Watson all getting into the thirties. Falconer and Fulcher then shared the wickets to dismiss Glamorgan for 168 in 97 overs, a testament to the quality of Norfolk's bowling. That first-innings lead of 76 was sufficient to win the Championship for Norfolk for, although the county collapsed in their second innings, rain interruptions prevented a positive result. This was an exceptional performance against a county who, eight years later, were elevated to first-class status and who on this occasion included a number of players who would represent them at that higher level.

In this championship-winning season, Falcon, Falconer and Watson took most of the wickets and the batting honours went to Falcon and Stevens, as usual, and to Popham. Reginald Popham had made his debut for Norfolk,

The 1913 Norfolk Championship-winning team. Standing (l to r): *R Falconer, LF Wynne-Wilson, AR Hudson, RF Popham, CBL Prior (Hon Secretary), E Gibson, H Watson.* Seated (l to r): *RW Collinson, GA Stevens, M Falcon, EJ Fulcher, RW Thurgar. A drawn match with Glamorgan ensured that they won the Minor Counties Championship.*

in a non-championship game, in 1910 at the age of 18 and, with a total of 1083 Minor County runs (at 25.78), gave good service before and after the First World War. He also played some first-class cricket for the MCC but was better known as a soccer player, collecting three amateur caps for England in 1914 and 1920.

Unfortunately, this on-field success was not matched by financial prosperity off it, and in August 1913 the Club had to report that their finances were still in an 'unsatisfactory position' and that £250 was needed to wipe off the existing debt and to meet the guarantee and expenses of the Glamorgan Match. A Shilling Fund was opened and the names of donors published in the *Eastern Daily Press*. The Fund was closed after a fortnight but although the response had been very positive it appears that the financial problems were not completely resolved.

By this time, however, war clouds were gathering over Europe to the extent that hostilities broke out before the 1914 season could be completed. Indeed, the home game with Staffordshire was cancelled because of the conflict, although other games were played after its outbreak. Norfolk had slipped to seventh in the championship table, but it did not really matter. By the following Spring, 22 county players had enlisted.

Three key players of the pre-war period who appeared in that 1914 season did not re-appear in the Minor Counties Championship after the War. Gibson took 307 Championship wickets for Norfolk an average of 16.82, taking five wickets in an innings on 25 occasions and five times taking ten wickets in a match; he also took 58 catches. In addition, when representing Garboldisham Manor against I Zingari (including two Test batsmen) in their 1906 Cricket Week, he captured all ten first-innings wickets for 35 runs. Falconer, in only three seasons with Norfolk, took 125 wickets at 11.25, with one exception easily the best average of any Norfolk bowler to take over 100 Championship wickets. Both would survive the war but not Ralph Thurgar who as a wicketkeeper made 95 dismissals as well as scoring 1108 runs.

The years leading up to the First World War had been remarkably successful for Norfolk, the more so given the parlous state they had been in only a few years previously. The decision to pull out of the Championship in 1902 had been amply justified; Norfolk were now at the top of the pile of second-class counties. The batting line-up was strong and at any one time there were three, if not four, bowlers capable of match-winning performances. Two players, though, stood out.

The first was the young captain. Making his Championship debut in 1907 but missing the whole of the 1909 campaign, Michael Falcon had by the end of 1914 seven seasons under his belt and he was already the outstanding allrounder in Minor County cricket. Like so many of the pre-war county side he had gone to a major public school – in his case, Harrow – and then on to Cambridge University. He won his cricket Blue in all his four years there (1908 to 1911) and was captain in 1910, this at a time when Cambridge, and Oxford, cricket was strong. Initially, he concentrated on his batting but by the end of his time there, and as his performances were already demonstrating, he was becoming a force with the ball. He played for Norfolk from his debut season in 1906 until 1946, captaining the county for all but the first six years. Moreover, his cricketing exploits did not stop with Norfolk. In 1913, he took six for 58 for the Gentlemen against the Players at the Oval, and in 1924 seven for 78 in the same fixture, at a time when this contest was one of the most prestigious in the cricket calendar. He also appeared occasionally for a range of all-amateur sides such as the Free Foresters and the MCC.

His two most celebrated performances, though, were against the visiting Australians. The 1921 tourists had taken all before them winning the first three Tests to follow their clean sweep in Australia during the previous winter. They had gone through the 1921 tour unbeaten until at Eastbourne they came up against a side put together by the former England captain, Archie MacLaren. Notwithstanding the visitors' total dominance at this time, MacLaren had said that he could select a side that would beat them. His chosen Eleven included Falcon and was made up entirely of amateurs with only the captain, ageing fast bowler Walter Brearley and the South African, Aubrey Faulkner, having Test experience to that point. MacLaren's amateurs batted first and were dismissed for a mere 43 but Falcon then took six for 67 to limit the Australian lead on first innings to 131. A much better second innings left the Australians with 196 to win but they fell 29 runs short of their target. It was an amazing performance in which the Norfolk captain played a leading part. Then, five years later and at the age of 37, he was selected to represent a Minor Counties' side in the tourists' opening fixture. On this occasion, he took seven first-innings wickets for 42 with his victims including Bardsley, Ponsford and Woodfull, three absolutely top-drawer batsmen.

All these performances helped to justify the plaudits he received during his career and afterwards. As examples, his obituary in *Wisden's Almanack* suggested that he would have played Test cricket if he had played for a first-class county, and the *Cricketer* magazine felt he should have been selected in the 1921 Ashes series. Later, in 1924, the same periodical expressed the view that he was the most difficult bowler in England stating that 'he has pace, can make the ball swing away from the bat and he can also send down a nasty off-break'. And, four years later, it opined 'a great bowler and greater cricketer, it seems a thousand pities that [he] has not been seen in international cricket both at home and abroad. His own modesty is possibly one of the causes of his absence from big cricket'.

His involvement with Norfolk cricket did not end when he retired. He was chairman of the County Club from 1950 to 1969 and President from 1969 to 1972. Previously, he had served from 1914 to 1938 on the Committee of the MCC, a substantial period that was all the more noteworthy given the famous cricketers and high-ranking people who also served at that time. Nor was he merely a cricketer. He was Member of Parliament for the East Norfolk Parliamentary Division from 1918 to 1923, Norfolk High Sheriff in 1943 and a Director of the Norwich Union Life Insurance and Fire Societies.

In summary, as a right-handed batsman he scored 11538 Minor County runs at 33.83 with 21 hundreds and 63 half-centuries and, as a fast-medium right-arm bowler, captured 690 Championship wickets at 16.49 taking five wickets in an innings on 52 occasions and ten wickets in a match nine times. In addition to 247 Minor County matches, he also played 89 first-class games in which he scored 3282 runs (at 25.25) and took 231 wickets (at 24.79).

The second outstanding Norfolk cricketer from this period was Geoffrey Stevens. His father had played for the old Norfolk and Norwich Club and his two older brothers also represented the county. Geoffrey himself attended Norwich Grammar School where he forced his way into the school team at the age of ten! In seven years in the School Eleven he had a highest score of 256, made against Ipswich School in 1908 by which time he was already establishing himself as a regular member of the county side. A prolific right-handed batsman and a fine slip fieldsman, he represented Norfolk until 1930. Unlike Falcon, though, he did not have days in the national headlines although he was a member of various Minor Counties' representative sides. Nevertheless, he was good enough for *The Cricketer* magazine in 1921 to describe him as one of the best dozen batsmen, amateur or professional, in English cricket which was high praise given the quality of the others. He was also said to have had Test Trial claims. In 158 Championship matches he scored 8122 runs (at 33.15) with 15 centuries and 44 fifties; there were also 137 catches and a stumping. After his retirement he served the County Club as secretary between 1952 and 1961. His son Bryan kept wicket for Norfolk during the period from 1937 to 1958.

# CHAPTER 8

# Golden Years
# (1919–1939)

The carnage of war left an indelible mark on British society. It would never be the same again with the names on the war memorials across the country, in almost every town and village, bearing witness to that. In Norfolk, those names included some who had played for the County Club. Second Lieutenant George Carter had made occasional appearances in 1913 and 1914 but in 1916, at the age of 19, he was killed in Mesopotamia. Captain Gervase Birkbeck, who had three county hundreds to his name, fell in 1917. Captain Ralph Thurgar, the batsman-wicketkeeper in those successful pre-war years and also football goalkeeper for Norfolk, was killed in the same year. Other county players who lost their lives included Captain Eric Penn, Captain Sydney Page and Major Vincent Hoare and all these names would be recorded on a memorial tablet unveiled by County Club chairman Ernest Raikes in the pavilion at the 1921 Lakenham Festival when Revd H.B.J. Armstrong, father of the future County Club secretary, conducted a brief service. Other former Minor County players who lost their lives were Corporal Thomas Wharton and Second Lieutenant Ronald Taylor and in addition to those killed in the war Geoffrey Colman was badly wounded and Basil Cozens-Hardy lost a leg.

The Minor Counties Championship did not resume immediately after the war. Rather, there were just a few informal matches in 1919, the most notable of which was the visit of an MCC and Ground eleven to Lakenham.

They included Douglas Jardine, then only 19 but later to win fame – or, in the view of some, notoriety – as captain during the Bodyline series of 1932–33. Michael Falcon dismissed him for a duck.

The Championship resumed in 1920, and the years that followed saw Norfolk retain their position as a leading Minor County and, at an individual level, continuing success for Falcon and Stevens. In that first post-war competition, in which they played just six Championship matches, Norfolk finished fifth (out of 16) with their captain leading the way at the head of both the batting and bowling averages with 480 runs (at an average of 60) and 46 wickets. Stevens hit 421 runs and Watson captured 39 wickets. Individual highlights were undoubtedly the recording of two of only eight double-centuries scored for the county in over one hundred years of the competition. Against Bedfordshire at Lakenham Stevens hit 222, including 4 sixes and 31 fours, in an innings that remained the highest individual effort for Norfolk until eclipsed by Carl Amos in 1998. And in the away fixture with Hertfordshire, Falcon scored 205 with 2 sixes and 20 fours. There was also a sole county hundred for his younger brother, Harry, against Essex Seconds. With the ball, Watson's figures included a hat-trick against Hertfordshire at Lakenham and in total Falcon and Watson took six wickets in an innings on seven occasions.

In 1921, Glamorgan joined the ranks of the first-class counties where they would struggle for some years. On the other hand, Norfolk continued their successful run in the second-tier competition with a fourth place finish. The batting was solid but not spectacular, and it was the bowling, again spearheaded by Falcon, that was chiefly responsible for six wins from the ten games played. Watson again provided admirable support as did two newcomers to the side: slow left-arm bowler Walter Beadsmoore (46 wickets at an average below 13 in his debut Championship season) and the professional Jack Nichols who, although born in Acle and representing Norfolk twice in 1898, had found his way back into the county side via pre-war spells on the playing staffs of Lancashire and Worcestershire before moving to Staffordshire where he had considerable success before the war. Soon afterwards, Falcon discovered him coaching at Bishop's Stortford College, declared that he was the man for Norfolk, and duly 'poached' him. Nichols also strengthened the batting. Thomas Raikes, the Club chairman's

Michael Falcon, *c.* 1920. *By this time, Falcon was considered to be one of the best fast bowlers in English cricket. He was not such a bad batsman, either!*

son, also broke into the side in a summer when, for Winchester School in a major public school fixture against Charterhouse, he hit 94 and then captured eight for 14 taking all his wickets before a run was scored off him.

The following season saw Norfolk return to the top of the Championship table with eight wins from the 12 games played; and in all the remaining four games the county won on first innings. Falcon again led the way with most runs (727 at an average of 38.26) and most wickets (60 at 13.35). Carrying all before them, the county were helped by substantial and regular contributions with the bat from Stevens, Richard Carter and Nichols with further support from Geoffrey Colman, Watson and Major John Wormald. In fact, Norfolk batted all the way down the order. The bowling returns were even more impressive with Beadsmoore (40 wickets), Nichols (39), Watson (59) and Raikes (27), together with Falcon, taking 225 wickets between them at a combined average of just over 13. Indeed, the all-round performances of the side led *The Cricketer* magazine to opine that the county would not disgrace themselves in the first-class competition.

Buckinghamshire finished runners up to Norfolk and exercised their right to challenge Norfolk for the championship in a play-off at Lakenham. Batting first, the visitors scored 225 to which Norfolk replied with 218. Colman's 98 was described as 'a masterpiece in timing and sound judgment' and he received support from Falcon and Carter. In the second innings, Buckinghamshire were dismissed for 90, with Falcon taking four for 18 and Watson 3 for 33. Left with 98 to win, Norfolk collapsed to 39 for five. Falcon and Carter then took the score to 81 – 18 runs to win with five wickets in hand. Unfortunately, the visitors' bowlers prevailed and Norfolk lost by 8 runs. At least, *The Cricketer* was able to report the sportsmanlike response of the Norfolk team and crowd at the end of the game

> 'Before they can leave the field the Norfolk eleven to a man are out and heartily congratulating the men of Bucks, and the spectators could not have accorded their own players a warmer reception than they did to the winners. What a grand match! We raise our glasses to winner, loser and spectator all in a single toast, and not forgetting the umpires. Cricket as it is and was and always must be, they all had a hand in it, whether it was playing, judging or appreciating. The real cricket. No cup, no medals, no hysterics. Just the indefinable, pleasant spirit which comes of the best and purest of games'.

Similar good reports about Norfolk's sportsmanship also followed their game in the same year against Cambridgeshire.

Norfolk's performances around this time prompted talk of elevation to the first-class championship. The issues were set out in an article in the *Eastern Daily Press* on 7 August 1922 under the heading 'Should Norfolk be a first class county?' It began by referring to the successes on the field and expressing the view that that playing-wise Norfolk could compete with many first-class counties. However, it went on to recognise that it would be necessary to add to the professional playing strength because the current amateurs would be unlikely to devote up to four months to playing cricket. Also, being an also-ran in the County Championship would be less attractive, if indeed it had any attraction at all. The article then raised the practical matters of finance and the need for properly equipped grounds and concluded by referring to the 'niggardly' support from the public even in the 1922 season. Falcon and County Club secretary Prior were amongst those who felt that Norfolk should retain their second-class status. Others, including the influential George Pilch, disagreed. In the event, Norfolk did not pursue higher status. As a postscript to this debate, Pelham Warner would shortly suggest the first-class county championship be divided into two Divisions with an opportunity for perhaps Buckinghamshire or Norfolk to join and it was against this background that there was a move to develop a cricket ground in Great Yarmouth that would be comparable to those in other seaside towns elsewhere in the country and be used for at least some Norfolk games. But nothing came of this, either.

Before the start of the 1923 season Eric Fulcher, at the age of 32, lost his life in a shooting accident. He had been an important member of the county side since 1910 and, with 2057 Championship runs (at 19.40) and 64 wickets, had made a number of valuable contributions with bat and ball. In addition to his games for Norfolk he had also been a member of Lord Hawke's MCC team that visited the Argentine in 1911–12 as well as making four first-class appearances for Kent and three for Lionel Robinson's Eleven. His best innings for Norfolk was perhaps one of 126 versus the MCC and Ground at Lord's in 1914.

It may be that this untimely death affected the county side because the success of 1922 was followed by a much poorer season that saw Norfolk finish 16th out of the 20 competing counties. The batting and bowling generally continued to rest on the same shoulders although Colman came to the fore. There were two main reasons for the decline: poor fielding and inadequate support for the leading batsmen. The only individual highlights were Falcon's 98 and eight wickets versus Hertfordshire, Colman's 125 versus Surrey Seconds and Beadsmoore's eight for 59 versus Bedfordshire. In the home game with Hertfordshire there was the curiosity of Nichols keeping wicket but taking off his pads to bowl; Stevens took over behind the stumps.

In each of the next two seasons Norfolk finished sixth. This improvement was largely down to the batting of Falcon, Stevens, Colman and Nichols and the bowling of Falcon, Beadsmoore and Watson and, in 1925 at least, Nichols. In each season the county lost only one game compared with a

Norfolk going out to field, 1923. *Geoffrey Stevens is in the middle of this photograph, hands in pockets. He was a Minor County batsman of the highest class and considered by many to be good enough to succeed at first-class level.*

combined total of nine victories. Individual highlights included the captain's 148 and eleven for 78 versus Surrey Seconds at Hunstanton in 1924; this being the first time a Minor County game had been played there. More unusual in 1924 was the appearance of Edward Long, a lob – that is under-arm – bowler; he was the last such bowler to play for Norfolk. Nichols' 127 out of 191 in the first innings of the 1925 away game with Staffordshire was also notable given that the opposition included Sydney Barnes in their attack and Nichols himself was now 47. In its review of the 1925 season, *Wisden's Almanack* recorded that several new amateurs appeared in the side during the season but 'no pronounced talent was discovered'. The county's amateurs also included Neville Tufnell who had made his Norfolk debut two years previously. Now 38, he was a middle-order batsman, at least at this level, and a wicketkeeper. Another Cambridge Blue, when he was a contemporary of the Norfolk captain, he had toured South Africa with the MCC in 1909–10 and in the Second Test had substituted as wicketkeeper when the original choice was injured; in doing so, he became the first substitute to make a stumping in a Test match. He played in the final Test of that series as the first-choice selection but then waited a further 12 years before playing his only county match for Surrey. He also once stumped five batsmen in one innings from the same bowler. However, he did not pull up any trees for Norfolk.

Financially, the County Club was now subject to the payment of entertainment tax introduced in 1916 as a wartime measure but to remain in place until 1960, and this made substantial inroads into their potential profit. For instance, for the 1924 season, on a turnover of approximately £1200, there was a net profit of £126 after a tax bill of £104.

Elsewhere, *The Cricketer* reported that there had been no improvement in the fielding or catching. This was perhaps not surprising given that a number of key players were beginning to age. For example, at the end of the 1925 season in which Norfolk conceded their highest ever Minor County score of 550 for five declared by Surrey Seconds, Nichols was 47, Tufnell 38, Falcon and Watson each 37 and Stevens 34. Good young players were not coming through, and unsurprisingly the County Club now entered a relatively unsuccessful period. In addition, for the 1926 season, Watson was now coaching at the Royal Navy College in Dartmouth and therefore unable to play. A new professional, right-arm fast bowler Reginald Covill from Cambridge, was engaged but he did not come up to expectations and left after two seasons in the county team; his subsequent career with the county of his birth was much more successful. The batting, apart from Falcon, Stevens and John Coldham, performed moderately and Colman could play just once. Only Geoffrey Mower of the bowlers provided effective support for the captain but all the bowlers were let down by the fielding. The outcome was that of the ten matches played five were lost and there were no victories.

The individual highlights were a century and five-wicket haul for Falcon against Kent Seconds; 104 not out (out of 190) by Stevens, batting at number seven, against Surrey Seconds; and a fine hundred by Coldham versus Hertfordshire. Coldham had first played in 1924 and appeared in the Minor County game against the touring South Africans in that year, doing much towards his side's success. He was a teacher, however, and this restricted his availability but when he could play he often scored valuable runs. The score-sheets for 1926 also included for the first time the name of Rought-Rought, a cricketing family from Brandon. There were three brothers altogether – Basil, Rodney and Desmond – and it was the first two who made their debuts in 1926. Thereafter, and certainly until 1939, their name was synonymous with Norfolk cricket. In addition, Rodney and Desmond won cricket Blues at Cambridge University.

At the start of the 1927 season, Norfolk engaged Albert Lord from Leicester as their county coach on a three-year contract. (His real name was in fact Albert Callington, but he decided to change it, apparently because, when he first joined Leicestershire, they already had players by the name of King and Knight and he too now wanted to be part of the aristocracy!). That year also saw the discontinuation of matches with Staffordshire because of the cost of making the long journey.

The county rose to mid-table in 1927, a season badly affected by wet weather. The main problem when play was possible was the batting where Falcon's average of 44 was more than twice that of the next best; he alone passed 80 in the ten games. On five occasions, out of 12 completed innings, they were dismissed for under 100; on three occasions, under 50 with a lowest of 36 against Buckinghamshire. They were not helped by Colman's absence for much of the season through ill-health. Beadsmoore was the most successful of the bowlers, and Rodney Rought-Rought chipped in with useful wickets. Fielding was still a problem, particularly in the slip area. The 1927 season was the last in which Harold Watson played for Norfolk. Altogether in the Minor Counties Championship, he captured 341 wickets at an impressive average of 17.23 as well as scoring 1403 runs and taking 54 catches.

The fixture list was starting to have a repetitive look with home and away fixtures with the Second Elevens of Kent, Leicestershire and Surrey and with Hertfordshire and Buckinghamshire, in a championship that, by 1928, had grown to 23 counties. Three victories were recorded compared with a total of one in the two previous years, and only one game was lost. Almost inevitably, the captain led the way, topping both sets of averages with impressive returns in both disciplines and a best match performance against Buckinghamshire when he scored 104 and took seven for 82 including a hat-trick; this being the first occasion on which a player had scored a century and taken a hat-trick in the same Minor County match. In addition, Rodney Rought-Rought began to fulfil his promise scoring 470 runs at an average of over 39 and taking 30 wickets at just over 24 each. Beadsmoore and Nichols provided variety in the bowling attack and were reasonably effective. *Wisden's Almanack* noted that the fielding 'reached a much higher level of efficiency' that probably was linked to the development of a number of younger players.

For the 1929 campaign Norfolk had dispensed with the professional services of Frederick Hyland although his only Norfolk appearance was as a substitute fielder. In addition, Lord had yet to qualify and would leave in 1930 before doing so. This left Nichols as the only paid player and, at the age of 51, he was awarded the home game with Hertfordshire as his benefit match. In total, his benefit raised approximately £220, a sum that was regarded as good for the times. The hope had been to engage another professional bowler but in the event only J. Cresswell, who contributed little on the field, materialised, and he made no greater mark than Hyland. As it was, Rodney Rought-Rought responded to the need by taking 59 wickets, including a hat-trick versus Buckinghamshire, at the impressive average of 12.94. Falcon, Nichols and Beadsmore again provided the necessary support. The batting was less consistent with only the captain and Stevens having good seasons. Falcon hit 189 against Leicestershire Seconds and in doing so put on 170 for the sixth wicket with wicketkeeper John Bally. Bally himself hit his only county hundred in the same innings.

Lincolnshire replaced Leicestershire Seconds in the fixture list for 1930, a season when Norfolk fell four places to nineteenth in the championship table. The batting in particular continued to let the county down – 39 in the first innings of the home game against Surrey Seconds being the low point – with only Coldham and Basil Rought-Rought enhancing their reputations. The latter scored his maiden Minor County hundred in the away game with Hertfordshire. Nichols was given a five-year coaching contract with Norfolk although he played only a handful of games. He did, though, return match figures of ten for 48 in that same Hertfordshire match. Walter Eagle who, like the Rought-Rought brothers, came from Suffolk, marked his debut season with six for 64 versus Kent Seconds, and overall was the most successful bowler. He played only three years for Norfolk but reappeared with Cambridgeshire between 1935 and 1939. The season marked the end of an era with the retirement of Geoffrey Stevens, and Geoffrey Colman also played his last Minor County game. The wounds he suffered in the First World War affected his health and, by 1930 and at the age of 38, he no longer felt equal to the strains of county cricket. Nonetheless, he had been a successful performer for Norfolk in the 1920s scoring 2379 Championship runs at an average of 30.50. Sadly, he died five years later, just after his 43rd birthday.

1930 saw the Minor County debut of three players who would appear regularly in the Norfolk side in the years to come. Batsmen Cedric Thistleton-Smith (2208 runs at an average of 23.00) and Harold Theobald (1650 runs at (22.30) and right-arm medium-fast bowler 'Jack' Lingwood (127 wickets at 18.44) all had their days of individual success in the years that followed.

That 1930 season marked a particularly low point in the county's fortunes but the following year saw Norfolk climb to tenth. More success would have come their way had the batting been stronger – only once, for instance, did they pass 210 in an innings and the highest individual score was only 73 not out. But the signs were encouraging and the County Club's membership of about 600 could look forward with some confidence. Basil Rought-Rought was maturing as a batsman and he easily topped the averages and had the highest runs aggregate. He also carried his bat through the first innings against Hertfordshire with 52 not out in a total of 110. His brother, Rodney, dominated with the ball with 55 wickets at 9.49 each including match figures of 14 for 73 versus Buckinghamshire. Eagle also made progress and Alec Utting showed promise with the ball, although Beadsmoore fell away. *The Cricketer* recorded that the 'brilliant wicketkeeping of Captain Pedder was one of the features of the season'. He had first played for Norfolk in 1913 and this was his last season. He also played one game for Gloucestershire in 1925. In the light of what was to come, it is worth noting that David Walker, at the age of 18, made his debut, scoring that 73 not out just referred to. He came into bat with the score at 7 for one and was still at the crease when the last wicket fell. Born in Loddon, he was educated at Uppingham School and won his cricket Blue in each of his three years at Oxford University (1933–1935). For this year Norfolk also had the services of three professional coaches with Nichols being joined by Lingwood and John Daley who in the event left within a year to take up a professional appointment with the Wisbech club and in 1939 took 46 wickets in his only season for Suffolk.

1931 was the last season in which two of the leading bowlers of the previous decade appeared in the Minor Counties Championship. Beadsmoore in the 12 years he represented Norfolk took 294 wickets at the impressively low average of 14.28 taking five wickets in an innings on 18 occasions. Nichols, too, hung up his Championship boots finishing with 3263 runs (at 24.35), 224 wickets (at 19.55) and 72 catches (plus a stumping) in exactly 100 matches.

There was a falling back in 1932, although the feeling was that the season would have been more successful with better weather and better luck with the toss. Again the batting was the weaker of the disciplines with only Basil Rought-Rought reaching three figures – 109 against Leicestershire Seconds. He had, again, the highest aggregate, too. However, there were useful contributions from Falcon, Walker (in the few games he played) and Bill Edrich in his first Minor County season. Walker and Edrich were both still teenagers. In the last fixture of the season Edrich, who had begun his championship career with two ducks, top-scored in both innings. Lingwood was the most successful bowler with 50 wickets and a best match performance of eight for 24 and eight for 50 in the opening fixture with Lincolnshire, that match return being bettered only by Charlie Shore's figures against Durham in 1897. He was well supported by Rodney Rought-Rought. However, the bowling averages were topped by 16 year-old Tristan Ballance who like Walker was at Uppingham School. His 16 wickets came at 11.75 runs each and included five for 28 on his debut. The quartet of exceptionally promising youngsters was completed by Wilfrid Thompson, described in his obituary as 'a bowler of explosive pace and a hitter of numerous sixes of quite prodigious carry'. He, too, went to school at Uppingham and was a fine all-round sportsman who also represented Norfolk at rugby and golf. He also served as a major in the Coldstream Guards in the Second World War.

As the new season dawned, there were genuine reasons for optimism within the county. The fixture list, with ten games, had a familiar look to it save that Cambridgeshire had replaced Surrey Seconds. Home matches were almost always played at Lakenham with three in the Festival Week although around this time Hunstanton would, with eight fixtures between 1924 and 1937, occasionally host a match. But King's

Lynn, apart from two matches in 1947 and 1948, had ceased to be used as a home venue. The opening game in 1933 was away to Lincolnshire where Basil Rought-Rought continued his good form of the previous season with 111 before the bowlers led the county to an innings victory. The next game against Hertfordshire saw Norfolk bowled out for 54 before Rodney Rought-Rought took eight for 24 including a spell of five wickets for two runs in eight overs. Rain on the second day prevented a positive finish. Away to Kent Seconds, Walker (179) and Edrich (68) put on 184 for the second wicket to lead Norfolk to a score of 459. Rodney Rought-Rought took nine wickets as the home side hung on for a draw. Two further wins on first innings followed in the games with Hertfordshire (when Nichols umpired) and Cambridgeshire. In the latter of these matches, Walker (139) and Edrich (71) took part in another big second-wicket stand, this time 166. The Lakenham Festival week featured games against Buckinghamshire, Lincolnshire and Kent Seconds. In a low-scoring match, Buckinghamshire were beaten by eight wickets with Rodney Rought-Rought capturing six second innings wickets for 20. Bill Edrich took four for 37 in the same innings before steering his side to victory with 55 not out. He was awarded his county cap on the same day. Next, Basil Rought-Rought hit his second century of the season in the Lincolnshire game, as Norfolk won by ten wickets. The third Festival fixture saw Norfolk pass 400 for the second time in that season against Kent Seconds with Walker again hitting a big hundred, this time 182 not out. Thompson took the bowling honours with six for 37 and 6 for 43. Next, Norfolk travelled to Buckinghamshire where they won on first innings, as they also did in the final championship match against Cambridgeshire. In that game, Thistleton-Smith opened in the absence of Walker and hit 174. There were also five first-innings wickets for Edrich.

At this point, Norfolk sat at the top of the Minor County table with a percentage of 72.00. There then followed a most unfortunate mix-up by the Minor County authorities. It was initially assumed that Yorkshire Seconds had finished as runners up, and, as such, they exercised their right to challenge Norfolk for the title. The match was played at Lakenham on 6 and 7 September. Norfolk never recovered from a bad start and, against a side containing future England Test captains Len Hutton and

The Norfolk team that played Yorkshire Seconds in the 1933 Challenge Match.
Standing (l to r): *DG Buxton (Hon Secretary), WS Thompson, DC Rought-Rought, RC Rought-Rought, BJ Wood, TGL Ballance, FD Cunliffe.* Seated (l to r): *WJ Edrich; BW Rought-Rought, M Falcon, DF Walker, JC Thistleton-Smith. This was the play-off match that wasn't! It was only after Yorkshire's victory that it was realised that they did not qualify to contest the game in the first place.*

Norman Yardley, lost by nine wickets. Falcon (45 in the first innings) and Walker (53 in the second) offered most resistance with the bat; Rodney and Desmond Rought-Rought shared seven first-innings wickets. And so, Yorkshire returned home as champions. Except that some seven weeks later, when the final table was being checked for insertion in *Wisden's Almanack*, it was discovered that a mistake had been made in the notification of the result of Yorkshire's match with Staffordshire and that they had in fact finished third behind Wiltshire! Yorkshire had had no right to challenge Norfolk in the first place. It was by then too late for Wiltshire to exercise their right to challenge, so it was agreed to treat the 1933 Championship as 'not decided' and to ignore the so-called Challenge Match.

This unsatisfactory position notwithstanding, it had been an outstanding season for Norfolk. Walker, with over 700 runs and topping the overall

Minor County averages, was the star performer with the bat and was ably supported by all the Rought-Rought brothers, Falcon, Edrich, Thistleton-Smith and Frank Cunliffe.

There was also a debut in 1933 for Michael Barton. Born in Dereham, Barton also played for Norfolk in the three seasons (1935 to 1937) he was studying at Oxford University. He appeared in two more games in 1947 but then joined Surrey where he captained the side from 1949 to 1951, helping to lay the foundations for the side that won the County Championship in seven consecutive years from 1952.

Rodney Rought-Rought took the bowling honours with 59 championship wickets but with significant contributions from his brother, Desmond, and Edrich. Significantly, the county was recognised as a good fielding side with John Wood showing promise behind the stumps in his first county season. He went on to play 68 Championship matches for Norfolk making 143 dismissals. As a postscript to the season *Wisden's Almanack* noted that membership had increased by several hundreds.

If those supporters feared a falling off in 1934 they were to be pleasantly surprised. Although Norfolk finished third behind Lancashire and Surrey Seconds, their percentage increased slightly and they were of course the leading truly 'minor' county. The batting improved a good deal with Walker again leading the way, this time with 3 more hundreds plus scores of 95 and 83 in only eight innings. His highest score was 190 against Hertfordshire, when he featured in partnerships of 155 for the second wicket with schoolboy and future England hockey international Fred Self and 168 for the third wicket with Bill Edrich. Walker's other three-figure scores came against Lincolnshire (157) and Kent Seconds (101 not out). Desmond Rought-Rought and Edrich recorded their first Championship centuries and Basil Rought-Rought, Thistleton-Smith and Falcon also made valuable contributions. The bowling continued to be penetrative with Edrich and Rodney Rought-Rought taking most wickets and heading the averages and support from Thompson and Rodney's brother, Desmond. Edrich followed up his hundred against Lincolnshire with six for 23, including a spell of five wickets for one run in 15 balls. He later took five for 9 in eight overs against Kent Seconds (all bowled) to add to his five for 63 in the first innings. Thompson's reputation as a big hitter was growing and *The Cricketer* described the fielding as 'a joy to watch' – a far cry from the performances a few years earlier.

Off the field, Alan Colman had stood down as secretary in 1932 having succeeded Prior ten years previously, and in 1933 Captain Desmond Buxton took up the administrative reins, a post he held until 1949 apart from a one-year break in 1945. The 1935 AGM noted that the full cost of the coaching provided by the County Club – essentially for its members and their sons – had now risen to just short of £400 but reassured itself with the thought that 'few clubs in Great Britain offered so many valuable privileges for one guinea only'. The cost of coaching notwithstanding, the County Club was able regularly to report a small annual profit around this time, no doubt helped by a reduction in entertainment tax liability.

1935 saw a continuation of the county's good run. Of the first six games, four were won outright and the other two on first innings. 152 from Bill Edrich and six for 27 from Thompson helped to easily defeat Hertfordshire. Kent Seconds were also well beaten with Desmond and Rodney Rought-Rought each taking five wickets in an innings and also together adding 114 for the ninth wicket, which remains the county record for that wicket. The home fixture with Lincolnshire saw no fewer than five batsmen pass 50 including Ronnie Gladden with 94. Desmond Rought-Rought's innings of 58 included a shot that brought him 8 runs. A loss on first innings against Buckinghamshire was followed by victory over Kent Seconds (again!). Up until the last week of the season Norfolk had an excellent chance of challenging the leaders but two drawn games deprived them of this opportunity. Nevertheless, it had been another good year. The batting relied on those who had scored well in the immediately preceding years and Gladden, who had first played in 1927 but had then given up county cricket for four years to concentrate on farming. There were also debuts for Eric Edrich and Harry Birkbeck.

The wickets were spread fairly evenly with Desmond and Rodney Rought-Rought, Bill Edrich, Ballance and Thompson sharing 154 wickets. The outstanding individual performance was Desmond Rought-Rought's 11 wickets against Hertfordshire. And again the fielding was praised.

The 'golden' years continued in 1936 when, for the consecutive fourth season and excepting the invalid challenge match with Yorkshire, Norfolk were unbeaten. The season was all the more remarkable because Rodney Rought-Rought was absent through injury and three of the 12 games were so badly interfered with by rain that there was not even a result on the first innings. The campaign opened with a ten-wicket win over Hertfordshire, with a hundred from Bill Edrich in his last season before qualifying for Middlesex, and 13 wickets for Ballance. Lincolnshire were then bowled out for 41 in a one-innings game with three wickets each for Desmond Rought-Rought, Bill Edrich and Falcon. Kent Seconds were beaten by an innings before rain saved Hertfordshire from certain defeat. The return fixture with Kent Seconds saw Norfolk hit up 405 for four with 210 from Walker; he added 109 for the second wicket with Edrich and 221, in two hours, for the third with Thistleton-Smith. Kent hung on for a draw. In the next game against Buckinghamshire, Ballance took nine second-innings wickets for 32 to take Norfolk to a nine-wicket win. Unfortunately, the final game with Cambridgeshire was only drawn, with the county in a strong position: Barton passed fifty in each innings and there was a maiden Championship hundred from Theobald. Altogether, nine batsmen averaged over 22 with Walker again leading the way. The bowling averages were headed by Ballance (42 wickets at 8.11 each) – he was considered to be almost unplayable on a rain damaged wicket – but with support from Falcon, Edrich, Thompson and Desmond Rought-Rought. The season's outcome was that Norfolk had a percentage of 78.57. Agonisingly, Hertfordshire's percentage was 78.78 but because the two had already played one another (with Norfolk overwhelmingly dominant in both games) there was no Challenge Match. Notwithstanding, Norfolk were entitled to feel that they were the best-performing county over the course of the season.

1936 also marked the opening of the new thatched pavilion at Lakenham in memory of Geoffrey Colman who had died in the previous year. This would be a special feature of the county ground until the move to Horsford in 2001.

The county slipped to tenth in 1937, a year in which Middlesex Seconds were added to the fixture list to give 12 Championship matches altogether. It was also the first season without Bill Edrich, now playing regularly for Middlesex. In addition, David Walker, who never played a full season because of other commitments, appeared in only four matches. Even so, five batsmen averaged over 40 and seven scored centuries. Of particular note, Eric Edrich started the season by taking 161 off the Hertfordshire attack and taking part in a fifth-wicket partnership for Norfolk of 171 with his evergreen captain. Basil Rought-Rought, who topped the averages with 757 runs, then hit 159 versus Lincolnshire. Against Kent Seconds, Norfolk ran up 526 for seven, their highest score in the Minor Counties Championship, with centuries from Desmond Rought-Rought and Theobald. Walker himself recorded hundreds against Cambridgeshire and Lincolnshire. Basil Rought-Rought (143) and Ballance (107) shared a county record seventh-wicket partnership of 196 against Buckinghamshire, and Theobald and Ballance added 142 together against Cambridgeshire. The seventh century-maker was Barton – 141 versus Middlesex Seconds. There was also some mighty hitting from Thompson, including 58 against Hertfordshire with seven fours and four sixes and 69 against Kent Seconds with five sixes and seven fours, including 23 from one over. Finally, Falcon's 456 runs should not be overlooked. The bowling, too, performed well with Rodney Rought-Rought back to fitness and taking 42 wickets. He was well supported by Lingwood, Thompson, Ballance, Falcon and Desmond Rought-Rought all of whom had at least one bag of five wickets in an innings. 'George' Pilch marked his first season as a county regular with 16 wickets.

In the following season Norfolk rose to eighth, again out of 23 competing counties. Of the 12 fixtures, only one was lost; three were won. Lancashire Seconds replaced Lincolnshire as opponents but unfortunately the county's first visit to Old Trafford was abandoned without a bowl bowled, the same fate as befell the Test Match there a week previously. Walker remained prolific with 765 runs, including three centuries, in 13 innings at an average of almost 70. Desmond Rought-Rought also passed 500 runs, and Eric Edrich hit the only other hundred. The innings of the season, though, may well have been Thompson's 93 in 66 minutes against Hertfordshire when he added 92 for the last wicket with Lingwood. His innings included 42 in two overs from one unfortunate opposition bowler. Theobald made useful runs including 86 in a third wicket partnership of 207 with Walker (158) versus Cambridgeshire. As to the bowling, Rodney Rought-Rought, again through injury, did not feature at all and it was left to his brother, Desmond, to lead the way with 38 wickets. The most impressive performance with the ball, though, came from Geoff Edrich – who was now assisting Nichols with the coaching – with match figures of nine for 53 against Buckinghamshire. Otherwise, the wickets were generally shared amongst the same bowlers as in the previous year. Eric Edrich, now established as the regular wicketkeeper, was described in *The Cricketer* as being 'much improved'.

So to the final season before the Second World War, played against an increasing threat of conflict. For 1939, the points system changed to one based on an average per game. Also, Durham and Northumberland replaced Lancashire and Middlesex Seconds as opponents. Walker again topped the batting averages with a highest score of 217 versus Northumberland and sharing in an opening partnership of 323 with Theobald, a record first-wicket stand in all Minor Counties Championship cricket to that time and not beaten until 2002 by Norfolk openers Carl Amos and Carl Rogers. Eric and Geoff Edrich and Desmond Rought-Rought all scored hundreds and Falcon, at the age of 51, topped 500 runs. Geoff Edrich's contributions included a stand of 112 with Rodney Rought-Rought for the ninth wicket against Cambridgeshire. On the bowling front, Rodney Rought-Rought took 30 wickets but the other two successes were newcomers. George Langdale, an off-break bowler, had played a handful of games for Derbyshire and would appear for Somerset after the war. In this season with Norfolk he took 22 wickets but although he was more successful in first-class cricket as a batsman he did not pass 50 in his 11 innings for Norfolk. Later, in 1953, he took 71 championship wickets for Berkshire including ten for 25 against Dorset. The other debutant was Cecil Boswell, a leg-break and googly bowler, who had played for Essex between 1932 and 1936 and was now qualified for his new county. He captured 38 wickets, a prelude to greater success when peace returned.

The combined effect of these performances was that Norfolk rose to seventh. However, the final matches were played out in a somewhat strange atmosphere and for the final two games the county were without the two players who headed their batting and bowling averages: Walker and Ballance. In fact, and although it was not known at the time, both had played their last Minor County game. In his eight seasons, David Walker

Norfolk going out to field, 1939. (l to r): *CSR Boswell, M Falcon, WS Thompson, DF Walker, EH Edrich, RC Rought-Rought, GR Langdale, HE Theobald, TGL Ballance, DC Rought-Rought. The missing player is almost certainly GA Edrich.*

topped the batting averages seven times. In July 1939 he was invited to lead Sir Pelham Warner's Eleven against The Rest in the Folkestone Cricket Festival in September although the match never took place. In 1940 *The Cricketer* opined that he 'would assuredly have been one of the leading amateur batsmen if he could have spared the time for first-class cricket'. However, by then he was serving in the Education Department of the Sudanese Government but he then joined up with the RAF and two years later, and aged 28, Flight Lieutenant Walker was dead, killed in operations over Norway. He was not only a fine cricketer; he had also won a hockey Blue at Oxford. Prior to the war, he was a teacher at Harrow School and it was this that in his later years with Norfolk restricted his appearances. His overall record for Norfolk was 3997 runs at an average of 63.44 and 13 hundreds. His average is exceptional by any standards.

Major Tristan Ballance was only 27 when he was killed in action near Naples, only three months after being awarded the Military Cross for gallant and distinguished service in North Africa. He won his cricket Blue at Oxford in 1935 and 1937 and, together with David Walker, would probably have been a key member of the Norfolk side for many years to come. As it was, he took 168 wickets at an average of only 17.14.

Rodney Rought-Rought had also played his last competitive game for Norfolk finishing with a Minor County record of 2039 runs (at 16.05) and 438 wickets (at 15.42). His brothers played for a short period after the War with Basil finishing with a Championship record of 4665 runs (at 23.68) and Desmond with 2948 runs (at 26.55) and 242 wickets (at 21.34). Between them, they represented Norfolk on 334 occasions in the Minor Counties Championship, with Basil leading the way with 140 appearances. Basil, as well as wicketkeeper Wood, spent four years in a prisoner-of-war camp in Germany.

And in 1943 Humphrey Master died. He played occasionally for Norfolk between 1905 and 1911 but then went on to serve on the County Club Committee for 29 years including 15 as Chairman.

# CHAPTER 9

# Ups and Downs
# (1946–1976)

For the period of the First World War it had generally been thought unpatriotic for adult cricket to continue. Not so between 1939 and 1945 when, although the first-class and minor county programmes were put on hold, recreational cricket was encouraged. Nonetheless, the loss of six seasons of competitive cricket slowed down the development of younger players who might otherwise have come through in that period. Certainly, at first-class level, this resulted in the backbone of the county elevens in the first post-war season comprising very largely of players who had appeared in 1939. Furthermore, most of those who did appear for the first time in 1946 played only a small number of games and did not feature again at that level. Amongst other consequences, the MCC sent an ageing party to Australia in 1946/47, and they were beaten easily. And an unusual situation arose at the Oval when a certain Nigel Bennett turned up before the start of the 1946 season to ask about the possibility of some second eleven games and was offered the captaincy of the Surrey first team in the mistaken belief that he was someone else of the same name!

Of course, too, the more tragic effects of war affected the county sides of 1946. In this respect, Norfolk, with the loss of David Walker and Tristan Ballance, together with four very promising young players in David Colman (at the battle of El Alamein), James Jackson (in a war-time accident), John Sale and Richard Kerrison, were probably hit harder than most; indeed,

Jackson and Colman had already represented Norfolk in the Minor Counties Championship. Also, there were no Edriches to strengthen the batting. The net result was that the Norfolk side of 1946 contained a mixture of players whose best days had either passed or were to come. This was illustrated in the reappointment of Michael Falcon as captain. He was now 58, and it had been 34 years since he first led the side. Norfolk played just six matches in this first post-war season, winning only the opening game against Hertfordshire when Thompson, Boswell and Peter Powell, on his debut, each took five wickets in an innings and the skipper scored an unbeaten 70. Gerald Mitchell, the Framlingham College captain, showed promise, hitting the highest individual score of 95 (out of 157 all out) in the return fixture with Hertfordshire. All in all, however, Norfolk did not have a successful season, finishing 14th out of 18 competing teams. It was a portent of times to come.

Michael Falcon retired at the end of that season, although he remained involved with the county club in various capacities including chairman and President. For the 1947 campaign the new captain was Wilfrid Thompson. The points system changed again but remained based on an average per match figure in order to reflect the fact that counties, again numbering 23 and including six Second Elevens of first-class counties, continued to play an unequal number of fixtures. Norfolk themselves played ten games, winning two but losing five. Young players were introduced, most notably Nigel Moore (aged 17), and altogether in that season they included six who were still at school in the summer term. 'George' Clements (who had debuted in 1938) posted the only hundred of the summer – 114 versus Hertfordshire – but the outstanding performance came from Boswell who in the home fixture with Hertfordshire took nine second-innings wickets for 90. The new captain headed the batting averages and also had the highest aggregate with 412 runs. Boswell did likewise with the ball – 52 wickets at an average of 15.55 – and was well supported by Frederick Pierpoint, a fast bowler who had played a few games for Surrey before and after the war. Unfortunately, after a reasonably successful 1948 season, his performances fell away and he left the county a year later. The final point to note for the 1947 season was the two appearances made by Michael Barton but they would be his last for Norfolk. By the following season, he had joined Surrey and by the end of that year was captaining the side. This time there was no mistaken identity!

For the next five years Norfolk languished near the foot of the Minor Counties Championship whose competing teams reached as many as 32 in 1950. Out of 50 games in those five seasons there were 21 defeats and just two wins. The batting throughout this period was generally inconsistent but there were exceptions, in particular Clements, who headed the 1948 and 1949 averages; Eric Edrich, who reached 1000 runs in the combined seasons of 1949 and 1950, including 170 not out away to Kent Seconds in 1949; and Powell scored a maiden Championship century against Suffolk in 1950 when he and Clements added 188 for the fourth wicket. Thompson, Mitchell, Moore and Bill Thomas also had their days with Thompson hitting 6 sixes in an innings of 84 against Kent Seconds in 1949 and Mitchell taking 139 off the same attack in 1950. However, that was one of only five centuries in the whole of this five-year period.

The bowling was also not at its strongest at that time. Thompson was no longer the force he had been before the war, and the county relied heavily on Boswell and the emerging Peter Walmsley, who would become the mainstay of the attack for most of the 1950s. For each of the seasons 1949 to 1951, the former took most wickets with 41 (at 19.53) in 1949 the best return. His particular highlights were 15 wickets for 127 versus Buckinghamshire in 1949 and figures of five for 8 in 16 overs against Suffolk in 1952, Norfolk's first win at Lakenham since 1946. Walmsley, a fast-medium left-armer, broke into the county side in 1950 and after two modest seasons took the bowling honours in 1952 with 31 wickets at an average of 18.38, including match figures of ten for 57 versus Suffolk. Clements also had some success, most notably three for 27 and seven for 20 against Kent Seconds in 1949. There were also five-fors in this period for John Fielding (in Boswell's 1952 benefit game with Essex Seconds), David Carter, Pierpoint and Moore, who was beginning to establish himself as the main allrounder in the side. He was a Cambridge golfing Blue but in his time there he played just three games for the University. His highlight at first-class level came when, representing the Minor Counties against the touring South Africans in 1960, he top scored in the second innings with 59, this off an attack that included Neil Adcock and Hugh Tayfield, both Test bowlers of the highest quality.

On a more positive note the wicket-keeping of Eric Edrich brought special praise with *The Cricketer* describing it as 'brilliant'. Statistically, Edrich stands second only to Doug Mattocks in the list of Championship dismissals with 149 (including a small number as a substitute fielder) to add to his 2531 runs (at 30.49).

During this period Thompson stood down as captain for business reasons to be replaced in 1951 by Laurence Barrett. Thompson continued to turn out occasionally for Norfolk and he finished his county career in 1955 with a record of 2323 runs (at 20.92) and 203 wickets (at 20.93). His successor was a fine all-round sportsman, and a good enough hockey player to have a trial for England. Like many others, he also served the County Club well after his playing days were over, including a spell as Chairman between 1969 and 1976.

There were two sadder notes. In 1952, Frank Inch, the County Club Secretary, was killed in a motor accident, to be replaced by Geoffrey Stevens who in turn served until 1961 when he stood down and was succeeded by Jack Read. And John O'Brien, who had shown promise with the bat in the 1950 season, lost his life in the Korean War. More happily, membership of the County Club reached four figures for the first time although, as would continue to be case, they were still heavily reliant financially on receipts from Test matches.

1953 proved to be Norfolk's most successful post-war season to this point, winning three of their ten matches outright and another two on first innings. As a result, they rose to 15th out of 26. The captain led the way in the first game against Essex Seconds, with 103 batting at number eight in the order. The batting highlight, though, was the opening partnership in the home fixture with Suffolk when Moore (122) and Powell (120) put on 244 thereby laying the foundations for one of the victories. Moore, with 506 runs, had the best aggregate and also the highest average of those who played regularly. The bowling attack continued to be spearheaded by Walmsley (45 wickets) and Boswell (33) but the only reliable support came from Moore and Mike Harrison. The bowlers came under a particularly heavy assault from Hertfordshire's sixth-wicket pair who added 333, the highest-ever partnership for any wicket against Norfolk in the Minor Counties Championship. In the penultimate game of the season, away to

Norfolk going out to field against Suffolk, 1952. (l to r): *PG. Powell, CSR Boswell, WO Thomas, PL Mason, LA Barrett, JL Fielding, NH Moore, BGW Stevens, PG Walmsley, JC Bate, WL Drinkwater.*

Future Test stars John Edrich and Peter Parfitt, *c.* 1955.

Buckinghamshire, there was a debut for a 16 year-old left-handed batsman from Billingford, near Dereham, about whom much more would be heard in the years to come – Peter Parfitt.

The promise shown in 1953 did not carry through into the following season when only one outright victory was recorded. Powell and Moore, together with Thomas, and Walter (but known as 'Bill') Drinkwater all averaged over 24, with centuries from Powell (149) and Thomas (104, his first Minor County hundred) in a second-wicket partnership of 203 in the home fixture with Suffolk. The batting averages, though, were headed by a 17 year-old left hander with a familiar surname, John Edrich. Parfitt had an unsuccessful season with the bat but showed promise with his off breaks, not least when, with Boswell, he bowled Norfolk to victory against Hertfordshire at Lakenham. The bowling averages, though, were headed by Walmsley with 24 wickets at 19.16. His best performance was a ten-over spell against Buckinghamshire when he took eight for 40. He and Moore also bowled out Hertfordshire for 54 in the away fixture at the end of the season. For this season, Derek Lambert, an experienced coach, joined the county as a professional, although he did not qualify to play until 1955. In the event, he never appeared in the Minor County side.

By 1955, John Edrich had joined the Surrey staff and topped the batting averages in their Minor Counties Championship winning side. Parfitt, who hit 401 runs at 57.28, replaced him at the top of the Norfolk averages. Still at school, he had a top score of 131 against Kent Seconds which led to him being awarded his county cap. He headed the bowling averages as well, as a result of taking seven for 44 in the away fixture with Hertfordshire. Nigel Moore also averaged over 50 with the bat, and considerable support also came from John Bate, Thomas (who had the highest aggregate with 560 runs including two hundreds), Powell, who had taken on the captaincy, 'Dick' Hoff (with 118 out of 143 for 2 against Hertfordshire and scored in 80 minutes) and Boswell. All of them averaged over 25. The bowling honours were more narrowly confined with Walmsley and Boswell taking 38 and 31 wickets respectively. In addition, David Thorne returned second-innings figures of six for 29 against Buckinghamshire. He went on to a career in the Army where he rose to the rank of Major-General and following the end of the 1982 Falklands conflict took over command of the UK forces there. His twin brother, Michael, also played for Norfolk. David Thorne first played for Norfolk in 1954 but a newcomer in 1955 was Andrew Corran, an 18 year-old allrounder from Gresham School who went on to win his cricket Blue in each of his three years at Oxford University and then play over 100 games for Nottinghamshire, captaining them in 1962. In his last season there, he took over 100 wickets. He was also a good enough hockey player to win his Blue in that sport. All that was in the future, though in 1955 it was this blend of experience and youth that saw the county rise to 11th place out of 30, their only top-half finish between 1946 and 1958.

1955 also saw the County Club signing up to the Eagle Club scheme. By allowing free admission to all members of the Eagle Club Norfolk received a donation of £42 from the boys' comic of that name. At the same time, the county membership rose to around 1100.

For 1956, the county fixture list increased to 12 games, with fixtures against the Second Elevens of Middlesex and Nottinghamshire. The season also saw a new professional with Ted Witherden replacing Boswell. The retiring professional had played 103 Minor County matches for Norfolk in which he took 329 wickets (at 22.02) as well as scoring 1921 runs. He remained involved with the County Club both as a coach and in an administrative role. Witherden was a right-handed batsman and off-break bowler who had played a number of matches for Kent in the early 1950s. He had also turned in some good performances for Kent Seconds against Norfolk in that period which no doubt registered with his new county when the time came to find a successor to Boswell. Even allowing for the increase in fixtures, his performances in his first year with Norfolk, and indeed the years that followed, were exceptional. His opening season saw him top both sets of averages with 658 runs at nearly 44 and 39 wickets at 13.33. Unfortunately, the only reliable support came from Moore and Powell, with the bat, and Walmsley, with the ball. The net result was the county finished the season one place off the bottom of the table with no wins. An all-out score of 38 in the final game against Hertfordshire was the lowest point. On the brighter side Henry Blofeld, aged 16 and an opening batsman and wicketkeeper still at Eton, made his debut and showed much promise.

There was no Peter Parfitt in 1956. He had joined Middlesex where he was a regular until 1972. Indeed, he was one of the most prolific batsmen in the country during this period, scoring almost 27,000 first-class runs, including 58 centuries, as well as picking up 277 wickets and 564 catches, mostly in the slips where he excelled. Following his Test debut on the 1961–2 tour to India and Pakistan he went on to play 37 times for his country scoring 1882 runs at the healthy average of 40.91. His scores included seven hundreds.

Norfolk barely improved in the next two, winless, seasons. This was despite the increasingly impressive performances of their professional who passed 800 runs in both 1957 and 1958, including a total of seven three-figure scores. Batting support came chiefly from Powell and, in 1958, Corran who hit his only Minor County hundred against Hertfordshire. Geoff Fiddler also began to make his mark. Nigel Moore, though, played only infrequently although against Buckinghamshire in 1957, he scored 163 not out and with Witherden put on 261 in an unbroken stand for the third wicket. (This partnership was followed immediately by the Buckinghamshire openers putting on an unbeaten 205 with not one wicket falling on the second day).

1957 was the last year in which the Recreation Ground at Hunstanton hosted Minor County games, to the chagrin of those in the west of the county but understandable in the light of attendances compared with those at Lakenham.

After a poor season in 1957, Walmsley returned to form the following year with 50 wickets at 14.42, including a best match return of 12 wickets for 91 against Middlesex Seconds and best single-innings figures of seven for 15 versus Nottinghamshire Seconds when, with Corran, they bowled out the visitors to Lakenham for 46. Witherden also performed usefully with the ball and Roger Schofield, a young leg spinner, showed promise. The bowling attack also now included Arthur Coomb who had previously played for many seasons with Bedfordshire. Although now in his late thirties, he turned in a number of good performances in his eight seasons with Norfolk, notably match figures of 11 for 141 against Nottinghamshire Seconds in 1957.

Bryan Stevens played his last game for Norfolk in 1958, having made 113 wicket-keeping dismissals in a county career that began in 1937. He, too, continued to serve his county in a range of roles as well as being the Eastern Daily Press sportswriter for many years. By the end of the following season Bill Thomas's Minor County career was also over; he had scored 2259 runs at an average of 23.77.

1958 was Bill Edrich's last year with Middlesex and for 1959 he returned to Norfolk to skipper the county side. His return heralded one of the more successful periods in Norfolk's history. In his first year back in the county of his birth he made an immediate impact leading Norfolk to seventh place and making major contributions with bat and ball. In a summer when generally batsmen dominated he was one of five county batsmen to average over 40. Top of the batting list was Witherden who scored 1031 runs at an average of 79.30 with three centuries. Even now, only 13 batsmen have achieved this four-figure milestone in Minor County history and Witherden himself stands eighth in the all-time list. Moore collected 566 runs (at 56.60) with two hundreds and Terry Allcock, the new wicketkeeper and Norwich City footballer, Blofeld, Powell and David Rossi, completed a strong batting line-up. Wickets were shared more evenly for although Walmsley took most with 33 dismissals, Coomb, Corran, Edrich, Schofield and Derek Godfrey all played their part.

That season was a foretaste of things to follow in 1960. Winning six of their ten games – against Hertfordshire and Nottinghamshire Seconds (both twice), Cambridgeshire and Suffolk – Norfolk finished at the top of the Championship. Leading the way was the skipper with 852 runs (at 53.25) and 43 wickets (at 16.10), although in both cases these aggregates were second, to Witherden (855 runs) and Corran (46 wickets) respectively. Edrich and Witherden scored the only centuries and had many fine partnerships together with the highest being the unbroken 180 they added for the fourth wicket against Cambridgeshire. They were well supported by Moore, Blofeld and Fiddler. In a wetter summer, though, it was the bowlers whom the county had most to thank for, in addition to Corran and Edrich, substantial hauls were achieved by Coomb, Walmsley and the two left-arm spinners, David Thorne and Joe Campbell Gibson. The most impressive individual performance, in a season when all of these bowlers had their day, was Corran's match return of four for 33 and eight for 102 against Buckinghamshire. There were also seven wickets in an innings for Thorne and Coomb in the home game with Hertfordshire.

The county's success in 1960 meant a Challenge Match against the runners-up, Lancashire Seconds, at Lakenham at the beginning of September. Unfortunately, Norfolk lost the toss and had to bat first on a rain-affected wicket. Against a side which included three players who were or would be Test cricketers and all of whom played first-class cricket at some stage in their careers, mostly on a regular basis, Norfolk did well to reach 153 in their first innings. Then, against the opening bowlers Walmsley and Corran, each of whom took four wickets, the challengers slumped to 44 for six. It was left to diminutive Harry Pilling, aged only 17 but in due course to be one of the leading exponents of batsmanship in one-day cricket, to lead the recovery with 79 not out. Lancashire were eventually dismissed for 206 and then Norfolk reached 70 for three in the second innings before the former Test offspinner Roy Tattersall took over with five for 17 in 30 overs as the county fell away to 131 all out. The visitors lost just one wicket in chasing the 79 required for victory. It had nonetheless been a fine season and one of which Norfolk could be proud.

It was at the end of the 1960 season that *The Cricketer* printed an article headed 'Norfolk shows the way', which opened with the statement that a 'spectacular new approach to two-day cricket has developed in the Eastern counties of England in the past few years'. Having referred to Norfolk's success in 1960, it went on to suggest, against a background of falling spectator numbers and a real concern about the future of the game in this country, that even more encouraging was the fact that, in some places at least, the new order had awakened some slight new interest among the watching public. Peter Powell was particularly praised for his positive approach notwithstanding that, before 1960, it had brought little success for the county. With a stronger side, Bill Edrich was able to go further in the quest for brighter cricket and positive results. The writer attributed Edrich's success to four principles:-

> 'Quick runs, with no thought at all for personal averages; a
> preference for letting the opposition bat first so that he can make
> the running from behind, as it were, with no serious thought for
> first-innings points; make positive efforts, when necessary, to
> ensure that the opposition is not shut out of the game with only a
> draw to fight for; and an all-round abhorrence of time wasting and
> other negative tactics, deliberate or otherwise'.

The Norfolk team that played Lancashire Seconds in the 1960 Challenge Match.
Standing (l to r): *EG Witherden, DC Thorne, AG Coomb, GG Fiddler, JJC Gibson, HC
Blofeld, LWJ Hart.* Seated (l to r): *PG Walmsley, PG Powell, WJ Edrich, NH Moore, AJ
Corran. Norfolk topped the Minor Counties Championship table but were defeated in
the Challenge Match by a very strong Lancashire side.*

Norfolk fell towards the foot of the Championship table in 1961.
This was largely due to the ineffectiveness of the bowlers who, in 12
games, managed to capture only 117 wickets between them. This was
not a recipe for success in a season when Norfolk often batted first, no
doubt in part due to opposition captains seeking to negate part of the
winning formula of 1960. Edrich topped the bowling averages and Tracey
Moore, with 20 in his first full season, took most wickets. The captain
also headed the batting averages with 558 runs at 79.71 and nine others
averaged 20 or better with Fiddler (467 runs) and Evan Hall (459 runs)
the other major contributors. Witherden's batting fell away although he
did score one of the three county hundreds; Edrich hit the other two in
the home game with Staffordshire. Towards the end of the season, Norfolk
turned to a group of younger players and in the final match, against
Lincolnshire, seven of the side were aged under 20. The new players

Clive Radley, *c.* 1967. *Radley's career with Norfolk was confined, as a seventeen-year old, to the 1961 season. He then followed the footsteps of Bill Edrich and Peter Parfitt to Middlesex and in due course into the England side.*

included a number who were to make their mark in the years to come: wicketkeeper batsman Doug Mattocks, allrounder and future captain David Pilch and a 17 year-old who soon followed Parfitt to Middlesex, Clive Radley. Hertford-born but educated in Norwich, Radley went on to score 26,441 first-class runs with 46 hundreds. He stepped up to Test cricket relatively late in his career playing eight matches and hitting two centuries. Following his retirement he became the MCC's Head Coach between 1991 and 2009. Hall had also joined the MCC Groundstaff for the 1962 season but with less success.

Norfolk's topsy-turvy form continued over the next few years. Four victories in 1962 saw a jump to 8th place out of 23. In a side with a blend of youth and experience it was Edrich who again topped both sets of averages with 587 runs at 41.92 and 39 wickets at 13.53, including 12 in the home fixture with Buckinghamshire. There was a final county hundred for Witherden in his last season with Norfolk and although otherwise he contributed little in that year he had altogether in his seven seasons scored 4794 runs (with 13 centuries and 22 fifties at an average of 45.65) and taken 104 wickets at 21.15. Rather, the batting relied on Fiddler, Nigel Moore and Powell to support the captain. Martin Wright, Tracey Moore and Gibson came to the fore with the ball although Walmsley fell away and by the end of the season he also had played his last county game. He had in his 13 years with the county side taken 329 Championship wickets at 21.19. Coomb also contributed little in this 1962 season and his county career was also effectively over.

The county slipped back in the following year notwithstanding more fine performances from the captain. He scored the only hundred – an undefeated 136 out of 211 for nine – in the second innings of the home game with Suffolk when, in a ninth-wicket partnership of 50 with Fiddler, his partner scored exactly nought! Pilch hit just under 500 runs. And in the home match with Hertfordshire, Mattocks (65 not out) and Wright (48) added 101 for the tenth wicket, which remains a county record. Gibson continued to develop as an allrounder and there was a promising first season from Billy Rose, primarily a slow left-arm bowler but who would make useful contributions with the bat. In the home game with Lincolnshire he returned match figures of ten for 73 and hit 41 in an innings win. For this 1963 season, the new professional was John Shepperd, a right-arm fast-medium bowler from Middlesex and holder of the MCC advanced coaching certificate. He came recommended by Bill Edrich and followed his 163 Championship wickets (at 23.60) with contributions as a coach and administrator, playing a significant part in the development of cricketers in Norfolk in the years that followed.

Peter Powell's long playing career with the County Club finished in 1963. Since his debut in 1946 he had played in 140 Minor County matches, scoring 5459 runs (at 23.63) and holding 100 catches. He had started his county career as a specialist spinner and tail-end batsman but soon worked his way to the top of the batting order by which time his bowling was no longer required. His post-playing years included a period as the National Cricket Association's Development Officer for the Eastern Region.

1964 was more successful with Norfolk winning four of its 12 games. Inevitably, Edrich again led the way, this time with 713 runs and, by now operating as a slow bowler, 28 wickets. Others who performed well were Ian Mercer (639 runs including a top score of 127 against Cambridgeshire), Rose (with 43 wickets) and Shepperd (37 wickets). Wright twice took six wickets in an innings. That year marked Nigel Moore's last in the county side; altogether he had scored 4761 runs (at 31.95) including seven hundreds and 28 fifties.

In the following year, when Norfolk dropped towards the foot of the table, it was again Edrich, Mercer, Rose and Shepperd who were the leading performers. Mercer, who was chosen to play for the Minor Counties Eleven to play the touring South Africans, scored the only hundred and Rose took 11 wickets against Suffolk but they had little support in a season made all the more disappointing by bad weather that significantly affected a number of games. Some comfort could however be taken from the policy, for the time being at least, of only selecting players associated with the county.

That 1965 season marked the final Minor County game for Henry Blofeld; since his debut in 1956 he had scored 1530 runs and made 65 dismissals. He had been a very promising schoolboy cricketer, good enough to be the Cricket Society's first Young Player of the Season in 1956, but a very serious bicycle accident whilst still at Eton proved a major setback and although he recovered sufficiently to win a Blue at Cambridge University it was as a cricket writer and commentator that he made his best and most well-known mark. He has entertained millions of cricket lovers over a period of 40 years in a style that is both individual and well-informed.

1966 brought an upturn with four wins. The same quartet of players again performed consistently over the season: Edrich scored 496 runs and took 29 wickets, Mercer hit 362 runs, Rose captured 33 wickets, and Shepperd added 253 runs to his 40 wickets. In addition, there were encouraging contributions from Pilch (489 runs) and Tracey Moore and Tony Bland with 28 wickets each. The only hundred came from Doug Mattocks, by now firmly established as the first-choice wicketkeeper, who hit 104 against Suffolk. Always reliable, he tended to alternate at this stage of his career between opening and the lower-middle order. The most exciting finish in the season came in the home game with Buckinghamshire when, chasing 234 and needing four off the last ball, Shepperd hit it for six. Earlier, Pilch and Edrich had added 179 for the third wicket. Fiddler's county career, in which he totalled 2996 runs at an average of 20.81 but without a century, ended in this year.

1967 saw a change in the secretaryship of the County Club with David Armstrong taking over the reins from Jack Read. Apart from a break between 1969 and 1972 he held this post until 1985. He also served as Secretary of the Minor Counties Cricket Association from 1983 to 2001. His contribution to Norfolk cricket can perhaps best be summarised in the tribute paid to him in the 1985 County Handbook where the Chairman wrote that he had 'spared himself neither time nor trouble over every problem both large and small which comes to him as Secretary. His has been an outstanding example of labour and love over some eighteen years'.

It was clear by 1967 that the batting was not strong enough to post competitive scores or chase down challenging targets, both necessary if the county was to be successful in the Minor Counties Championship. Bill Edrich was also now less effective as a bowler. To remedy this, and as a reversal of recent practice, Norfolk engaged two players released by first-class counties. Graham Saville was a 23 year-old right-handed batsman who had played for Essex between 1963 and 1966. Ronnie Bell, on the other hand, was a slow left-arm bowler who after a handful of games with Middlesex in the early 1950s had then spent eight years with Sussex and had close to 400 first-class wickets to his name. Their impact was immediate. Saville hit 940 runs, the highest aggregate in the whole of the Championship that year. Mercer again scored well (498 runs) and David Stockings and James Donaldson had good seasons with 510 and 470 runs respectively. Bell, for his part, headed the bowling averages with 34 wickets at 15.14 although Tracey Moore took most wickets (42) including four for 56 and eight for 71 in the away game with Hertfordshire. Shepperd, now paid on a match-by-match basis and separately for his coaching, had a good season with 39 wickets. The outcome was that Norfolk won five of their 12 games and rose to fifth, and in doing so recovered the ability to chase successfully against the clock. 208 for seven in 113 minutes brought a win against Lincolnshire; and for the second season running Shepperd hit the last ball of the match for six to beat Buckinghamshire, this time the ball improbably going through the hands of the fielder at third man.

Norfolk were further strengthened for the 1968 season by another former first-class player, this time allrounder Richard Jefferson. He was to make his mark both on the field and, later, in his contribution to youth cricket in the county. He came with the pedigree of a Cambridge Blue and six productive seasons with Surrey and was a very welcome addition to the county ranks. The combination of four former first-class players and solid contributions from such as Mercer, Tracey Moore and Pilch ensured that Norfolk continued to prosper in 1968 when they rose to fourth. Jefferson's performances with the ball (38 wickets at 8.34) enabled him to finish second in the overall Minor County averages, behind an emerging fast bowler from Yorkshire, Chris Old. Highlights included nine wickets for both Bell and Jefferson in a win against Buckinghamshire when Saville and Edrich added 137 for the sixth wicket and six wickets in each innings for Jefferson against Cambridgeshire. Indeed, the county would have qualified for the Championship play-off had they won their final game with Buckinghamshire. Instead, following the loss of the first day to rain, they lost by 40 runs in a one-innings game.

Bell left at the end of the 1968 season in which he also acted as the County Club's coach, but with Saville scoring 758 runs and Jefferson (now captain) and Tracey Moore taking 58 and 53 wickets respectively he was not missed. This time, Jefferson's figures were enough to see him head the competition's bowling averages, just ahead of former West Indian Test bowler Sonny Ramadhin, now with Lincolnshire. On three occasions he took ten wickets in a match. Rose, who had been displaced by Bell, returned to the side and bowled well, with a best innings return of seven for 59 versus Buckinghamshire. The batting was still largely dependent on Saville with Edrich and Mercer and, to a lesser extent, Pilch providing most support. A young left-hander also made his debut: Quorn Handley, but known as 'Fred', would become a regular in the county side for the next 22 seasons during which he played many match-winning innings and always batted attractively.

1970 was Bill Edrich's last full season with the county side and he marked it by heading the batting averages for the fifth and final time since his return to Norfolk. The only century, though, came from Handley's bat – exactly 100 against Suffolk. Mercer, Philip Mindham, Gerald Goodley and

Paul Borrett also scored valuable runs. Rose was the leading bowler with 43 wickets and was supported by the veteran Edrich and Tracey Moore; both Rose and Moore each took ten wickets in a match. Without Saville's runs – he had been re-engaged by Essex after scoring 2275 runs in his three seasons with Norfolk at an average of 44.60 – and the bowling of Jefferson, the county slipped to 12th place. This, though, was to be their highest position until the end of the new decade.

It was now becoming more common for Minor County clubs to engage either Test or seasoned county championship players coming to the end of their careers. For 1971, for instance, Lincolnshire had Ramadhin, Cambridgeshire had Terry Jenner, the Pakistani Nasim-ul-Ghani was with Staffordshire, Derek Shackleton with Dorset and Dave Halfyard at Durham. A county's success became linked to the quality and performances of their import(s). Norfolk had none in 1971 and finished outright last (out of 22) for the first time. There were no individual hundreds although Donaldson (who had his best season with 527 runs and carried his bat for 77 not out against Cambridgeshire), Robin Huggins, Mercer (who had taken over the captaincy when Jefferson stood down during the 1970 season and in his nine seasons with Norfolk recorded 3688 runs at 31.79) and Pilch were reasonably consistent. The bowlers, though, captured only 91 wickets between them in the 12 games to which Moore contributed 44.

It was a similar story in 1972 although the batting was strengthened, albeit only for that season, by the arrival in Norfolk of Ken Taylor to take up a teaching post. He had enjoyed a successful career with Yorkshire that included three Tests, 13,000 runs and 131 wickets and had been an integral member of their championship-winning sides of the 1960s. In the event, and apart from two games in 1974, he was to play just this one season for Norfolk but he made such a mark that his 831 runs at an average of 63.92 and including four hundreds and another score of 99 not out, were sufficient to place him at the top of the Minor County batting averages and make him Norfolk's first winner of the Wilfred Rhodes Trophy inaugurated in 1955 and awarded to the leading batsman in the competition. Huggins and Mattocks offered most support but the greater weakness continued to be on the bowling front where, again, only Moore with 38 wickets achieved any great success.

Norfolk remained near to the foot of the Championship table in 1973 although for the first time in three years they managed to win a game, against Hertfordshire. This was due to Moore returning second-innings figures of seven for 62 on his way to 36 wickets for the season. He did however have support from Keith Rudd and Neil Beacock. Without Taylor, the batting struggled to compete although Pilch, the new captain, enjoyed a good season with 443 runs. Huggins and Handley also performed with credit, but the highest individual score was posted by a returning Allcock, with 82 against Cambridgeshire.

Two wins, from ten games, in 1974 pointed to an improvement with Colin MacManus heading the batting list and scoring the only century, against Hertfordshire. Pilch's match figures of ten for 53 against Suffolk represented the bowling highlight of the year and Beacock, with 20, captured most wickets.

Whilst there was a falling back to last but one in 1975, the games were generally reasonably close with some exciting finishes. The averages were topped by two relative newcomers, Graeme Wilton and Ted Wright, although Huggins with 593 scored most runs and Mike Oxbury, with 26, took most wickets. For this and the following season the county had the services of New Zealander Ross Ormiston, a young right-handed batsman and leg-break bowler who provided some backbone to the batting without really dominating but who on his return home played over 50 first-class matches. However, to be fair to middle order batsmen, the points system now in place for the Minor County competition meant that first-innings points were decided on the score after 55 overs with the result that they were under pressure to get on or get out. 1976 was a similar story. The captaincy had now passed from Pilch to Moore and the former responded by having his best season with the bat – 585 runs at 34.41 with a maiden Championship hundred (102 not out) against Cambridgeshire. Handley hit the other century, against Buckinghamshire, and in both of these games the opponents were left hanging on at the close with one wicket to fall. Handley also passed 500 runs, and Ormiston was only eight short. Ted Wright took most wickets (33) with 25 from the captain and 29 from Barry Battelley.

It had now been nearly 40 years since Norfolk had been consistently successful on the cricket field but this was about to change.

# CHAPTER 10

# The Modern Era
# (1977–2014)

There were already signs before 1977 that the County Club's fortunes were improving, but that year saw a step change in their progress. Not least amongst the reasons for the revival was the engagement of two players of proven quality: ex-Yorkshire batsman Phil Sharpe and left-arm pace bowler Terry Barnes from Lincolnshire. Sharpe, with over 22,000 first-class runs to his name had also played 12 times for England for whom he scored 786 runs at an average of over 46. He was also recognised as one of the genuinely all-time great slip fieldsmen and, like Ken Taylor, he had been a member of the very successful Yorkshire team of the 1960's. Barnes, although not of the same pedigree, was one of the best opening bowlers in Minor County cricket and a match-winner. Indeed, in their first season it was Barnes who made the greater impact with 32 wickets, including eight for 45 against Buckinghamshire. The best individual performance with the ball, though, came from Rose with eight Hertfordshire wickets for 41. Moore, Wright and Battelley also chipped in with useful wickets, with the last-named taking seven for 83 versus Cambridgeshire. Handley again passed 500 runs for the season although the batting averages were headed by Mattocks, who also had 28 dismissals behind the stumps. John Barrett also began to make his mark with the bat.

For the following season, Norfolk's ranks were further improved by the acquisition of Stephen Plumb, a right-handed batsman and slow-medium bowler who had played a couple of games for Essex. He would be a major figure in the Minor Counties Championship for the next 18 years, helping to win many matches for his county. In this, his first season, though, he performed modestly; instead, the leading batsmen were again Handley (568 runs, including two hundreds, against Hertfordshire and Suffolk) and Barrett, but now joined at the head of the averages by Sharpe. Barnes took most wickets (37) and Pilch and Wright each topped 20 dismissals. A particular highlight was the finish to the home game with Hertfordshire when, with the visitors needing 12 to win from the last ten balls and having three wickets in hand, Pilch took a hat-trick. 1978 also witnessed the rarity of a home game away from Lakenham when Lancashire Seconds were entertained at Barton Turf because the county ground was unable to accommodate the fixture. Tracey Moore played his last Minor County game that season thereby closing a county career that in 169 Championship games brought him 474 wickets at an average of 25.28, a total second only to Michael Falcon.

The steady improvement continued into 1979 under the reins of the new captain, Sharpe. John Edrich returned for this one season and, 25 years after his debut for the Norfolk, was awarded his county cap. Notwithstanding the presence of these two accomplished Test batsmen, the real batting success was Plumb – 604 runs including one century and six fifties. The other county hundred came from the bat of Handley when steering Norfolk to victory over Lincolnshire. The averages, though, were headed by Robert Bradford. Wright and Barnes again led the bowling attack, and overall the county were unbeaten for the first time since 1936, resulting in an eighth place finish.

There was further progress, and a rise to seventh place, in 1980. For the first time in the county's history four batsmen scored over 500 runs – Handley (691 with one hundred), Plumb (674 with two hundreds), Sharpe (557) and Huggins (517). The highlight was Plumb and Handley's opening partnership of 193 in 39 overs away to Buckinghamshire, when both reached three figures. The match itself culminated in a tie with the hosts losing their last wicket to a run out on the last ball, the last over itself being a wicket maiden bowled by Barnes. Barnes (40 wickets) and Wright (36) were again the leading wicket-takers, but there was increasing support from Plumb, including nine wickets in the away game with Lincolnshire when Barnes also took five in each innings. Wright returned the best individual figures with seven for 39 against Cambridgeshire in an innings when someone who would become very familiar in Norfolk cricket, Alan Ponder, hit 111 out of a total score of 155 all out. The next highest individual score was 10! The season also marked the 200th appearance of David Pilch for the county. On the wider arena, Plumb was honoured by selection for both the Minor Counties Eleven versus the touring West Indians and the winter MCC tour of Bangladesh.

The county's fortunes continued to improve in 1981 with the ingredients for success being very much those evident in the previous season. Four batsmen again passed 500 runs: Huggins (629), Handley (607), Plumb (593) and, topping them all, Parvez Mir with 836 runs. Parvez had played three One Day Internationals for Pakistan and would end his first-class career with almost 4000 runs and 192 wickets in 80 games. Initially, combining his appearances for Norfolk with professional duties in Lancashire he had a major impact on cricket in his adopted county.

In that 1981 season, Huggins, Parvez and Plumb all scored centuries as did Nigel Cook and Bradford. Barnes again took most wickets with 32, including figures of four for 10 in 19 overs against Lincolnshire, and was closely followed by Parvez (30) and Plumb (25). Both Parvez and Plumb were emerging as match-winning allrounders and Wright and Pilch also chipped in with useful wickets. As a result of performances in which all the regulars played a significant part, the county rose to second, with four wins from 12 games. This record could easily have been better still. In the opening game versus Hertfordshire, Norfolk finished two runs short of victory with one wicket in hand; and against Suffolk the scores were level with Norfolk nine wickets down when stumps were drawn. Second place entitled Norfolk to challenge Durham at the beginning of September. Both sides were without key players, with Norfolk missing Sharpe and Handley; Mattocks captained instead. The opening two days were interrupted by rain and saw Durham reach 244 all out after recovering from 65 for six. Norfolk replied with 170 for nine, Plumb top-scoring with 43. Durham then lost two early wickets but were steered to a match-saving and championship-winning score by current Pakistani

The 1981 Norfolk team. Standing (l to r): DJM Armstrong (Hon Secretary), SG Plumb, PJ Mir, PA Motum, FLQ Handley, TH Barnes, RD Huggins, H Wright (Team Manager and Scorer). Seated (l to r): E Wright, DE Mattocks, PJ Sharpe, DG Pilch, BA Meigh. Runners up in the Minor Counties Championship, Norfolk then drew the Challenge Match with Durham.

Test allrounder Wasim Raja with 166. Left with 350 to win in very little time the match petered out into a draw.

Norfolk slipped back in 1982. Only one win, against Lincolnshire when Barnes returned match figures of 11 for 65, saw to that. The batting generally held up with Plumb having the highest aggregate and best average (640 runs at over 53). There was a maiden century for Tyrone Powell with 115 against Suffolk and a first-wicket partnership of 159 between Plumb and Handley in the home fixture with Buckinghamshire. Barnes captured 42 wickets at an average of exactly 15, a return which was sufficient to place him at the head of the Minor County bowling averages and win for him the Frank Edwards Trophy, an award introduced in 1970 for the leading bowler in the Championship. Parvez and Plumb again provided most support. The season marked Phil Sharpe's last as captain, being released at the end of the campaign because of the limit on the number of professionals a county could engage. He had made a valuable contribution in his six seasons with Norfolk, not just with his 2038 runs (at 30.87) but also through his leadership in the last four of those years. It was also Ted Wright's last season of a Minor County career that began in 1969 and saw him take 215 wickets at an average of 25.39.

1983 saw not only a new captain, Fred Handley, but a new form to the Minor Counties Championship. The 20 competing teams – 19 counties and Somerset Seconds – were divided into Eastern and Western Divisions, with each playing nine games. Winning two of their matches, and losing only one, Norfolk finished fourth. Both victories, against Cambridgeshire and Cumberland, came in run chases. In the second of these games, the county had been set 267 to win and reached this target thanks to a captain's innings of 101 not out from 67 balls. Over the season as a whole, Plumb again led the way with 726 runs including one century and five other scores over 60. Huggins and Parvez provided most support in a season when Norfolk only batted first in the last of their nine games – shades of the early 1960s and Bill Edrich. It was perhaps as well, as Barnes, after taking 212 Championship wickets at an average of 21.27 in six seasons with Norfolk, was no longer available and the bowling was increasingly reliant on Plumb and Parvez. However, there was an end-of-season debut from David Thomas who joined his older brother, Peter, in the county side.

Parvez was very much the star of the following season. He headed the county's batting and bowling lists – 503 runs at 38.69 and 59 wickets at 12.67 – this being the first 'double' since Falcon's in 1923. The bowling return was sufficient to follow Barnes as the winner of the Frank Edwards Trophy. His best figures, seven for 36, were in the fixture with Durham, who went on to win the Division and then the Championship. On this occasion, though, Parvez was instrumental in securing a six-wicket win for Norfolk. Over the season, he received most support from Don Topley, a member of the MCC groundstaff, who in his first year with Norfolk took 27 wickets. Huggins contributed 465 runs with the bat but here were no centurions. 1984 was also notable for the retirement of David Pilch. In 225 Minor County games for the county he scored 6333 runs at an average of 20.42, and took 222 wickets (at 25.27) and 145 catches. Only Michael Falcon, with 247 games, has made more Championship appearances.

1984 saw the setting up an Under-25 county side, under the auspices of John Shepperd, the team manager for the County Club. Replacing the Club and Ground elevens, initially they played mainly against club sides but in due course fixtures were arranged with similar sides from other counties. Ten years later, the Under-25 side was replaced by a Second Eleven and then, in 2000, the Development Team was established.

There was then a major slipping back in the four seasons from 1985 with two eighth places and on two occasions finishing last in the Eastern Division. The 36 games played in this period yielded just two successes and contained a run of 31 winless games. There were reasons for this. Firstly, a change in the registration rules meant that after 1985 Parvez was no longer eligible to play for Norfolk. He went out on a high by topping the Minor County batting averages with 332 runs at 66.40 and in winning the Wilfred Rhodes Trophy he became the first person to win both Minor County awards in successive seasons. In his five seasons with Norfolk he played 42 Minor County matches scoring 2458 runs at an average of 41.66 and taking 167 wickets at 21.19. To take Parvez out of the county side was clearly going to leave a massive gap to fill.

Secondly, the batting, apart from Plumb who took over the captaincy in 1987, was inconsistent. Plumb himself scored over 2400 runs in the four years from 1985 to 1988, including 204 not out against Cumberland in 1988 – the first double-century in the Championship for 27 years. A measure of his pre-eminence and the county's reliance on him is that apart from Parvez in 1985 and Huggins in 1988 no one scored more than 300 runs in a season between 1984 and 1988. There were, though, some bright performances, not least in the 1986 fixture with Bedfordshire when Plumb became only the second county player, after Bill Edrich, to hit hundreds in each innings. And in the second innings of that game Plumb shared in an opening partnership of 225 with John Carter who also reached three figures. Plumb also hit not-out scores of 131 and 70 as Norfolk just failed to beat Bedfordshire in 1987.

The bowling in this period generally performed better than the batting. Plumb continued to bowl steadily in an attack in which David Thomas, who in 1988 was chosen to represent the Minor Counties against the touring Sri Lankans, was increasingly making his mark. (Plumb himself led the Minor Counties team in that match and scored 59 and 108, a performance that confirmed his position as a leading non first-class player of the generation).

However, Topley had by 1985 left to pursue a first-class career with Essex (in which he took 367 wickets at an average of 27.64) and Nasir Zaidi, a leg spinner, who joined the county in 1985 following his release by Lancashire and was seen as a long term replacement for Parvez, had little success apart from six for 46 versus Hertfordshire and had played his last game for Norfolk by the middle of the next season. Rodney Bunting had most success in this period before also leaving in 1988 for a first-class career, in his case with Sussex. In the three years preceding his departure he took 67 wickets at an average below 20 with best match figures of 11 for 71 against Northumberland in 1986. Ray Kingshott, a left-arm spinner who, like Plumb, played his club cricket away from Norfolk came into the side in 1987 and by the following year was heading the list of wicket-takers with 28, including five for 30 against Bedfordshire.

1987 saw a change in the secretaryship. David Wild, who had kept wicket for Norfolk in a few games in the early 1970s, stood down after two years although he remained heavily involved with the County Club, as chairman between 1998 and 2002 and most recently as President. His successor was Stephen Skinner, still in post after completing 27 years of dedicated service.

The green shoots of recovery were emerging in 1988, not least in increased player availability – something that had been a matter of concern around this time. The 1989 County Handbook also reported a 'marked upsurge in team spirit'. For that new season the County Club engaged a player-coach for the first time since Ronnie Bell in the late 1960s. The chosen player was Roger Finney, a right-handed batsman and left-arm bowler who had played 114 games for Derbyshire between 1981 and 1988. So began a Derbyshire connection that has served Norfolk cricket well in various capacities. Finney made an immediate impact scoring 659 runs at an average over 41 and with a top score of 125 versus Durham. There was also a resurgence in form from Fred Handley with 609 runs and although Plumb did not have such a productive year both Steve Dixon and Danny Stamp passed 350 runs. The bowling was strengthened by the addition of Andy Mack, a left-arm pace bowler originally from Aylsham but who had played first-class cricket with Surrey and Glamorgan. In this, his only full season with Norfolk, he took 38 wickets at an average of 15.21 with an innings-best of seven for 52 versus Bedfordshire. Kingshott captured 35 wickets and Thomas, with 20 at 11.05, had the best average, sufficient for him comfortably to win the Frank Edwards Trophy. Most significant, though, was perhaps the fact that the county were now able to field a settled side with seven players appearing in all nine games and two others in eight. The outcome was a very satisfactory second place finish in the Eastern Division, only three points behind Hertfordshire. It could easily have been top spot for in the final game, versus Cambridgeshire, Norfolk were only two wickets short of victory.

1989 marked the end of Robin Huggins' playing career with Norfolk. He had made his debut in 1965 and, apart from 1969, had played in every season until his retirement. In all, in 157 matches, he scored 6883 runs with two hundreds and an average of 27.64. He, too, continued to serve the County Club in a non-playing capacity.

A closely contested Eastern Division in the following season saw Norfolk slip back to sixth but nonetheless there were encouraging signs. Stamp hit most runs with 505 and Finney, now with a three-year contract and a responsibility to develop his coaching role, again scored well. Topping the averages, though, in his first year in the county side was Carl Rogers with 487 runs including five scores over fifty. Kingshott took 35 wickets for the second successive season with a match best of 12 for 105 (eight for 47 and four for 58) against Northumberland in the last Minor County fixture of the 100th Lakenham Festival. Jimmy Lewis, who had broken through in the previous season, collected 27 wickets, including six for 62 versus Suffolk and Mark Ellis also had a six-wicket haul (against Bedfordshire).

1990 marked the last season in the county eleven for Fred Handley. He had decided to retire after 22 successive years representing Norfolk. His 7800 runs, with ten hundreds, in 162 games only partly describes his contribution for he will be remembered as much for the entertaining way he compiled them as for the bare statistics. There was also his contribution in the field where he held 121 catches.

Plumb relinquished the captaincy at the end of the 1990 season, to be succeeded by David Thomas. There was an immediate and dramatic resurgence in the former skipper's batting form – 992 runs at an average of 90, with ten scores over 50 including two not-out centuries against

Hertfordshire, 150 not out versus Northumberland (when he also took eight wickets) and two 90s in the fixture with Lincolnshire. Unsurprisingly, this return won for him the Wilfred Rhodes Trophy as the Minor County batsman with the best average. Those two hundreds against Hertfordshire meant that he became the first, and only, batsman to achieve the feat twice in the Minor Counties Championship, and his season's aggregate was the second highest for the county, behind Witherden's 1031 from one more match in 1959. Most batting support came from Finney, Dixon, Rogers and Stamp (who shared in an opening partnership of 182 with Plumb as Norfolk chased down a fourth innings target of 276 to beat Hertfordshire by nine wickets). Rogers hit his maiden Championship hundred against Bedfordshire adding 182 for the second wicket with Steven Taylor. Kingshott again took most wickets (30), including match figures of ten for 158 against Staffordshire, followed by Plumb (21) and Lewis (19). The 1991 Cumberland game was notable for two reasons. It was the first time that North Runcton had hosted a Minor County game, and it marked the final county appearance of Doug Mattocks. He had made his debut in 1961, played 212 Championship games, scored 3482 runs and made 459 dismissals – 399 catches (an all-time record in the Minor Counties Championship) and 60 stumpings.

Norfolk rose from fifth to fourth in 1992. Plumb, Rogers and Finney led the way with the bat together with Richard Farrow in his first full season. There were no individual centuries but all the regular players, even the bowlers, averaged over 20. The bowling attack was considerably strengthened by the return of Bunting who collected 30 wickets at under 22. Kingshott took 28 wickets and Neil Fox, an off-spinning allrounder, made valuable contributions with bat and ball. Sadly, the close season saw the death of Sir Charles Mott-Radclyffe. He had been chairman for 13 years from 1976 and in this, and his succeeding Presidency, had served the County Club well.

1993 heralded the arrival of Steve Goldsmith in the county side. Formerly with Kent and Derbyshire, he made an immediate mark with 917 runs at 70.54, including eight fifties and a score of 200 not out in a memorable innings at Lakenham against Cumberland when he and Finney added 290 in an unbroken third-wicket partnership, a county record for that wicket. He and Rogers also steered Norfolk to a nine-wicket victory against Hertfordshire with a stand of 172. Three others, Finney, Plumb and Rogers, all passed 500 runs for the season and the first two named also hit hundreds. In the circumstances it was unsurprising that there was little opportunity for the other batsmen. On the bowling front, Kingshott had left at the end of the previous year – his six seasons with Norfolk brought him 174 wickets – and the attack was now largely in the hands of Bunting (36 wickets), Thomas (24) and Plumb (21) with the skipper finishing as the runner-up in the overall Minor County averages to Paul Newman of Staffordshire. The captain's figures included a best return of six for 36 to help set up a convincing win over Suffolk. Overall, Norfolk finished second in the Eastern Division, behind Staffordshire.

The following year saw Rogers, with 775 runs and two hundreds, have his best season to date. Plumb and Goldsmith also exceeded 500 runs and there was a promising first full season from Carl Amos that heralded a career in which he scored 5737 runs (at 35.63 and with ten hundreds) in 16 years. However, it was the captain who headed the batting averages with 461 runs and, helped by nine not-out innings, an average of 76.83. This helped to place him second in the overall Minor County averages, just a year after he had secured a similar position in the bowling list. Yet the outstanding performance of the season was perhaps that of opening bowler Adam Cole. Going in as nightwatchman at the end of the first day's play in the game with Buckinghamshire he carried on the following morning adding 168 for the second wicket with Plumb and ending up with 102. The bowling averages were again headed by Bunting (44 wickets at 19.34) including a match return of nine for 51 in an emphatic win over Northumberland when he and Cole with four wickets each bowled out the north-east county for 56 in their second innings. Plumb added 28 wickets to his runs, and all the bowlers received excellent support from new wicketkeeper Stephen Crowley with 30 dismissals.

1994 was Finney's last season in the Championship side although he continued to be involved as the county coach. In his six seasons he had scored 2855 runs in the Minor Counties Championship at an average of 36.13. However, for the following year Norfolk were reinforced by the signing of Neil Foster, the former Essex and England opening bowler with

29 Tests and over 900 first-class wickets to his name. In this, his only season with Norfolk, he captured 29 wickets and was part of a bowling attack in which Bunting (24 wickets) and Mark Powell (25) also stood out. Slow left-armer Powell best figures were six for 69 in Staffordshire's second innings, a return which laid the basis for openers Rogers and Plumb to hit off the 230 runs required for victory without being parted. Both these batsmen again had consistent seasons with the latter scoring three hundreds, but the batting honours went to Goldsmith – 816 runs at 58.29, including three centuries and a 99, with a highest score of 156 not out against Suffolk at North Runcton. This innings included 6 sixes and 19 fours and was described in the County Handbook as 'a quite amazing innings'. 1995 also saw promising debuts from two young bowlers: Martin Saggers and 17 year-old Paul Bradshaw. The net result was that Norfolk finished second in the Eastern Division, only two points behind the winners.

The portents were not necessarily good for 1996. Bunting had retired, having taken 201 wickets (at the impressive average of 21) in his two spells with the county side, and Foster had moved on. Also, Plumb, after 18 seasons as professional, was not offered new terms and he joined Lincolnshire. In his 146 Championship games with Norfolk he scored 10,067 Minor County runs, including 17 hundreds and 67 half centuries, at an average of 43.77 as well as taking 283 wickets and 75 catches. He also played 47 matches over 13 seasons for the Minor Counties side in the Benson and Hedges competition, scoring 827 runs at an average of 20.67. To replace this wealth of experience Norfolk engaged Tim Boon, the former Leicestershire county captain and opening batsman with 11,820 first-class runs (in 248 games) to his name, and Paul Newman, previously with Durham and Staffordshire but before then an opening bowler with Derbyshire. In 135 first-class matches he captured 315 wickets.

Newman immediately took on the captaincy, but it was Boon who grabbed the headlines with 902 runs (at 64.43) including four centuries and three other scores over fifty. Goldsmith, described in the Chairman's annual report as 'so talented that I can hardly bear to watch him', was second in the averages with 618 runs. Rogers and Thomas also provided solid support. The new captain took most wickets (29) and Goldsmith and Thomas had good returns. There was also a promising first season from

Martin Saggers. *Saggers played his early cricket at North Runcton and had two seasons in the Norfolk side before joining Durham. Test recognition came following his move to Kent.*

19 year-old Mark Thomas, David's nephew, who helped to compensate for the loss of Saggers to Durham. King's Lynn-born Saggers later moved on to Kent and during his time there that earned his three Test caps. Overall, his first-class career brought him 415 wickets in 119 matches at an average of 25.33. 1996 saw Norfolk record four outright wins and finish in top place in the Eastern Division. The play-off final involved a trip to Devon, the winners of the Western Division. The hosts opened up with 259 for five in their fifty allotted overs to which Norfolk replied with 165 for seven. Devon declared their second innings at 251 for six (Newman took five for 69) so setting Norfolk 346 to win. The county were bowled out for 197 with most resistance coming from Boon with 55. It was a disappointing end to the season but nonetheless Norfolk had had a most successful year.

The make-up of the 1997 team was largely unchanged although Boon, in his last season with Norfolk, played in only four of the nine games.

However, as had been the case throughout the 1990s, the side was generally very settled. Goldsmith and Rogers both scored over 600 runs and David Thomas over 400 runs but the best performances came from Amos with 712 runs and eight half-centuries. Goldsmith and Newman took 24 and 22 wickets respectively although the leading bowler was Mark Thomas with 35 wickets at 15.29. But perhaps the outstanding performer was wicketkeeper Matthew Boyden with 36 dismissals, a new county record in the Minor Counties Championship beating Eric Edrich's 33 victims in 1939. The blend of youth and experience saw Norfolk have another successful year, this time finishing third to add to their one-day triumph.

1998 saw the introduction of two more young players into the squad in the form of Robert Moyser and James Walker. Both showed promise, but the leading batsman was Amos with 632 runs at 57.45. This included three hundreds the biggest of which was 226 not out against Lincolnshire at Lakenham, the highest-ever score for Norfolk beating Geoffrey's Stevens' 222 against Bedfordshire in 1920. In compiling this record-breaking innings he shared in a partnership of 191 for the third wicket with Goldsmith. The match itself was one of three games played that season under 'grade rules'. These were essentially first-innings games of 120 overs per side although they would continue into a second innings if time allowed. It was a two-year experiment, discontinued after 1999. Amos's double hundred was not the only impressive individual batting performance for in the second innings of the game against Hertfordshire Goldsmith hit 157 not out, adding 195 for the fourth wicket with Rogers. The bowling highlights were two seven-wicket hauls, by David Thomas and Goldsmith. But generally, the bowling was not as penetrative as in the preceding years.

With three wins, Norfolk rose to second in their Division in 1999. A wet summer was essentially the reason why no batsman scored more than 400 runs and the highest individual score was Rogers' 84 not out against Cambridgeshire. Goldsmith had the highest aggregate (365) and also took most wickets (21) although the best figures were returned by Mark Thomas with six for 31 in the game with Hertfordshire – reduced to one innings a side after rain delayed the start until after lunch on the second day – when the opposition were reduced to 50 for eight before being dismissed for 104, with Norfolk then reaching their target in 18.1

overs. In similar vein, Suffolk collapsed to 14 for seven before reaching 124 all out. The performance of the season, though, was probably in the Grade match against Bedfordshire when Norfolk chased down the target of 341. Struggling at 223 for six, the county were steered to victory by an unbroken seventh-wicket partnership of 118 between Fox and Newman. Amos's good form for the county was recognised in his selection for the Minor Counties representative eleven to play the MCC at Lord's. The season also marked David Thomas's last in the county side. In a county career going back to 1983 and comprising 122 Minor County games he scored 3002 Championship runs at an average of 27.80, took 198 wickets at 21.73 and held 84 catches.

Despite the acquisition of ex-Sussex and Buckinghamshire leg spinner Andy Clarke, Norfolk fell back in 2000. No batsman passed 300 runs and only Amos posted a three-figure score. He also represented the England and Wales Cricket Board in the European Championships. Goldsmith, Newman and Clarke each captured over 20 wickets and Newman, now player-coach, performed the hat-trick against Cambridgeshire. In hindsight, perhaps the most significant events of a rain-affected season were the debuts of three young players, allrounder Chris Borrett, wicketkeeper Luke Newton and slow left-armer George Walker.

Around this time, it was not the on-field activities that dominated the cricket headlines in Norfolk. Circumstances meant that the County Club had no choice but to move away from Lakenham, and their Committee took the decision to relocate to Manor Park at Horsford in time for the 2001 season. There were also differing views on who should lead the county side. Together, these issues ensured a lively Annual General Meeting in December 2000 at which the move to Manor Park was endorsed and the re-appointment of Paul Newman confirmed. Whatever the rights and wrongs of the respective arguments, it is a credit to cricket in Norfolk and to the County Club that these difficulties were resolved without lasting damage to Norfolk cricket.

So, the 2001 season saw the county's home venue move to Manor Park, and it speaks volumes for those involved with the Club and at Horsford Cricket Club that this was successfully achieved. In addition, Norfolk cricket must be grateful to all those who supported the move financially.

If the re-location had not been enough of a change, the format of the Minor County competition was altered again, this time to involve the ten teams in each Division playing only six games, but of three days duration. From now on, individual records and performances need to be seen in that different light. Andy Clarke had departed in the close season, to be replaced by the signing of Chris Brown, an off spinner who had been on Lancashire's books and who in his first year with Norfolk took most wickets with 21 victims. Amos was the leading batsman with 405 runs and a top score of 138 against Staffordshire.

The success in the 2001 one-day competition followed through into the next year. Winning three of their six games, Norfolk easily headed their Division, so qualifying for the Championship play-off. In seven matches, including the title decider, Goldsmith and Rogers each passed 550 runs. Amos had another consistent season and Borrett made significant progress. Brown again led the way with the ball – 30 wickets at just under 21 – with most support from Bradshaw and Goldsmith. There were also a number of fine individual performances, in particular from Amos (180) and Rogers (153) in putting together a first-wicket stand of 335 against Hertfordshire. It was the highest Norfolk partnership for any wicket and the highest opening partnership in the whole of the Minor County competition. Goldsmith also stole the headlines with 167 from only 157 balls versus Northumberland. The play-off final was away to Herefordshire who won the toss and batted first. They were bowled out for 302 with Brown taking four for 98. In reply, Norfolk totalled only 217 for eight in their 70 allotted overs; five batsmen reached the thirties but no further. The hosts then set Norfolk the impossible target of 331 in what turned out to be only 45 overs. The loss of early wickets meant a rearguard action and thanks to 51 from Borrett Norfolk salvaged a draw and a share of the Championship. Whilst this was not the outcome hoped for, it had still been a successful season.

Bradshaw took over the captaincy in 2003, leading a side that was increasingly home-grown. Although the county slipped to seventh there were impressive performances, not least, from Amos and, in his last season in the county side, Goldsmith (599 runs at 66.56). In the game against Staffordshire the pair put on 180 for the second wicket to lead a successful run chase to a target of 314; this after the opposition had opened up with

Carl Amos and Carl Rogers in front of the scoreboard detailing their record first-wicket partnership of 335 against Hertfordshire in 2002.

451 for four declared. Brown was the leading bowler with 36 dismissals and in the fixture with Suffolk he added an unbeaten 118 to his nine wickets, his innings including a ninth-wicket partnership of 103 with Matthew Goodrham. Michael Eccles took 20 wickets in this, his debut season.

Steve Goldsmith's Championship record over his 11 seasons in the Norfolk side deserves to be recorded. In 90 matches he scored 6063 runs (at 44.25 and including ten centuries and 39 fifties), took 181 wickets and held 49 catches.

For the following 2004 season, Norfolk recruited Tony Penberthy, previously with Northamptonshire, but unfortunately a back injury restricted his Minor County career to just one game. More successful was the signing later in the year of Trevor Ward, a right-handed batsman who had played 248 first-class games for Kent and Leicestershire scoring 13,876 runs, including 29 hundreds, at an average of 34.43. The absence of a regular professional enabled locally-bred batsmen to flourish, most notably Amos (556 runs with two hundreds), Borrett and Rogers who both passed 450 runs. Borrett hit his maiden Championship century with 111 versus Lincolnshire. Although Norfolk failed to record a win there were two outstanding batting partnerships. Amos and Rogers, each with a century, put on 191 for the first wicket against Cambridgeshire; and Rogers and Matthew Wilkinson added an unbroken 151 for the fifth wicket in the game with Buckinghamshire, just 20 short of the county record established in 1937. Brown returned the best bowling figures over the course of the season with 26 wickets at 25.69 with most support coming from Eccles whose best figures of four for 71 and seven for 74 came in the tied game with Staffordshire.

2005 was an altogether better year with three outright wins from the six games and a third place Divisional finish. The outstanding performer was Rogers with 779 runs amongst which were three centuries and four 50s. His average of 86.55 was sufficient for him to win the Wilfred Rhodes Trophy so following in the footsteps of Taylor, Parvez and Plumb. His season's achievements included sharing in a county record partnership of 223 for the second wicket with James Spelman in the fixture with Northumberland. There was also a match double of 64 and 141 not out against Hertfordshire. Amos, with 529 runs at just over 48, was reliable as ever; his scores included 157 out of 461 for eight against Bedfordshire. Ward, Spelman and Borrett completed a formidable top five in the batting order. Brown was the most successful bowler with 44 wickets at 18.27, including match figures of five for 53 and eight for 65 versus Bedfordshire and another nine wickets against Buckinghamshire. Skipper Bradshaw took 26 wickets at 20.69 with at least one wicket in every innings in which he bowled.

Another consistent year, again with three victories, followed in 2006. Rogers again dominated the batting with 618 runs (at 77.25) and two centuries, a return made all the more impressive because, with Bradshaw injured for the whole year, he also took on the captaincy. Six other batsmen averaged over 34 with Borrett, Spelman and Ward all scoring hundreds. Spelman's 144 came in an opening partnership of 282 with Rogers in the fixture with Bedfordshire, a game in which Brown bowled Norfolk to victory with seven for 120 after both sides forfeited an innings. Brown was again the outstanding performer with the ball (35 wickets at 22.22) with most help coming from Ian Slegg (24 wickets at 21.33).

Bradshaw returned to lead the side in 2007 when Norfolk rose to second. Runs were less easy to come by but nevertheless Ward and Borrett both hit just under 400 runs. There was also a promising debut season from Jaik Mickleburgh, soon to join the Essex staff where he has become a consistent opening batsman in the first-class game. Yet again, Brown was the leading wicket-taker with 29 at 22.03, supported by the captain (19 wickets at 19.32), Slegg and Eccles. Of the three wins, the most convincing was against Buckinghamshire when Brown had match figures of 11 for 78.

This was Paul Bradshaw's last season in the Minor Counties Championship; in 82 matches he took 175 wickets at an average of 27.54. For 2008, Rogers was the new captain and Brown the county coach. As a whole, though, the campaign was not one of the county's better years with Ward's aggregate of 398 being twice as many as the next highest. Walker emerged as a leading bowler with 23 wickets at 28.66 and Stephen Gray took over from Newton as the regular wicketkeeper as well as scoring useful runs. There was also a first game in the fixture with Buckinghamshire for Sam Arthurton who, at 16 years and 26 days, became the youngest player to appear for Norfolk in the Minor Counties Championship, to be equalled exactly to the day by Callum Taylor in 2013.

Results improved in 2009 with two wins and only one defeat lifting Norfolk to third place in the Eastern Division. Ward again headed the batting list – he and Spelman each topped 400 runs and there were maiden Championship hundreds from Ben Patston against Staffordshire (in a match that finished with the scores level and Norfolk having two wickets in hand) and Ashley Watson versus Hertfordshire, with the latter coming in between tours of duty with the Royal Air Force in Afghanistan. Walker and Brown dominated the bowling averages with 41 and 31 wickets respectively; no one else took more than eight. They each took nine wickets in the win over Lincolnshire but the individual highlight was Walker's figures of nine for 48 and seven for 48 against Cambridgeshire. The first-innings return was the best for the county for over 70 years and the match figures the third-best in Norfolk's history. 2009 also marked Chris Borrett's last season in Norfolk's Championship side; his 2546 runs at an average of 32.22 included 2 hundreds and 17 fifties.

In the following season Norfolk fell to seventh place with only one win and four draws in their six games. That sole victory came against Staffordshire when Ward scored a hundred in each innings. He and Arthurton, who hit his maiden Championship century, added 204 for the third wicket in the first innings of that game. Both Ward and Spelman cleared 600 runs with the former reaching three figures on four occasions altogether and the latter three times. Brown (26) and Walker (23) again took the lion's share of the wickets.

Walker took over as captain for 2011 when, with two games won and three drawn (in two cases with the opposition eight and nine wickets down in the fourth innings), there was again a seventh-place finish. Rogers (556) and Spelman (505) had the highest run aggregates with the former hitting two hundreds including 173 against Northumberland. Brown, with 35 wickets, was the pick of the bowlers in a season that marked the six-wicket debut against Bedfordshire of 17 year-old fast bowler Oli Stone; his ninth-wicket partnership of 104 with Rogers (172) in the same match against Bedfordshire was also crucial in securing a victory by one run.

One win and five draws in 2012 resulted in a rise to third place. Three games were badly affected by the weather with the consequence that individual returns were less impressive than in other years. Arthurton, whose commitments with Essex were now restricting his Norfolk appearances, did however hit 158 and 92 against Bedfordshire. Those with most wickets were Brown (20) and Eccles (18). This year also marked Rogers' retirement at the end of the Festival matches. In 159 Championship games he scored 10,186 runs at 38.73 with 19 centuries and 61 fifties. There was also the small matter of 148 catches. Altogether, this was a phenomenal record compiled over 23 seasons and was suitably marked at the close of his final game. Walker relinquished the captaincy at the end of the season, to be replaced by Brown.

Although following heavy defeats in their first two games (in which Harry Bush's 148 against Cambridgeshire was the high spot) Norfolk dropped one place in the following year, the remaining matches brought three highly impressive wins. Following Spelman's first-innings 181 against Northumberland, when he and Ward added 183 for the third wicket, the county then chased down 260 in 41.5 overs to secure a four-wicket victory with 16 year-old debutant Callum Taylor steering Norfolk over the line with 48 not out. Lincolnshire were beaten by 259 runs when Peter Lambert hit 80 from only 47 balls in the second innings.

Norfolk's home at Manor Park, Horsford since 2001.

The season was rounded off by a six-wicket win over Staffordshire when Ward (123 and 82 not out) and Taylor (127 and 76 not out) stole the show with partnerships of 172 (a Norfolk record for the fifth wicket) and an unbroken 115 and Nathan Perry-Warnes had set up the victory with six second-innings wickets.

Overall in 2013, the leading performers with the bat were Spelman and Ward with each passing 500 Championship runs, and Brown, for his part, increased his tally of wickets to 381 (at an average of 22.89), the fifth highest for Norfolk in the Championship. That final match against Staffordshire marked Ward's retirement. In his nine seasons as Norfolk's professional he scored 3705 runs at an average of 48.12 and with ten centuries and 20 fifties.

For the 2014 season Norfolk recruited the former Durham and Derbyshire batsman Garry Park to replace Ward, and he captained the side in the three matches that Brown missed through injury. The team's performances were mixed and resulted in an eighth place finish with the only victory being a convincing home win over Suffolk. The batting highlights were two centuries from both Park and Arthurton, but no bowler took more than Ben France's 18 wickets. Spelman, if not quite so prolific as in previous years, increased his Minor Counties' aggregate to 3494 runs, with nine hundreds and an average of 36.78. Brown, for his part, increased his tally of wickets to 381 (at an average of 22.89) the fifth highest total for Norfolk in the Championship.

Any disappointment in these results could be tempered by the fact that some of their younger players were not always available for selection because of their cricket commitments elsewhere, notably Arthurton with the MCC groundstaff and Taylor at Essex. In addition, Norfolk can take pride in the first-class careers being forged by Jaik Mickleburgh at Essex and Robert Newton and Oli Stone at Northamptonshire. All of which reflects on both the quality of coaching in Norfolk and the opportunities that good young cricketers have to develop.

# CHAPTER 11

# Over in a Day

The early 1960s saw a number of significant changes introduced into English county cricket. In 1962, the first-class counties agreed to abolish the amateur status. No more Gentlemen and Players; instead, in future all those playing first-class cricket would be called cricketers. Those who were previously labelled amateurs could now be paid in the same way as the professionals rather than either not at all or, as was often the case, by means of appointment to a paid post within a county club.

Two inter-related innovations were introduced for the 1963 season, in the form of a one-day knock-out competition between the 17 first-class counties together with sponsorship for that competition. Strictly, neither was new. The very first English cricket tour to Australia in 1861 had been sponsored by a firm of Melbourne caterers. Having tried unsuccessfully to entice Charles Dickens to visit on a lecture tour, they turned to a group of English cricketers who proceeded to make a handsome profit for their sponsors. Then, in 1873, the MCC attempted to promote a knock-out competition amongst the leading counties of the time. In fact, only one game was played, a two-day fixture between Kent and Sussex. Thoughts of a similar competition, involving three-day matches, returned in the early 1940s as the MCC prepared for the resumption of cricket after the war, but nothing came of it. It was, however, revisited in 1960 at a time when attendances at county matches were dropping markedly. The outcome was the birth of one-day county cricket, and with a sponsor!

**Gillette Cup (1963–1980)**

In its first, 1963, season, the Gillette Cup was contested only by the first-class counties. Initially, matches comprised 65 overs per side with bowlers able to bowl up to 15 overs each, though for 1964 this was reduced to 60 and 13 (and later to 12). Also, to begin with, there were no special fielding restrictions. For 1964, it was agreed to invite the five leading Minor Counties of the previous season, and this continued up until the end of Gillette's sponsorship in 1980. It will be gathered from Chapter 9 that Norfolk's championship record around this time restricted its participation in the competition to its early years.

Norfolk's first appearance was in 1965 and involved a first-round tie with Hampshire at Southampton. The hosts, who included most of the side which had won the County Championship for the first time in 1961, batted first and made 295 for 7 in their 60 overs. Peter Sainsbury top scored with 76 and there were useful contributions from all who batted. The bowling honours went to Tracey Moore (two for 45 in his 13 overs) and David Pilch (three for 44 in 8 overs). Unfortunately, Norfolk's opening batsman, Revd 'Claude' Rutter, dislocated his jaw whilst fielding which meant that Henry Blofeld opened with Ian Mercer. They put on 87 for the first wicket, with the former hitting 60, but unfortunately the innings fell away in the face of Sainsbury's slow left-arm spin (seven wickets for 30) and Norfolk were beaten by 148 runs.

Norfolk's second appearance came in 1968, and on this occasion they were drawn against another Minor County, Cheshire. Scoring was difficult on a damp Macclesfield wicket but Norfolk reached 208 all out with five balls remaining of their 60 overs. The innings was built around Graham Saville (73) and Richard Jefferson (55, including 4 sixes) and at one point the county's score was 158 for two. The bowling of John Shepperd, Tony Bland and Jefferson reduced Cheshire to 70 for five but the home side recovered to such an extent that when the ninth wicket fell they needed three runs to win. Then, with two balls left, a hit for six took Cheshire over the finishing line.

The next season brought a first-round match at home to Yorkshire. Rain delayed the start until 4.30 pm and then Tracey Moore (six for 48) and Jefferson (two for 15 in nine overs), dismissed the reigning county champions for 167. Only John Hampshire, with 55, scored freely. Sadly, Norfolk could only reply with 78 against an accomplished and varied bowling attack that included Chris Old, Richard Hutton, Tony Nicholson, Don Wilson and Brian Close. To put the defeat in context, the winners fielded ten past or future Test players and went on to win the Gillette Cup that year.

Norfolk's final appearance in the competition came in 1970, with a first-round trip in late April to Lord's to take on Middlesex. Rain prevented any play until the last of the three allotted days whereupon Middlesex batted first and reached 264 for 5. Eric Russell top scored with 80 and Tracey Moore was the pick of the bowlers with two for 41 in 12 overs. Norfolk again fell short, being dismissed for 117. There was however opportunity for a few minutes of high entertainment from Bill Edrich on his return to the scene of so many personal triumphs earlier in his career. He ended his innings of 36 with 22 from six balls – 2,4,4,6,0 and 6.

Disappointing as Norfolk's record was, to put it into context in the 18 years of the competition a Minor County only beat a first-class county on three occasions.

## NatWest Bank Trophy (1981–2000)

The National Westminster Bank took over the sponsorship of the 60 overs competition in 1981. For the time being there continued to be five Minor Counties, and now Ireland, competing with the first-class counties. However, this was changed in 1983 when the competition was expanded to include the 13 leading Minor Counties (out of the 20 competing in the two Divisions) as well as Scotland and Ireland: 32 teams altogether.

Norfolk's first season in the new competition came in 1982 when they were drawn away to Leicestershire. Batting first, Norfolk reached 164 for seven in their 60 overs with Parvez Mir top scoring with 55. The home side had little difficulty reaching their target, winning by eight wickets with 12 balls to spare. Top-scorer, with 65 not out, and Man of the Match was David Gower, now fully established in Test cricket.

In the extended competition of 1983, Norfolk played host to Glamorgan. The Welsh county posted 202 for nine with all the bowlers returning good figures, most notably Andy Agar (12 overs for 22), Parvez (three for 43 in his allotted overs) and David Pilch (three for 15 in four overs). Norfolk started well with thirties from Stephen Plumb, Parvez and Nigel Cook taking them to 136 for three. Rodney Ontong then captured four wickets to add to his 45 runs and Norfolk's innings ended 25 runs short with three overs left. It had been a close-run thing.

The 1984 season saw Norfolk again host a first-round match, this time against Hampshire. The *County Handbook* records that the game was played in front of the biggest crowd at Lakenham since the old August Bank Holiday Mondays. Paul Whittaker opened up with a spell of 7–4–5–1 before pulling a muscle and the visitors eventually reached 239 for eight. A typically attacking innings of 40 from 48 balls from Fred Handley gave Norfolk brief grounds for optimism but they were dismissed for 121 with Nigel Cowley taking five for 24 with his off-breaks.

Norfolk were again drawn at home in 1985, this time to Leicestershire, and again before a large crowd. Good bowling and fielding restricted the visitors to 213 for eight with Gower again leading the way with 41. All the bowlers either took wickets or bowled economically with David Thomas returning figures of three for 50 and Plumb bowling his 12 overs for just 19 runs. Norfolk's batsmen were unable to match the efforts of their bowlers with only Robin Huggins, with 29, offering significant resistance. Altogether, their completed innings total of 73 used up 46 overs with Test player Peter Willey returning the analysis of two for 4 in his 12 overs and Les Taylor four for 14 in 11.

The county's next appearance in the competition came in 1990 with a visit to Headingley. Unfortunately, Norfolk did not do themselves justice, being dismissed for 104. Yorkshire's opening pair of Martin Moxon and Ashley Metcalfe knocked off the runs in less than 21 overs.

1991 brought with it a first-round tie away to Gloucestershire. Following a rain delayed start, the first-class county reached 237 for seven with Mark Ellis (two for 33 in his 12 overs) and Plumb (one for 36 in his full complement) the pick of the bowlers. As in the previous year, Roger Finney offered most resistance as Norfolk totalled only 84. This reply was not helped by more overnight rain and then a hostile spell of five for 17 from David Lawrence, at the time the great hope of English fast bowling who later in the summer took five for 106 in the Fifth Test against the West Indies.

Leicestershire, this time without Gower, hosted Norfolk in the following year and whilst they again prevailed the county turned in an improved performance compared with the two previous years. Batting first, the Midlands county reached 293 for seven with Plumb and Ray Kingshott each bowling 12 tight overs. Norfolk responded well with Carl Rogers hitting 51, the second half-century for the county in this competition, and leading his side to an all out score of 161.

In 1993, Norfolk hosted a visit from Warwickshire, their first home game in the competition since 1985. A century from Dominic Ostler was the foundation for the visitors' score of 285 for nine, with three wickets each for David Thomas and Rodney Bunting. Then, and not for the first time, Norfolk were undone by an off spinner, this time Neil Smith with five for 17. Steve Goldsmith top scored with 32 in an innings total of 142.

Norfolk again provided the home venue in 1994 with Worcestershire the visitors and as in 1993 temporary stands were erected to accommodate spectators. The rules of the competition allowed them to include John "the Dentist" Maynard, a West Indian fast bowler then playing with Vauxhall Mallards and he accounted for Graeme Hick for 6. However, Worcestershire reached 309 for eight with 98 from Gavin Haynes and 78 from Tim Curtis. Norfolk replied with 172 to which Plumb contributed 57. In a game interrupted by bad weather and running over to the second day, Worcestershire won by 137 runs and, like Warwickshire in 1993, went on to win the competition.

The first-round draw for the next year paired the county with Lancashire, at Old Trafford. Against a team containing ten players who won international honours in one form or another, Norfolk began uncertainly but Goldsmith (47), Neil Foster (36) and Stephen Harvey (39) took the score to 188. Mike Atherton and John Crawley were then dismissed relatively cheaply but an unbeaten century from Jason Gallian steered Lancashire to an eight-wicket win.

In 1996, Norfolk travelled to Hampshire where they played their part in a splendid day's cricket. The first-class county opened up with a first-wicket partnership of 269 between John Stephenson and Jason Laney but four wickets from Goldsmith then helped to peg Hampshire back to 322 for six in their 60 overs. After losing two early wickets, Norfolk recovered through Goldsmith (43) and Thomas (41) before Neil Fox (68) and Mark Powell (37) added 99 in 54 minutes for the seventh wicket, the stand representing the highest partnership to date in Norfolk's contests with the first-class counties. Norfolk were eventually dismissed for 223.

Norfolk qualified again for the following year, when they visited Edgbaston to take on Warwickshire. As had been the custom, the first-class county batted first but the start of the innings did not follow the normal script. In an inspired opening spell skipper Paul Newman removed three batsmen by the time the total had reached 5. A run-out and two wickets for Paul Bradshaw then reduced the home side to 25 for six before Andy Moles and Ashley Giles led a recovery which eventually took Warickshire to 207. Newman (four for 23) and Bradshaw (three for 42) were Norfolk's bowling heroes. The county's response (127 all out) was creditable but ultimately they were undone by Allan Donald and Ashley Giles with the latter capturing five wickets. So, in the end, the upset of the season that had been threatened in the first hour did not materialise but Norfolk had given their first-class hosts the fright of their lives.

1998 saw another creditable performance, this time at home to Durham. Norfolk batted first, reaching 198 for eight. David Thomas hit 59 and there were significant contributions from Rogers and Mark Thomas. Durham began their reply slowly and lost their first two wickets for 54, but then David Boon, the Australian Test batsman, took over and led his side to an eight-wicket win with 80 not out. Paul Bradshaw was the pick of the bowlers with one for 19 in nine overs.

For the 1999 season, a number of changes were introduced to the competition. Games were reduced to 50 overs per side but the competition itself was expanded to include all the Minor Counties, rather than the highest-placed 11 from the previous season, as well as teams representing the County Boards within the first-class counties. Norfolk were paired with the Surrey County Board eleven and a high-scoring game at Cheam resulted in a 23-run defeat. Carl Amos (76) and David Thomas (70 not out) took the honours for Norfolk.

2000 brought with it Norfolk's first win in this competition. Drawn away to Cornwall in the first round, the home side were restricted to 170 for six, with three wickets for Goldsmith and two for Bradshaw. Carl Rogers then led his side to a four-wicket victory with 83 not out, an innings that earned him the Man of the Match award, also the county's first in this competition. For the second round Norfolk travelled again, this time to play Dorset. Unfortunately, after restricting the home side to 181 for eight, with Goldsmith again returning the best figures, they could only manage 71 in reply.

## Cheltenham and Gloucester Trophy (2001–2006)

At the end of the 2000 season NatWest ended their sponsorship and were replaced by the Cheltenham and Gloucester Building Society. In the first year of the new sponsorship Minor Counties Wales came to Manor Park for the first county game there after it became Norfolk's home venue. The day began with the opening of the new scoreboard and, after a rain delayed start, the visitors reached 186 for eight with slow bowlers Robbie Austin, Chris Brown and Carl Rogers bagging most of the wickets and at an economical rate. In reply, it was Rogers who held the innings together with 45 but there was insufficient support and Norfolk finished 35 short.

The plethora of domestic cricket meant that the 2002 competition began in September 2001 when the first two rounds were played. In the first of these, Norfolk entertained Holland who had just qualified for the 2003 World Cup and posted 245 for three in their 50 overs. Again leading the way was Rogers who carried his bat for 139 and was supported in a second-wicket partnership of 180 by James Walker (76). The Dutch lost early wickets to Bradshaw who finished with four for 30 in his 10 overs but recovered to the extent that they needed 15 runs from the last 12 balls with one wicket in hand. That tenth-wicket partnership took the visitors' score to 245 but the last wicket fell at that score to a run-out as Holland's last pair went for the winning run from the final ball of the innings. Norfolk went through because they had lost fewer wickets. A fortnight later, the Somerset County Board side came to Manor Park for the second-round tie. Batting first, Norfolk reached 173 with Carl Amos top scoring with 42. After 22.1 overs the Somerset Board's score stood at 61 for two but then the rains came and prevented any further play, even on the following, reserve, day. Norfolk had won through by virtue of a faster scoring rate although if the Duckworth/Lewis method (already introduced for matches involving first-class counties) had been in force for this game the visitors would have won through. The reason it was not applied was because the ECB dared not let scorers with non-first class teams wrestle with its complexities! The third round followed over eight months later, again at home, but this time against first-class opposition in the shape of Kent. The visitors batted first scoring 341 for six. Norfolk's reply began well with Rogers and Amos adding 64 for the first wicket but, not for the first time at this level, the innings fell away with Kent winning by 191 runs.

The same, somewhat odd, scheduling continued for the next season. Norfolk received a bye in the first round and then travelled to Berkshire. Batting first, the county were dismissed for 119, a score which the hosts passed less than 28 overs for the loss of four wickets. For the 2004 competition, started in August 2003, Norfolk were drawn at home to Lincolnshire who, batting first, reached 228 for nine with three wickets for Bradshaw, Newman and Josh Marquet, an Australian in the county that year as professional at the Norwich Club. This proved too stiff a target for Norfolk and despite 47 from Goldsmith, they finished 52 runs short.

2005 brought with it a more streamlined competition, comprising 32 sides of which only ten were Minor Counties. As a result, Norfolk did not qualify. For the 2006 season, the competing teams were again reduced, this time to the 18 first-class counties plus Scotland and Ireland. And so ended a period of 40 years during which the Minor Counties had their only opportunity to pit their skills against their first-class counterparts. Although the Minor Counties rarely prevailed in these contests, they nevertheless were a highlight of their cricket calendar and, in Norfolk at least, were eagerly awaited by players and spectators. It is a shame that they are no longer part of the English cricket scene. Fortunately, though, there have been other opportunities for Norfolk to achieve one-day success, and in this respect the county have very much made their mark.

### English Industrial Estates Trophy (1983–1985)
The growing popularity of one-day cricket amongst the first-class counties inevitably meant that in due course a competition would be established purely for the Minor Counties. All that was required was a sponsor and

one duly came forward in 1983 with English Industrial Estates. Played on a knock-out basis over 55 overs a side, and with a prize of £1,500 for the winners in that first year, Norfolk's opening tie was at home to Berkshire in a game played not at Lakenham but on Norwich Union's ground at Pinebanks in Norwich. Norfolk batted first and Handley (65) and Plumb (49) laid the basis for a score of 224 for eight. Plumb then took four for 37 as the visitors were dismissed for 143. The quarter-final round involved a trip to Wiltshire who passed Norfolk's score of 223 for 9 relatively easily for the loss of only three wickets.

For the 1984 season, the sponsors were known as English Estates but the competition itself was unchanged. Norfolk began with a qualifying round game at home to Suffolk (again played at Pinebanks), in a match which was reduced by bad weather to 30 overs per side and then played in what was at times heavy rain. In an exciting finish, Norfolk won by four wickets with Parvez Mir clinching victory, and reaching his own half-century, with a six off the first ball of the final over. This brought a first-round tie at the same venue with Bedfordshire who, largely through the efforts of Plumb (three for 10) and Thomas (four for 20) were dismissed for 110. Parvez again steered Norfolk home, this time with five wickets in hand. The quarter-final draw paired the county at home again, this time with Dorset, but played at Lakenham. Fifties from Plumb and Parvez took Norfolk to a score of 204 for seven, and Dorset fell 30 runs short. The semi-final, also at Lakenham, was a one-sided affair in which Northumberland were skittled out for 100 with wickets for all five bowlers. Again led by Parvez, Norfolk won by eight wickets to set up a final at Fenner's against Hertfordshire. On a drying pitch, the county struggled to 106 all out with half the runs coming in Handley and Plumb's opening partnership. Whittaker and Parvez reduced the opposition to 10 for three, and at 36 for five Norfolk were in with a chance, but the opposition captain, Collyer, rode his luck and with a score of 68 not out led his side to a three-wicket victory. Norfolk's success in reaching the final was, though, a foretaste of things to come.

The 1985 draw saw the county paired with Hertfordshire in the first round. Missed catches allowed the southern county to reach 251 all out and despite 110 from Plumb – the first century by a Norfolk player in a one-day competition – his side only reached 225.

**Holt Cup 1986–1992)**

English Estates short-lived sponsorship came to an end in 1985, to be replaced by the Holt Cup (Vernon Holt being the then President of the Minor Counties Cricket Association) although the format remained the same. Norfolk opened up with a qualifying round match away to Cambridgeshire who were bowled out for 167 and comfortably beaten by seven wickets. There were solid performances from both batsmen and bowlers and six catches for wicketkeeper Doug Mattocks. Horsford hosted the first-round tie with Suffolk and after a poor start Norfolk reached 194 for six thanks largely to Robin Huggins (63) and Mattocks (48 not out). All the five county bowlers, with two wickets each, then combined to dismiss the visitors for 171. The quarter-final tie was played at Swardeston and saw Norfolk hit up 336 for five with Plumb scoring 164 and sharing a second-wicket partnership of 251 with Huggins (96). The bowlers then ensured a comprehensive victory by dismissing Lincolnshire for 237. Back to Horsford for the semi-final against Oxfordshire and on a rain-affected wicket the visitors did well to reach 174 for eight. However, Plumb continued his excellent form by carrying his bat for 55 and Huggins hit 42 as Norfolk reached the final with a seven-wicket win. The final was at St Albans against their conquerors of the two previous seasons, Hertfordshire. Their opponents won the toss and asked Norfolk to bat. Solid contributions from Huggins (53), Thomas (46), Handley and Plumb (30 each) and John Carter (28) were responsible for a score of 223 for eight in the 55 overs. After losing two early wickets to Geoff Roff (two for 28 in 11 overs) the home side recovered to 165 for three before Rodney Bunting and Plumb, each taking three wickets, engineered a collapse that resulted in the last seven wickets falling for 28 runs and a Norfolk victory by 30 runs. Mattocks also claimed five catches as Norfolk won their first title for 73 years.

The next few years were less successful. In 1987, after beating Suffolk on the toss of a coin in a rain-ruined match, the county were easily beaten by Cambridgeshire in a game reduced to 40 overs an innings by more bad weather. The same opposition were victorious at the first hurdle in 1988 when, in another tie reduced to 40 overs a side, Norfolk collapsed to 87 all out and were beaten by ten wickets. The county batted better in the first-round game in the following year but still lost by four wickets as

Bedfordshire chased down the target of 240 with eight balls to spare. And in 1990, following a one-run win against Cambridgeshire in a game reduced by the rain to 12 overs a side, Norfolk lost by 79 runs to Lincolnshire despite 73 from Danny Stamp. 1991 brought a qualifying round win over Suffolk by nine wickets with Plumb hitting 87 not out, to be followed by an 11-run win against Cambridgeshire but Hertfordshire ended the run in the quarter-finals.

Norfolk went one better in 1992. Skipper Thomas, with runs and wickets, led his side to a three-wicket win over Cambridgeshire, and this was followed by a five-wicket success against Suffolk when there were four wickets for Jimmy Lewis and 66 from Rogers. The semi-final saw Norfolk welcome Devon to Lakenham in what was the first meeting between the two counties. Before a large crowd, Devon totalled 207 for eight, and then Finney led the reply with 53 but with 11 runs required from the final over Norfolk finished agonisingly one run short.

## MCC Trophy (1993–1998)

For 1993, the competition became known as the MCC Trophy. Norfolk, though, did not get past the preliminary round, losing in a high-scoring contest with Bedfordshire. Chasing a total of 270 for seven, Norfolk were indebted to a seventh-wicket partnership of 105 between Thomas (89) and Neil Fox (37) but in the final event they lost by 21 runs. The 1994 campaign began with a one-wicket victory over Cambridgeshire, the winning run coming from the last ball of the final over. Goldsmith was top-scorer adding 70 to his ten economical overs. However, Norfolk went out of the competition at the next stage, losing by 31 runs to Bedfordshire. Norfolk's only game in the next season resulted in a four-wicket defeat to Herefordshire in a match after fifties from Goldsmith, Amos and Thomas helped to post a total of 327 for eight. But in a match that yielded 655 runs Norfolk had played their part. The same could not be said of the preliminary-round match with Staffordshire in 1996 as Norfolk were beaten by 106 runs. However, this defeat was the prelude to a glorious series of performances in the competition.

The 1997 competition began with a trip to Wiltshire who batted solidly to reach 238 for seven with Mark Thomas taking two for 34 in his 11 overs.

Rogers and Amos (run out for 98) then put on 174 for the first wicket before the middle order steered Norfolk to a six-wicket win. The quarter-final victory away to Northumberland was less decisive for, following 75 from Tim Boon and 60 from David Thomas, the home side were in a reasonable position before the rain came with Norfolk only marginally ahead on overall scoring rate. The county continued to clock up the miles in the semi-final round as they travelled to Dorset. Defending a score of 200 for eight, Norfolk's bowlers made early inroads into the opposition batting reducing them to 23 for four. They recovered, but only to 161 all out. There were three wickets each for Bradshaw and Rogers. And so to Lord's for the final and a first-ever game with Shropshire. Rain caused a number of disruptions in Norfolk's innings but this did not prevent their openers adding 137 for the first wicket. Amos was then dismissed for 56 but Rogers batted through the innings for 119 not out. Building on this foundation, Norfolk reached 279 for four, and when the game resumed on the second day Goldsmith took over by removing five of the top six in the Shropshire order for 42 to leave Norfolk comfortable winners by 52 runs.

The format changed for 1998 with the County Board Elevens of the first-class counties joining the competition and the early rounds being played on a regional group basis. The games themselves reverted to 60 overs per side. Continuing their success of the previous year, Norfolk won all their four group games with particular highlights the 151 from Rogers against Suffolk in a total of 401 for five, fifties from Goldsmith, Stephen Livermore and David Thomas and an economical bowling spell from Newman. The quarter-final round saw Norfolk away to Oxfordshire who batted first and totalled 244 for six. Unfortunately, the early order, which had performed so well in the group matches, failed and despite a spirited fight back led by Livermore (64) the county finished 10 runs short.

## ECB 38 – County Cup Competition (1999–2002)

The opening matches in 1999, when the competition was re-named the ECB 38 County Competition (but with the MCC Trophy still at stake) and innings were reduced to 50 overs, opened with convincing wins over Cambridgeshire and Suffolk with Goldsmith playing major parts with bat and ball in both games. The third game, away to the Northamptonshire

Board, was awarded to Norfolk after heavy rain and the subsequent dangerous conditions, brought about by the home side's failure to protect the run-ups overnight in contravention of the competition rules, ruled out any possibility of play. By this stage, Norfolk were heading their group but a five-wicket defeat in the final match against the Essex Board meant that top place and the opportunity to progress were forfeited to their conquerors.

Norfolk's strong record in the group stage continued into the new millennium with a 15-run win over Bedfordshire – 92 for Amos and three for 30 for Andy Clarke – followed by a 168-run victory against Cambridgeshire – Nigel Llong hit 90 and Goldsmith took four for 24 – and an eight-wicket success in the game with the Leicestershire Board, when Amos and Goldsmith each scored hundreds and featured in a second-wicket partnership of 217. The final group game resulted in a win by 18 runs against the Northamptonshire Board and confirmed a quarter-final versus the Surrey Board. A century opening partnership between Rogers and Amos set up a 3-run win and a semi-final against Cheshire in Norfolk's final match at Lakenham but on this occasion they were well beaten. The Man of the Match was the visitors' off spinner, Chris Brown, whose performance did not go unnoticed by the Norfolk Committee.

Norfolk's increasingly impressive run of success continued into 2001. Bradshaw and Goldsmith began by bowling the county to a 2-run win over the Northamptonshire Board, to be followed by much more convincing victories against Bedfordshire, Cambridgeshire and the Leicestershire Board. Amongst these wins were a century for Amos and wickets and tight bowling from Chris Brown, now with Norfolk. The first of the knock-out rounds resulted in a 38-run victory in a low-scoring game on a difficult wicket against the Kent Board when Goldsmith hit 68 and Bradshaw took five for 14 in 8 overs. The semi-final draw brought a trip to Durham to face their Board Eleven and a seven-wicket victory built on wickets for Bradshaw, Newman and Brown and consistent batting from the top order. The reward was Norfolk's third one-day final and another trip to Lord's. Their opponents were Devon who, on winning the toss, asked Norfolk to bat. Rogers again batted well at the Headquarters of cricket, hitting 54, and was well supported by James Walker, Livermore and Chris Borrett. Still, a score of 202 for nine was not necessarily a winning one, at least not until the county bowlers got to work. Bradshaw and Newman struck early blows before Brown took four middle-order wickets for 15. The result was that Devon were bowled out for 88 and Norfolk had won their third final. Borrett with 33 and one for 19 in seven overs was named the Man of the Match.

Norfolk began their 2002 campaign with wins in the group stages, against the Leicestershire Board (by three wickets in a low-scoring game) and the Northamptonshire Board (where the bonus of 65 extras, including 40 wides, ensured victory on a faster scoring rate in a rain-curtailed match) but defeat to Lincolnshire meant that Norfolk did not progress further despite a convincing win in the final group game against the Huntingdonshire Board.

## MCCA Trophy (2003–present)

2003 brought a return to a purely knock-out format without the County Board Elevens. In that year Norfolk easily overcame Cornwall in the first round before losing to Cambridgeshire on a faster scoring rate. In 2004 Norfolk fell at the first hurdle despite an unbeaten 118 from 111 balls by Borrett against Dorset.

Norfolk began the 2005 competition with a home fixture with Berkshire and, batting first, made 277 for eight in their 50 overs with Trevor Ward (83) and Borrett (75) leading the way. Berkshire struggled to 160 for seven before their tail wagged to the extent that they finished only 9 runs short of victory. Bradshaw (four for 42) was the most successful bowler. The next round saw Norfolk paired with Herefordshire and this time the county's innings of 243 for nine was built around Rogers' 86. At one point in their reply, their opponents were 97 for two but they collapsed to 146 all out in the face of deadly pace bowling from skipper Bradshaw who in 9.1 overs took seven for 15, including a hat-trick. It remains the best-ever return by any bowler in the competition. The reward was a semi-final match away to Northumberland where again Norfolk recorded a comprehensive victory. Fifties from Borrett and wicketkeeper Luke Newton helped to post a score of 244 that the home side never looked like threatening, Rogers taking four for 24. And so to the final, against Wiltshire. It was originally due to be played at Lord's but rain prevented a start. Although in these circumstances the rules provided for the trophy to be shared this was not a popular outcome with the result that the game was quickly re-arranged for a few days later at Slough. Three wickets each for Bradshaw, Rogers and Mark Thomas helped to dismiss Wiltshire for 134, a total which Norfolk overtook in 27 overs for the loss of four wickets, Chris Borrett with 37 leading the way. Bradshaw took the Man of the Match award.

For 2006 the competition reintroduced a group stage but with no success for the holders. Defeats in three of the four group games – the other was abandoned – ensured that the county did not progress to the knock-out stage. The only highlight was a century from Rogers in the match with Suffolk. Despite winning two games in 2007, the outcome was the same. The most noteworthy performance came in the match with Bedfordshire when Ward hit 154 from 101 balls with 9 sixes and 15 fours in a score of 337 for six before Newton claimed six dismissals behind the stumps. This match was also notable for the appearance of a woman umpire, Lorraine Edgar, for the first time in a competitive Norfolk game.

A longer run followed in 2008. Norfolk began with a convincing win over Hertfordshire followed by a closer one against Suffolk and then defeat to Staffordshire. A victory by 5 runs in the final group game against Northumberland with fifties for Darren Robinson (in his only game for Norfolk) and Stephen Gray and four wickets for Mark Thomas led to a quarter-final tie away to Lincolnshire. 'Bud' Bailey, on his competition debut, took five for 40 as the home side was restricted to 235 for nine. Trevor Ward with 106 not out steered Norfolk home supported by Borrett's 53. The semi-final at home to Devon was an anti-climax after the bowlers, particularly Rogers with five wickets, restricted the visitors to 190. In reply, Norfolk never really recovered from the loss of early wickets and only Jaik Mickleburgh (75) provided any real resistance. The result was a defeat by 52 runs.

The 2009 campaign began with a group game against Northumberland who were easily overcome by 70 runs with Ben Patston top scoring with 76 and slow bowlers Brown, Walker and Rogers sharing the wickets. A reversal to Staffordshire followed but Norfolk then edged to an 8-run win in a high scoring tussle with Suffolk. Rogers, Ward and Borrett all passed 60. A much easier victory over Hertfordshire when Ward hit 71 and Walker took four for 20 guaranteed a quarter-final game against Lincolnshire in which a solid all round performance, to which skipper Rogers contributed 60 runs and two wickets, saw Norfolk victorious by five wickets. The semi-final was at home to Oxfordshire. Norfolk batted first and reached 235 – Ward hitting another half-century – before Eccles and Walker with three wickets each led the way in dismissing the visitors for 78. The final was played at the Riverside ground in Chester-le-Street where, after a rain delayed start, Rogers (91) and Patston (65) put on 105 for the first wicket. Spelman then hit 43 not out to take Norfolk to 257 for six in their 50 overs. In reply, Staffordshire, were soon 32 for five, with four wickets for Eccles and although the lower order rallied they were dismissed for 153. Eccles, with five for 34 in his ten overs, was named the Man of the Match and Norfolk had won their fifth knock-out title, thereby continuing the sequence established in 1997 of winning the competition every fourth year.

2010 was less successful with two defeats and an abandoned match in the group stage ensuring that Norfolk did not progress further. The solitary win came against Berkshire when Ward scored 92 and Bradshaw took four wickets. This season also saw Rogers complete 2000 runs and 50 wickets in Minor County knock-out cricket.

The 2011 results were also disappointing with defeats in all four group matches. The major highlight was Sam Arthurton's 133 not out versus Lincolnshire when Ward also contributed 92. Bradshaw passed 100 wickets in one-day matches for Norfolk, the first bowler to do so. The 2012 campaign was disappointing in another way with all four games abandoned due to the weather, two without a ball being bowled and a third after less than four overs, so ensuring no further progress that year.

After an easy win over Wiltshire in the first 2013 group match, thanks to fifties from Spelman and Arthurton and five inexpensive wickets for both Brown and Harry Bush, there were three close games all with exciting finishes. Suffolk's 290 for eight proved to be five runs too many for Norfolk despite an unbeaten 106 from Arthurton and 91 from Spelman. A solid team performance then saw Lincolnshire defeated by 7 runs before Bush (54) and Bradshaw (five for 66) led the county to a 12-run victory against Suffolk. Qualifying for the quarter-finals, Norfolk were drawn away to

MCCA Trophy winners 2009. Standing (l to r): *JM Spelman, MA Addison, SK Gray, PJ Bradshaw, SS Arthurton, TR Ward.* Kneeling (l to r): *H Bush (12th man), CR Borrett, CJ Rogers, BJ Patston, C Brown.*

Northumberland where despite 77 from Ward they suffered a 95-run defeat in a high-scoring game.

The 2014 group stage began with a batting collapse and defeat to Cambridgeshire but a 30-run victory over Bedfordshire (in which Arthurton and Garry Park added 145 for the third wicket) and exciting two-wicket wins against Suffolk and Hertfordshire (with the winning runs in each case coming in the final over) ensured a quarter-final tie away to Wiltshire. However, Norfolk lost a low-scoring game by three wickets despite three wickets in an economical spell from Ashley Watson.

Notwithstanding, Norfolk's record in this competition over the years has been second to none and their four cup-winning years are achievements of which the county can be proud.

## Other major one-day games in Norfolk

This chapter has concentrated on the one-day matches played by Norfolk. In addition, sides representing the Minor Counties have played the following matches in the county, all in the zonal round of the Benson and Hedges competition and all played at Lakenham.

**1st June 1974 Minor Counties (North) v Nottinghamshire**

Minor Counties (North) 138/9 Nottinghamshire 140/3 (Garry Sobers 69*)

**8th May 1976 Minor Counties (East) v Essex**

Essex 294 / 4 Minor Counties (East) 154

**30th April 1977 Minor Counties (East) v Middlesex**

Minor Counties (East) 92 Middlesex 93/4

**28th and 29th April 1997 Minor Counties v Derbyshire**

Minor Counties 256/7 Derbyshire 260/4

**5th May 1998 Minor Counties v Lancashire**

Minor Counties 52 Lancashire 53/3

**6th May 1998 Minor Counties v Warwickshire**

Minor Counties 111 Warwickshire 112/4 (Brian Lara 30*)

In addition, the statistical section includes a list of those Norfolk players who appeared for Minor Counties' representative teams in the Benson and Hedges competition.

# PART THREE

# A Short Miscellany

# CHAPTER 12

# The Edrich Family

There have been many famous cricketing families. At the beginning of the last century no less than seven brothers from the Foster family played for Worcestershire causing the county to be known as 'Fostershire'. More recently there have been the Chappells, Pollocks and Mohammads to name some of the more well-known. But right up there with these illustrious families are the Edriches of Norfolk five of whom played first-class cricket: the brothers, in order of seniority, Eric, Bill, Geoffrey and Brian and their younger cousin, John.

The brothers' grandfather was Harry Edrich, who farmed firstly at North Burlingham and then at Lingwood and was himself an active cricketer. On moving to Lingwood in 1900, he founded a club there, long since folded. Harry was struck down by poliomyelitis in 1903 but retained a keen interest in the game. Harry's son, also known as Bill, was born in 1890 and, as well as following his father's footsteps as a farmer, was a good enough cricketer to play, together with his brother Edwin, for Norfolk Club and Ground, a sort of county second eleven. Edwin also represented his county in a friendly fixture in 1919. Bill senior farmed in and around Lingwood and, briefly in the 1930s, in east Yorkshire before returning to his native county. He founded teams at Upton and Cantley and, following his return to Norfolk, played for Ingham until his late sixties. He also fathered four sons and a daughter.

Although not the eldest, Bill junior was certainly the most famous of those four sons. Born in Lingwood in 1916 he attended Bracondale School in Norwich where he won his school colours at the age of 13 and was captain in the following year (1930) notwithstanding his youthfulness. In that season he put in two particularly outstanding performances: ten wickets (all clean bowled) for 18 runs in 49 balls against Norwich High School and 121 (out of 168 for six declared) followed by eight for 20 against Diss Secondary School.

In 1931 he dominated his school's averages with 477 runs – more than 300 more than the next highest – and 71 wickets at an average below five. His most notable performance in that year was his 149 not out against the City of Norwich School when the next highest score was 5. Inevitably, performances such as these did not go unnoticed and he moved quickly into adult and representative cricket. At the age of 15 he was selected for the Norfolk Senior Colts match scoring 57 out of a total of 110.

The big step forward came in the 1932 season when, not long past his 16th birthday, he was picked for Norfolk, not in any ordinary game but against the touring All Indian side at Lakenham. Less than a month before the tourists first-ever Test Match, and against an attack including fast bowler Mohammad Nissar who was to take six wickets in that inaugural Test, young Bill alone stood firm in the first innings scoring 20 out of 49, as well as 16 in the second innings. He even took a wicket, that of Nazir Ali, one of the batting successes of the tour. *Wisden's Cricketers' Almanack* remarked at the time that 'Edrich, a schoolboy, batted in promising fashion for Norfolk'. In the Minor County competition that season Bill also batted and bowled promisingly.

About the same time he had a couple of games for Norwich City FC but it was his cricket career that was really taking off. Staying on at Bracondale School as a boarder when his father moved to Yorkshire, 1933 saw him as a consistent performer in Norfolk's table-topping side – 293 runs at an average just under 21 and 23 wickets at just over 20 being ample justification for a growing reputation. Again batting at first-wicket down, there was also a competent performance against the West Indian tourists. Bill himself commented in his autobiography how the first ball he received, from a particularly quick West Indian paceman, actually whistled through his hair – and this in the days before helmets. 35 runs in over two hours at the crease, in his only innings, was a precursor of even grittier performances still to come both on and off the cricket field.

It was inevitable that Bill's performances would attract attention further afield, and by now he was considering the possibility of playing cricket professionally rather than pursuing his original ambition of school teaching. With help from Michael Falcon, he went to Lord's in April 1934 for a trial with a view to joining the MCC groundstaff and qualifying for Middlesex, at the same time continuing to play for Norfolk. His cricket development continued and in that 1934 season he played his first first-class matches scoring half-centuries against both Cambridge and Oxford Universities. Still only 18, he finished third in the Norfolk batting averages with 527 runs, including his first Norfolk hundred, at an average of just under 48 and topped the bowling list with 40 wickets at 12.87. *Wisden* observed that 'Edrich, progressing as a run-getter, developed into their cleverest all-rounder and, bowling much faster than in previous years, took twice as many wickets at smaller cost'. In 1935, and still not qualified for Middlesex, he scored a further 488 Minor County runs as well as taking 27 wickets; and in the following year he hit 397 runs and captured 16 wickets. On top of these figures was his magnificent 111 not out against the 1935 South African tourists. Bill Edrich was now clearly a player to watch out for.

An administrative hiccup delayed Bill's qualification for Middlesex until after the end of the 1936 season. However, he made up for lost time in the following year by scoring over 2000 runs in his first full season. This led to his selection for a tour to India led by Lord Tennyson in a strong party most of whom played Test cricket at some stage in their careers. Bill opened the batting in all the matches in which he played and headed the batting averages with 876 runs at 46.10. An even more successful English season began with Bill joining the very select company of those who have scored 1000 first-class runs before the end of May. He also earned Test Match recognition with three games against Don Bradman's touring Australians. Unfortunately, his six innings yielded only 67 runs and although he was selected for the winter tour of South Africa his unsatisfactory introduction to Test cricket continued with 21 runs in five innings making 88 in eleven altogether. His bowling was used intermittently and although he often shared the new ball on that tour it was not strong enough to cement his place in the side. Then, in the final Test of that tour –the famous Timeless

Test in Durban – it all fell into place. After another failure in the first innings and with his Test career on the line, and with England chasing an improbable 696 to win in the fourth innings, he hit 219 to take his side to within 42 runs of victory before the game was called off as a draw in order to allow the tourists to catch their boat back to England. This was not enough to retain his Test place for the following summer although another successful county season led to him being named one of *Wisden's* Five Cricketers of the Year.

Then came the Second World War. The bravery shown in facing the West Indies at Lakenham in 1933 and later demonstrated after 1945 was eclipsed by his war record. Trained as a pilot, in 1941 he joined the 107 Squadron based at Little Massingham to fly twin-engined Blenheim bombers. He rose from the rank of Pilot Officer to Acting Squadron Leader in the space of 19 days, itself an indication of the heavy losses suffered by aircrew during the war. By the end of 1941 he had been promoted to Flight Commander and had won the Distinguished Flying Cross for his part in the daylight raid on Cologne in August of that year. Other heroics followed until he finished his flying duties in 1943. Most Blenheim airmen, though, did not survive. Bill's wartime experiences bring to mind the response of the legendary Australian allrounder Keith Miller when asked about the pressures of playing Test cricket. Miller, who himself had spent some of the war stationed at Great Massingham, replied that pressure was 'having a Messerschmitt up your __ , playing cricket was not'. One guesses that Bill Edrich shared that sentiment.

Peace brought with it a return to first-class cricket and, for Bill, a continuation of the fine batting form he had shown before the war. In 1946, and for the first time, he also made his mark as a fast bowler with 73 wickets at an average of 19.28; statistically his best-ever return although for the next six years he averaged over 40 wickets a season. He also took 29 catches as he developed into a very safe slip fieldsman. His Test place regained, he toured Australia for the first time over the following winter, establishing himself as his country's number three batsman. He performed well but the best had not quite arrived.

England in 1947 was still in the early stages of recovery from the war and this had not been helped by the bitterly cold winter just passed. This was the cue for Bill and his Middlesex and England team-mate, Denis Compton, to re-write the cricket record books. Their total runs aggregates of 3816 (Compton) and 3539 (Edrich) remain the highest ever recorded in a season. More remarkable was that a very high proportion of their runs were scored in partnership as they batted at three and four for both county and country. To give a few examples of the way they demolished bowling attacks in this long, hot summer they added 277 together in 130 minutes against Leicestershire, 287 in 165 minutes against Surrey and 370 in the Second Test versus South Africa.

For the years that followed Bill continued to be prolific, rarely failing to pass 2000 first-class runs in a seaon. His touring days were all but over, though. He declined one tour for business reasons and was controversially omitted from the 1950–51 Australian trip apparently for over-celebrating during a Test Match earlier that summer. Indeed, he did not return to the England side until 1953 when he helped his country to regain the Ashes lost 19 years previously. This secured his place on the 1954–55 tour to Australia where his solid rather than exceptional performances helped to win the series. And that was the end of a Test career in which, in 39 Tests, he had scored 2440 runs at an average of exactly 40, taken 41 wickets and held 39 catches. Good figures by anyone's standards, particularly at a time when Test matches were played less frequently than today and when there were no cheap runs.

His county career continued until 1958 having captained Middlesex for seven years from 1951, in the first two of those seasons jointly with Compton. But although aged 42, Bill had not finished with cricket. In 1959 he came back to Norfolk to take over the captaincy of the county side. This was not just a parting shot – he continued to represent the county of his birth until 1971 and was captain until 1968. In those 10 seasons leading Norfolk they won 35 games compared with 12 in the 13 previous years, a clear testament to his adventurous, positive approach to leadership. Chapter 9 gives the details of those seasons suffice to say here that in this second spell with the county, he scored over 6,000 runs in the Minor Counties Championship and captured 298 wickets, increasingly with off-spin and a willingness to buy wickets in the interests of seeking victory. This was a magnificent record at any stage of a career but remarkable for someone of his age.

And, so, at the age of 55 his career in representative cricket came to a close. His first-class record comprised 36,965 runs, 86 centuries, 479 wickets and 529 catches. And for Norfolk in the Minor Counties competition he totalled 8034 runs, 415 wickets and 151 catches, in that last case a Norfolk record.

None of this is to say that Bill's three brothers were not themselves capable cricketers. The eldest, Eric, was born two years before Bill. He also went to Bracondale School and graduated into adult cricket to play with his father at Upton and Blofield and with his Uncle George for East Norfolk. In 1932, he was selected for the Norfolk Club and Ground side but the next year moved with his father to east Yorkshire. There, his cricket developed and when he and his family returned to Norfolk to take up a farm at Heacham in late 1934 – incidentally, Bill was occasionally referred to in his younger days as the 'Heacham cricketer' – Eric's consistent run-getting brought him to the attention of the Norfolk selectors. He played in two county games in 1935, performing promisingly. Following that first season, he appeared with increasing regularity for Norfolk in the years leading up to the outbreak of war, scoring well. Also, having started his career as a medium-pace bowler, he turned to wicketkeeping, firstly with Heacham and West Norfolk and then in 1937 in the Minor Counties Championship. In that year he also scored his first century for Norfolk – 161 against Hertfordshire. The next year saw him make his first-class debut, for a Minor Counties representative side against Oxford University.

Farming was a reserved occupation during the War so Eric stayed at home. For much of the conflict this meant Buckinghamshire where his father had relocated following the sale of the farm he managed at Heacham. In deference to his three brothers who all served in the Armed Forces Eric played little wartime cricket but immediately following the end of the war he had a few friendly games for Northamptonshire. However, and together with Geoffrey, he was pointed in the direction of Lancashire where he spent three seasons playing 34 first-class games, scoring 918 runs and making 53 dismissals. His most notable performance was scoring 121 in the 1948 Roses match at Headingley putting on 150 for the fourth wicket with Cyril

Washbrook, a regular colleague of Bill's in the England side. However, at the end of that season he decided not to accept a new contract but instead retired to Norfolk where he shared professional duties with Cecil Boswell. He played three more seasons for the county although by 1951 his runs were starting to dry up; his wicketkeeping, on the other hand, remained of the highest standard. Thereafter, he took a coaching appointment elsewhere in the country and soon emigrated to New Zealand only to return later.

Geoffrey was two years younger than Bill and the third-born of the brothers. He also attended Bracondale School and was awarded his school colours in 1932.but when his family moved to Yorkshire in 1933 Geoffrey went with them. This, though, did not hinder his cricket development and on returning to Norfolk he also joined the Heacham club where he scored heavily. This run-scoring and, no doubt, his name brought him to the attention of the County Club and prior to the start of the 1937 season, still only 18, he was offered the opportunity to become the county's assistant coach to Jack Nichols. His responsibilities involved bowling at the County Club members for 15 hours each week, playing for the Club and Ground side and helping with the coaching. He also played a few games in the Minor Counties Championship and although initially his performances were modest he steadily improved in the following two years, scoring over 600 runs in 1939 at an average of 47.23 with two centuries. Both he and Eric performed well in Norfolk's game against the visiting West Indians that year, and he was also now bowling with some success.

That 1939 season turned out to be Geoffrey's last with Norfolk. Following the outbreak of hostilities he enlisted with the Royal Norfolk Regiment and this led to him going to Singapore following the Japanese attack on Pearl Harbor. He was captured and spent the final three years of the conflict as a prisoner of war including two years working on the laying of the notorious Thailand Railway into Burma. Indeed, he had been assumed to be dead. Returning to England in 1945 and, like so many others, much weakened by his experiences – his weight had reduced to six and a half stones – he had to decide on a career. Cricket appealed, and after many months spent regaining his strength, he joined Eric in approaching Lancashire. He was also offered a contract and for 11 seasons was a regular member of the Red Rose county side scoring over 15,000 first-class runs and 26 hundreds. There were also 333 catches. In eight of those years he topped 1000 runs with a season's best of 2067 in 1952. His consistency led to an invitation to join a Commonwealth team to tour India over the winter of 1953–54 and although his performances in the unofficial Tests did not do justice to his ability overall on that tour he batted well in a party almost all of whom played Test cricket at some stage in their careers.

Geoffrey's last years at Lancashire saw him successfully captain the side for part of the 1956 season and then skippering the Second Eleven where he was much respected and admired by a promising collection of younger players. Sadly, though, a difference of opinion within the Club over discipline at the beginning of the 1959 season led to him leaving Lancashire. He then played for Cumberland for three years before coaching at Cheltenham.

Brian Edrich never played for Norfolk. Born in 1922, he was only ten when the family moved north but on his return to the county he began playing for Heacham and by 1938 he was a member of their first team, bowling off breaks and batting in the middle to lower order. He was also learning to train greyhounds for a living. His break came at the end of that summer in a match between the Edrich family and a side put together by the owner of Barton Hall, Michael Trubshawe. Aged just 16, he scored an accomplished 60 and in doing so impressed to such an extent that a spectator mentioned his name to Kent County Cricket Club. Within a few weeks Brian had received a letter from Kent's secretary asking if he was prepared to join the county staff, this without even a trial. Brian readily accepted and, with Kent having found him winter work and also the relaxation of the registration rules that had delayed Bill's debut in the County Championship, he was registered in time for the 1939 season. In that first year, when he did not reach 17 until August, he played a handful of games, performing promisingly for Kent Seconds.

At the outbreak of war Brian was still below the age for call-up so at that point he returned to Norfolk and then moved to Buckinghamshire with his father when the farm he managed was sold. In 1942 he joined the Royal Air Force as a trainee pilot. This took him to Canada and then to India and Ceylon (now Sri Lanka). He left the RAF in 1946, initially to return to farming and then, a year later, to resume his cricket career with Kent. Over the next ten years he played 180 first-class games scoring 5500 runs at an average just over 20 and taking 130 wickets. The highlights were his four centuries including a highest score of 193 not out against Sussex in 1949 and seven for 41 versus Hampshire in the same year. He also passed 1000 runs in 1951. However, a poor 1953 season saw him released by Kent. He joined Glamorgan, playing his last three years of first-class cricket with the Welsh county but with limited success. The end of his playing career at this level saw him appointed as Glamorgan's coach but the need for economies forced them to curtail their coaching scheme in the early 1960s. Brian took up a coaching appointment at a school in Oxford and between 1966 and 1971 represented Oxfordshire in the Minor Counties Championship on 47 occasions.

Bill Edrich senior had a number of brothers the youngest of whom was Fred. His first son was born in June 1937 and christened John Hugh. Given his age, he had a somewhat quieter war than his cousins and his autobiography records that he spent much of this time being coached on the concrete wickets created by his father and Uncle George in their gardens in east Norfolk. In due course John also went to Bracondale School and in time captained the First Eleven, averaging 106 with the bat and opening the bowling. Representative cricket soon came his way with selection for Norfolk Junior Colts at the age of 13 and skippering them in 1952 when his team-mates included Peter Parfitt. The following year saw him playing with some success for Norfolk Club and Ground and earning a full county trial. By 1954 he was playing for CEYMS who were led by Laurie Barrett, then the county captain. That same year, and just turned 17, he was picked for Norfolk for the first time. His first two games, against Essex and Kent Seconds, were disappointing but by the end of the season he was at the head of the county's batting averages. In eight games he scored 240 runs at an average of 34.28 with a top score of 56 against Buckinghamshire and another half-century versus Suffolk.

Keen to follow his cousins into the first-class game he approached Lancashire but by this time they were recruiting only from within the county. Instead, Surrey – then in the middle of a seven-year winning run in the County Championship – offered him a contract and in his first season (1955) he topped their Second Eleven batting averages with 762 runs at an average just under 45. National Service followed, and although he continued to turn out for Surrey's second string he did not make his debut in the first team until 1958 when, in his one first-class game that year, he top-scored with 24 as Worcestershire bowled out Surrey for 57. 'Apart from John Edrich', *Wisden* reported, 'no one else batted confidently'. 1959 was the year he broke through. Indeed, opening the batting in his first match that year and only his sixth first-class game, he scored hundreds in both innings against Nottinghamshire at Trent Bridge. Five more centuries followed in a season's total of just under 1800 runs (average 52.91). He was even more prolific in the next three seasons with 2482 in 1962 his best-ever aggregate, again averaging over 50.

At a time when England were struggling to find a settled and reliable opening pair it was only a matter of time before John's performances were rewarded with a Test call-up. This duly came in 1963 against the strong West Indies tourists whose attack included the fearsome opening bowlers Wes Hall and Charlie Griffith, the incomparable Garry Sobers and off spinner Lance Gibbs. Initially, his scores were reasonably consistent rather than eye-catching but in the following year, after a winter tour to India where he suffered more than most with illness, he hit his first Test hundred – 120 against Australia at Lord's. Notwithstanding this, he initially failed to hold down a Test place. However, after being omitted for eight Tests he was recalled in 1965 for the Third Test against New Zealand when he hit 310 not out, the fifth-highest Test score ever made by an England batsman. This innings came during a particularly productive period in John's career when, but for an injury caused by a Peter Pollock bumper in the First Test against South Africa, he was on course to score 3000 runs in that season, a feat not subsequently ever achieved. He was, however, fit to take his place on the winter tour to Australia when he hit two more Test hundreds.

He continued to score highly in county cricket and after again dropping out of international cricket in 1966 and 1967 he re-established himself as a Test player in the years from 1968 to 1972 when he was an integral member of Ray Illingworth's successful England elevens. In particular, his 648 runs at an average of 72 were a significant contribution to England regaining the Ashes on the 1970–71 tour. And on his third visit to Australia in 1974–75, when England were confronted by Denis Lillee and Jeff Thomson at their quickest, he headed the batting averages with a series of gritty performances and had the honour of captaining his country in the Fourth Test. He played the last of his 77 Tests in 1976 against the West Indies when he and Brian Close, with a combined age of 84, were selected to open the batting in that summer's Third Test against a particularly hostile fast bowling attack that included Andy Roberts and Michael Holding. Their second innings partnership of 54, and the bruising they each suffered, are still remembered by those who witnessed it, and their innings were a testament to the courage of both batsmen. This was a cue for John's Test career to end, one that brought 5138 runs at an average of 43.54 and 12 centuries seven of which were scored against Australia including a highest score of 175 in the 1975 Lord's Test. He continued playing for Surrey until 1978 accumulating altogether in his first-class career 39,790 runs at an average of over 45, with 103 hundreds. These figures confirm that he was one of the very best batsmen of his generation.

He played his final season of competitive cricket back in Norfolk where in 1979 he scored 236 runs in his ten innings: a relatively modest conclusion to an enormously successful career in which he performed with great ability and courage at the very highest level in the game.


The Edrich family's contribution to Norfolk cricket was not limited to these four brothers and their cousin. Brief reference has already been made to the influence of the brothers' grandfather and their Uncle George. In addition, in the period following the First World War, their father and his brothers were well known in local cricket circles. Bill senior was a wicketkeeper-batsman; Edwin a fast bowler and attacking batsman; and George a batsman. As already noted, Bill senior played in the Norfolk Club and Ground side although not in the Minor Counties Championship. It has been suggested that a reason for this was that the County side tended to play its matches in the summer holidays when preference was given to younger players from the universities and colleges. And then there was Alice Edrich, aunt to the four first-class cricketing brothers. Alice was a fast bowler and fine bat who captained the Norfolk Ladies team in the 1930s and after subsequently emigrating to New Zealand coached cricket there.

The cricketing strength of the Edrich family in the 1930s led to them playing occasionally as a family team, so emulating the Colman side of the 1840s. The first such recorded match was in 1931 when in July at Blofield a family side played against East Norfolk in aid of the Blofield and District Nursing Association. The Edrich eleven comprised eight brothers and three sons with two other members of the family acting as umpire and scorer – the scorer was Alice. Unfortunately, the rains came and the match abandoned part way through the first innings. The next documented occasion was at the end of the 1938 season when, again at Blofield, they played a Norfolk team captained by Michael Falcon. The match was to be in part broadcast on national radio with the proceeds going towards the provision of a new recreation ground. The All-Norfolk side batted first with Falcon declaring their innings closed in time for the radio to broadcast the innings of Bill, fresh from an Ashes Test match. Unfortunately, though, he was dismissed first ball before the match went on the air! Soon afterwards, the rains came and the match abandoned. Not to be deterred the game was rearranged for the following Sunday at Barton Turf when Bill redeemed himself with a century.

The Edrich team for the first of the 1938 games comprised, in addition to the four brothers, William Arthur (farmer), Edwin Harry (farmer), George Herbert (auctioneer), Harry Macdonald (haulage contractor), Arthur Edwin (hospital attendant), George Charles (auctioneer's clerk) and Alan Walter (engineer). Altogether, with Bill and his brothers, this was four of old Harry's sons and seven of his grandsons. There were some 30 members of the Edrich family present with grandfather Harry, in his wheelchair, the proudest of them all. Alice was again the scorer.

Other similar games followed. For instance, in 1947 the family eleven, showing only one change from the 1938 game – Peter (who himself made

The four Edrich brothers at Lakenham, 1947. (l to r): *Eric, Bill, Geoff, Brian.*

two Minor County appearances for Norfolk in 1951) for Alan – featured in a match in aid of the RAF Benevolent Fund. Later games were played for the benefit of such as the National Fund for Poliomyelitis and the Norfolk Playing Fields Association. In addition, in 1955, the Edriches played against a Norfolk side in aid of Geoffrey's Testimonial Fund.

Until 1962, the fixtures were against other local elevens but in the following year the Lords Taverners formed the opposition for the first time. For a number of years, teams comprising well-known cricketers and personalities from the entertainment and wider sporting worlds came up to Norfolk in September to take on the Edrich team, drawing crowds of up to 8000. (In similar vein, an annual Sunday fixture in Yarmouth in the 1950s and 1960s involving celebrity entertainers there for the summer season sometimes attracted over 10,000 spectators, with 15,000 reported as attending the 1961 game). By the end of the 1960s, this particular highlight on the Norfolk cricket calendar had run its course; indeed the 1970 side that played an East Anglian eleven contained only five Edriches. Nonetheless, the games had over the years provided great entertainment, raised much money for good causes and in their way helped to put Norfolk cricket in the national limelight.

# CHAPTER 13

# Visitors from Overseas

Over the years Norfolk have played host to a number of overseas touring sides. Usually, these have been played at Lakenham with the opposition featuring either the County Club or a Minor Counties representative eleven. In addition, there was a short series of matches that served to bring cricket in the county to the attention of the wider cricketing world. This Chapter describes the visits to Norfolk made by Test-playing countries as well as a small number of other representative sides.

## Australian Aborigines (1868)

The first overseas cricket tour took place in 1859 when a team of 12 English professionals undertook a short visit to North America. The first English tour to Australia followed in the winter of 1861–2 with another visit two years later, this time also including New Zealand.

The financial success of the two Australian tours demonstrated that cricket had taken root there and it was not long before plans were being made for a reciprocal visit. However, unlike the tours that followed, the first Australian tourists were, with the exception of their captain, all Aboriginal. Following a three-month long boat trip they arrived in England in May 1868 and over a period of five months played 47 matches, none of them first-class. They met with mixed success on the cricket field but nonetheless proved to be very popular with spectators not least because in addition to their cricket they gave exhibitions of spear and boomerang throwing and other indigenous 'sports'.

That was certainly the case when they came to Norwich to play the Carrow Club on 23 and 24 July. Several marquees were erected at their Lakenham ground in preparation for the visit and the fixture was attended by Norwich's Mayor and Deputy Mayor as well as the gentry of the city and county. Carrow batted first and scored only 82. The tourists replied with 235, Johnny Cuzens top-scoring with 87, and other names on the scorecard included Tiger, Twopenny, Dick-a-Dick, Mosquito, Bullocky and Jim Crow. Carrow fared only marginally better in their second innings, managing 101 and going down to an innings defeat. Charles Lawrence, the tourists' captain, took eight wickets to add to his four in the first innings. The match report in the *Norwich Mercury* referred to the visitors creating 'a little sensation' by their play, appearance and 'novel performance with some of their native weapons and implements of the chase'. It also expressed concern that the attention paid to them would make them think they were the celebrities of their age and therefore spoil them for any industrious pursuit. At the end of the match, there were foot and hurdle races between some of the tourists and members of the Norwich Gymnastic Society, followed by the usual spear and boomerang throwing. The overall conclusion in the *Norwich Mercury* was, in words that today would be rightly regarded as patronising or even offensive, that 'the black gentlemen were decidedly an attraction worthy of attention'.

### Parsis (1888)

It was another 20 years before a touring team next came to Norfolk. Then, in 1888, a team of Parsi cricketers embarked on their second tour of England. The Parsi community were in fact the first Indians to play cricket. Originally from what we now know as Iran, and Zoroastrians by faith, they settled in and around Mumbai and by the middle of the 19th century they had begun to play serious cricket. By the time of this tour, over 50 Parsi cricket clubs had been established in that area with between 2000 and 3000 members. They had first planned to come to England in 1876 but that fell through and ten more years passed before their inaugural tour. In terms of results that tour was not a success but building on the experience gained from it their next, and last, visit to these shores in 1888 produced eight victories from 31 games. Their fixtures were generally against sides of 'Gentlemen', often representing their respective counties. So it was that on 6 and 7 August they played the Gentlemen of Norfolk at Lakenham.

The Parsis batted first and were dismissed for 78 with Ernest Raikes taking five for 31. Revd Arthur Davies led the Gentlemen's reply with 41 steering them to 136 all out. The tourists reached 129 in their second innings leaving the home side to score 72 to win. They struggled, not least against the underhand 'daisy cutters' of captain Pestonji Kanga, to the extent that when the ninth wicket fell eight runs were still required. However, Walter Rix and Revd Wickham saw the Gentlemen home. An hour still remained, so the Parsis went in for a third time finishing on 45 for four. The attendance was good with approximately 1000 paying spectators and 1200 to 1300 altogether, sufficient for the Parsis to take as their share of the gate money more than the £25 their captain had indicated was the most they had received up to that part of the tour. This support led the *Eastern Daily Press* to opine that it 'speaks volumes for the increasing interest in cricket in the county'.

## West Indies (1900)

The West Indies first toured England in 1900. They were not then the power in world cricket that they were to become in the last quarter of the 20th century and they won only five of their 17, all second-class, games. Their final match of the tour, on 10 and 11 August, brought them to Lakenham for a game with Norfolk. The hosts batted first scoring 117 to which opening bat Philip Fryer and number 10 Gerard Blake were the main contributors with 29 and 26 respectively. 'Float' Woods (five for 38) and Percy Cox (four for 44) shared all but one of the wickets. The tourists replied with 165 with Lionel D'Ade top-scoring with 68 not out. Charlie Shore was the only professional in the Norfolk side and, as he so often did, took the bowling honours with five for 64 including the dismissal of the tourists' star opening batsman, Charles Ollivierre, for a duck. Having restricted their opponents to a first-innings lead of 48 Norfolk then collapsed in the face of hostile bowling from 'Tommy' Burton who, in 10.4 overs, dismissed eight home batsmen for just 9 runs. The County Club mustered only 32 and lost by an innings and 16 runs.

## West Indies (1906)

Six years later, the West Indies returned to England, and to Lakenham. This time, 13 of their 19 fixtures were given first-class status, though not the fixture with Norfolk on 10 and 11 August. On this occasion the tourists batted first and put together the formidable score of 375 with a top score of 88 from Percy Goodman and other useful contributions from most of the side, including Lebrun Constantine, father of the more famous Learie. James Worman was the pick of the county bowlers with four for 94. In reply, Norfolk totalled only 91 with Oliver Layne returning figures of five for 14. Following on, the hosts made a better fist of it, reaching 166 with 48 from Basil Cozens-Hardy and 43 from Cyril Dunning. However, this was not enough to prevent another innings defeat. Layne took another four wickets but Sydney Smith did most damage with five for 48; he was to remain in England to qualify and play successfully for Northamptonshire. From Norfolk's perspective, the game was perhaps most notable for the debut of Michael Falcon. With scores of 0 and 5 and five wicket-less overs it was an inauspicious start for the 18 year-old.

## Australia and South Africa (1912)

1912 was the year of the Triangular Tournament in which both Australia and South Africa toured England with each of the three countries playing each other three times on a League basis. England won. The tournament was regarded as a failure largely because of the weakness of the opposition and the poor weather.

Both sets of tourists visited Norfolk. At the end of August, the Australians played a first-class game at Lakenham against an England Eleven. The first day's play was lost to the rain that had fallen continuously for 17 hours and caused such devastating flooding across the county. Play actually started at half past two on the second day but the rain returned with the tourists on 72 for five. The final day saw uninterrupted play in which the Australians took their overnight score to 136 all out with their prolific opener Warren Bardsley top-scoring with 47 and Sydney Smith, now playing for the home side, taking four for 37 and Alfred Morris, the Durham professional, capturing four wickets for 50. The England Eleven, which was in no way representative but which did include five players with Test match experience at that time, could only manage 79 in reply with the left-arm medium-fast bowler Bill Whitty taking seven for 40. The tourists declared their second innings at 79 for six and then Whitty took four more wickets to leave the England Eleven at 68 for four when stumps were drawn. Norfolk's representatives in the England Eleven ranks, Michael Falcon and Revd George Raikes, made only very minor contributions as did wicketkeeper Neville Tufnell who many years later would play a few games for the county.

Eight days after the finish of the Australian match the South Africans played their first ever game in Norfolk. However, unlike the previous tourist fixtures, this was not played at Lakenham but in the rural setting of Old Buckenham Hall, near Attleborough. As already mentioned in Chapter 3 the Hall had passed into the ownership of a wealthy businessman, Lionel Robinson, whose interests extended to cricket and led to him raising an Eleven to play the South Africans. The side he put together was, if anything, stronger than that which took on the Australians a few days earlier. In particular, it included four Test players in Patsy Hendren – the third-highest ever scorer in first-class cricket with 51,000 runs – his Middlesex colleague Bernard Bosanquet and two Test players from Lancashire in Jack Sharp and Harry Dean as well as the Australian all rounder Frank Tarrant. Falcon and Tufnell also appeared. Lionel Robinson's Eleven, which was their title, batted first and struggled to 153 with Michael Falcon justifying his selection with the second highest score of 29 after the first five wickets fell for just 30. Sid Pegler, one of a number of good leg spin and googly bowlers coming out of South Africa at that time, took six for 45. The tourists made a worse start to their first innings – at one stage they were 16 for five – as Falcon destroyed the cream of their batting, finishing with six for 47 in 18 overs. His wickets included Dave Nourse, the 'Grand Old Man' of South African cricket, and all but one were amongst the top six in the batting order. With a first innings lead of two runs the 'local' Eleven reached 255 in their second innings to which Hendren contributed a rapid 80. Pegler added five wickets to a tally that reached 189 by the end of the season. It then rained and, set 258 to win, the tourists collapsed on a drying wicket to 66 all out; Harry Simms, from Sussex, and Tarrant shared the wickets equally.

## Australian Imperial Forces (1919)

There were no more tours of England before the First World War but when peace returned and first-class cricket resumed in 1919 the tourists took the form of an Australian Forces team raised and financed by the military authorities. They were a success, losing only four of their 28 first-class matches. They also provided valuable experience for a number of young Australians who over the next few years were members of one of the very best Australian Test sides that first reclaimed and then twice retained the Ashes.

The tourists' first match brought them to Old Buckenham Hall and a 12 a-side fixture with a side again put together by Lionel Robinson. For this fixture he recruited a number of Kent players, most notably Frank Woolley, as well as the England allrounder and next captain, Johnny Douglas. South Africans Herbie Taylor and Sid Pegler also played and Norfolk representation was in the shape of aggressive middle-order batsman Eric Fulcher. The hosts batted first scoring 147 to which Fulcher contributed the second-top score; Cyril Docker returned figures of five for 34. The Forces Eleven replied with 227 with future Test skipper Herbie Collins leading the way with 87 and Pegler taking five for 54. The magnate's side fared much better in their second innings, declaring on 362 for eight with the Kent pair of Gerard de Hough and 'Wally' Hardinge scoring 87 not out and 72 respectively. Fulcher hit 31. Set 283 to win in three and three quarter hours the visitors finished nine runs short on 274 for nine with Johnny Taylor making 66. The Australians were offered the opportunity to play the game to a finish but declined.

## Australia (1921)

Tourists returned to Old Buckenham in early May 1921. Again, the home side was raised by Lionel Robinson and the visitors on this occasion were the all-conquering Australians. They had just completed a series whitewash over England in Australia – the first Tests after the end of the war – and were now starting out on what would prove to be a highly successful tour of this country. Indeed, they are reckoned to be one of the strongest touring sides ever to come to these shores. To counter this formidable line-up Robinson gathered together an eleven captained by semi-retired Archie MacLaren. Together, the two sides comprised the finest array of talent ever seen at one time on a cricket field in Norfolk. The full sides were

| LIONEL ROBINSON'S ELEVEN | AUSTRALIANS |
|---|---|
| J.B. Hobbs | W. Bardsley |
| D.J. Knight | H.L. Collins |
| V.W.C. Jupp | C.G. Macartney |
| E. Hendren | J.M. Taylor |
| A.P.F. Chapman | W.W. Armstrong (capt) |
| J.W.H.T. Douglas | J.M. Gregory |
| P.G.H. Fender | J. Ryder |
| G.E.C. Wood | H.L. Hendry |
| C.H. Gibson | H. Carter |
| J.C. White | E. McDonald |
| A.C. MacLaren (capt) | A.A. Mailey |

Unfortunately, the match was ruined by the weather although *The Cricketer* reported that at one point play continued through a hailstorm. Batting first in those particular conditions, the visitors were bowled out for 136, their lowest total of the tour. Warwick Armstrong alone offered any serious resistance against an attack in which Johnny Douglas, with six for 64, was the pick. In reply, the home team lost the early wicket of

Lionel Robinson's Eleven versus the touring Australian team at Old Buckenham, 1921. *The Australian captain, Warwick Armstrong, is batting*

Donald Knight before Jack Hobbs and Vallance Jupp added 117 for the second wicket. Hobbs, in his only first-class innings in Norfolk, hit 85 before retiring with a snapped thigh muscle, an injury that kept him out of cricket for seven weeks and thereby reduced further England's chances of regaining the Ashes that summer. It was an innings described in *The Cricketer* as 'a delightful an exhibition of batting as the Norfolk people will ever see'. Jupp also retired hurt, in his case with a badly bruised thumb, after scoring 59. Douglas then hit 41 not out before MacLaren declared on 256 for eight. The weather allowed Robinson's team enough time to take one wicket for 25 but the match ended tamely in a draw. Nevertheless, this was one of the few occasions that year when the Australians did not dominate their opponents.

Given the weather, the attendances were excellent with 2000 spectators present on the rain-interrupted first day and, in the opinion of the *Eastern Daily Press*, between 5000 and 6000 on the second day although some estimates put it higher with 10,000 or even 12,000 spectators being claimed. Either way, it was easily a record attendance for a 'serious' match in Norfolk.

This was the last occasion on which tourists of this standard played at Old Buckenham.

## West Indies (1923)

The West Indies returned to Lakenham in late August when they were entertained by the Norfolk County side. This was not one of Norfolk's better seasons and although the visitors were yet to gain Test status they easily overcame their hosts. The West Indies batted first, totalling 204 to which Harry Ince contributed 72. Michael Falcon took the bowling honours with four for 61 including the wicket of George Challenor, the tourists' star batsman, for 7. In reply, the county side reached 94 all out. George John and Victor Pascall each took four wickets and the 21 year-old Learie – later, Lord – Constantine, son of the 1900 and 1906 tourist, claimed two inexpensive victims. The West Indies then declared on 206 for four in their second innings with Challenor making amends for his first innings failure with 101, an innings described by *Wisden's Cricketers Almanack* as 'a brilliant display'. Set 317 to win, Norfolk were bowled out for 85 with Geoffrey Colman batting well for 40 not out in the face of hostile bowling from John (seven for 38). In bowling Falcon in the first innings John sent a bail 48 yards.

## South Africa (1924)

South Africa toured again in 1924. Their fixture at Lakenham on 20 to 22 August was originally to have been against Norfolk but in the event was fulfilled by a Minor Counties eleven picked by the Norfolk County Club and captained by Falcon. Nevertheless, Norfolk provided seven of the home side in what turned out to be an exciting and hard-fought match. Batting first, the Minor Counties reached 196, John Coldham top-scoring with 40 and Sid Pegler again the tourists' most successful bowler with five for 46. In reply, the South Africans, who included nine of the side that in their immediately preceding game had contested the final Test, could only muster 149, succumbing to the right-arm spin bowling of Jack Meyer, later to captain Somerset and in the wider world to found Millfield School. He took six for 60 with Falcon returning figures of three for 48. In their second innings the Minor Counties reached 272 with Charles Titchmarsh, the Hertfordshire opening batsman, contributing 80 and Percy Chapman, who two years later would lead England to an Ashes victory but who was currently playing for Berkshire, hitting a particularly attractive 68. Requiring 320 to win, Dave Nourse led the challenge with a solid 91 but the tourists lost wickets and with only two minutes left the last batsman was brilliantly caught in the slips. The Minor Counties had won by 25 runs with the two Norfolk bowlers Falcon and Beadsmoore taking five for 103 and four for 53 respectively. All but one of Falcon's victims were top-order batsmen. The local contribution to this memorable victory – which also included batsmen Colman, Coldham and Stevens, wicketkeeper Pedder and bowler Watson – had been significant. And it had been well supported by the Norfolk public with 2000 in attendance on the first day and 3000 on the second.

## New Zealand (1927)

Three years later, it was the turn of the New Zealanders, for the first time, to visit Norfolk, and Lakenham. It was the start of a sequence in which the county side entertained the touring side nine times in the 13 seasons leading up to the Second World War. The visitors on this occasion had not yet entered the Test arena and this, their first tour of England, involved games against a mixture of first-class and second-class opposition. After an uncertain start to their tour, their confidence and successes grew and they were unbeaten in 22 matches when they arrived in Norwich at the end of August for a two-day game. The tourists won the toss and asked their hosts to bat. Unfortunately, they were bowled out for 104 with Bill Merritt, the leading New Zealand bowler on this tour, capturing six wickets for 34 and no one scoring more than 20. The visitors' response was led by Roger Blunt (96) and Charles Dacre (99) who together added 169 for the fourth wicket. The innings closed at 312 with Rodney Rought-Rought returning figures of five for 102. Second time around, Norfolk managed only 111 with Jack Nichols, now aged 49, hitting 53. This time, Herb McGirr took the bowling honours with five for 16. The tourists had won by an innings and 97 runs.

### West Indies (1928)

The West Indians were back in England for the 1928 season in which they played their first Test matches. Unfortunately, they had a poor tour, losing all three Tests by an innings and generally failing to fulfil the expectations raised by their performances five years previously. Norfolk entertained them early in the tour, on 23 and 24 May. Frustratingly, the first day was completely washed out so that there was little hope of a result when the game eventually started. When it did, however, Norfolk dismissed their visitors for 149. George Challenor, who had first toured 22 years previously, top-scored with 28 and Beadsmoore was the pick of the bowlers with five for 37 in 21 overs. In all, Norfolk sent down 83.5 overs, but to be fair to the tourists, batting was naturally difficult on a drying wicket. Norfolk did not find batting any easier and closed on 123 for nine. Frederic Bell, who had previously played a few games for Durham, and Falcon with 38 and 27 respectively added 55 for the third wicket but no one else reached double figures. Allrounder Cyril Browne collected five wickets for 27.

### South Africa (1929)

The 1929 South African tourists were a young, inexperienced side who, although not overly successful, performed sufficiently well to promise better things to come. Their premier batsman was again the evergreen

The Norfolk and South African teams at Lakenham, 1929. Back row (l to r): *HG Owen-Smith, BW Rought-Rought, EL Dalton.* Standing (l to r): *HB Cameron, HF Low, JH Bally, AJ Bell, WA Beadsmoore, Q McMillan, GA Stevens, RH Gladden, AL Ochse.* Seated (l to r): *JA Christy, JE Nichols, HW Taylor, S Christopherson (NCCC President), M Falcon, HO Frielinghaus (South African tour manager), CL Vincent, B Mitchell.* On the ground (l to r): *FR Bell, GN Scott-Chad, EA Van der Merwe.*

Herbie Taylor whilst the leading bowler was slow leg-break bowler Quintin McMillan. They visited Lakenham on 26 and 27 June immediately before the Second Test and, batting first, reached 420 in less than five hours. The main contributor to this formidable score was Taylor with 170, scored out of 285 in just over two and a half hours and including 2 sixes and 23 fours. Cyril Vincent's innings of 62 included 4 sixes. Falcon returned figures of three for 65. In reply, Norfolk totalled 126 with 30 from Basil Rought-Rought; 'Sandy' Bell took five wickets for 37. Following on, the home side fared much better with Bell (69) and Ronnie Gladden (50) helping Norfolk to 250 but still resulting in an innings defeat. The wickets were shared amongst five South African bowlers.

## New Zealand (1931)

The New Zealanders returned to England in 1931 when they played their first Test matches in this country. It was a wet, miserable summer that helped to contribute towards the tourists drawing 23 of their first-class matches. 'Stewie' Dempster was their leading batsman and Bill Merritt, as in 1927, took most wickets. Their two-day, non first-class match against Norfolk began at Lakenham on 20 August when, batting first, they lost four early wickets before Dempster led a recovery with 93, steering his side to a total of 225. The Norfolk opening bowlers, Walter Eagle and Rodney Rought-Rought, each claimed four wickets. One wicket down overnight, the hosts lost their remaining 19 wickets on the second day. In their first innings of 97 Merritt took six for 40 with the only significant resistance coming from David Walker, aged 18, who coming in on the fall of the first wicket batted two hours for 31 not out. Following on, the county could only reach 66 in their second knock.

## All India (1932)

After a break of 21 years the Indians toured England in the following year when they played their inaugural Test match. They were officially captained by the Maharajah of Porbander, an appointment made on social class rather than cricketing grounds with the result that he played in only four first-class matches. In his place, CK Nayudu, their most successful player, led the side in the major games. Norfolk played host to the tourists on 2 and 3 June when, batting first, the visitors struggled to 101; only Nayudu passed 20. Alec Utting and Bill Lingwood returned the exceptional figures of 28–8–34–4 and 24–8–28–3 respectively. Norfolk's response lasted only an hour and a half as they were dismissed for 49. Mahomed Nissar, the tourists' fine fast bowler, took six wickets for 14 and Nazir Ali four for 26. The only resistance of any substance came from a schoolboy just past his sixteenth birthday whom *Wisden's Cricketers Almanack* listed in their match scorecard as 'Mr W.J. Edrich'. He scored 20. The Indians fared better in their second innings declaring on 204 for nine; Phiroz Palia hit 56 and Utting claimed another four wickets. Set 257 to win, Norfolk managed only 128 with Nissar bowling six of his eight wickets and taking 14 wickets in the match for 57 runs. This was one of the best bowling performances ever seen at Lakenham.

The Norfolk and All India teams at Lakenham, 1932. Standing (l to r): *JE Nichols (umpire), Jahingir Khan, ECW Ricketts (All India tour manager), Mohammad Nissar, JC Thistleton-Smith, PE Palia, NL Foster, Amar Singh, WJ Lingwood, BE Kapadia, HE Theobald, S Nazir Ali,, GJ Rye (umpire).* Seated (l to r): *SHM Colah, AG Utting, S Wazir Ali, BW Rought-Rought, KS Ganshyamsinjhi of Limbdi, M Falcon, Joginder Singh, GN Scott-Chad, CK Nayudu, DC Rought-Rought.* On the ground (l to r): *ND Marshall, AW Tyler, Naoomal Jeoomal, Ghulam Mohammad, WJ Edrich. This match marked Bill Edrich's Norfolk debut.*

## West Indies (1933)

The West Indies were the next tourists to visit Norwich. In the fine summer of 1933 they met with mixed success on the field. Their batting was led by the prolific George Headley, who scored 2320 runs in first-class matches on the tour at an average of more than 66. With the ball, 'Manny' Martindale, the very quick opening bowler, collected 103 wickets. However, because of his League commitments with Nelson in Lancashire, Learie Constantine was only available for five games and did not appear in the Lakenham fixture at the beginning of August. On that occasion, the match was dominated by Headley's innings of 257 not out. In all, he batted for five and a half hours and hit 33 fours and 1 five and did not give a chance. Clifford Roach gave him most support with

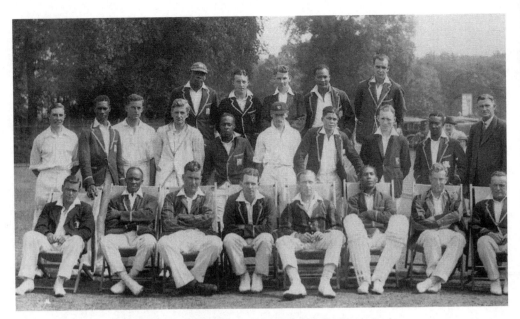

The Norfolk and West Indian teams at Lakenham, 1933. Back row (to r): *EA Martindale, WJ Edrich, RM Beresford, E Achong, CA Merry.* Middle row (l to r): *AW Tyler, VA Valentine, DC Rought-Rought, TGL Ballance, BJ Sealy, WJ Lingwood, CM Christiani, HF Low, G Headley, ELG Hoad.* Front row (l to r): *DF Walker, HC Griffith, RC Rought-Rought, GC Grant, M Falcon, CA Roach, BW Rought-Rought, CA Wiles.*

103, sharing a second-wicket partnership of 186. The tourists declared on 496 for eight, leaving Norfolk with little choice but to bat out for a draw. This they did quite easily compiling a first innings score of 257 with Basil Rought-Rought top-scoring with 57 and Bill Edrich, batting at number three, and Falcon, 28 years his senior, contributing 35 and 40 respectively. The tourists did not enforce the follow-on, instead batting out time to reach 35 for two.

### South Africa (1935)

Continuing the pattern established in 1926, the 1934 Australians did not play in Norfolk. However, in the following year the South Africans returned to Norwich. They proved to be a strong side with batting and bowling in depth. Only two matches were lost on the whole tour and they surprised most in the game by winning the Test series thanks to an impressive victory in the Second Test at Lord's. Against this background, Norfolk's performance against the tourists in mid-July was particularly creditable.

Batting first, the county side lost two early wickets but Bill Edrich, now aged 19 and in the process of qualifying for Middlesex, played a fine innings of 111 in two and three quarter hours, adding 146 for the third wicket with 20 year-old Michael Barton who scored 59. Coming in at the fall of the seventh wicket Frank Cunliffe hit 55 not out as Norfolk reached 325. Bob Crisp returned the best bowling figures with four for 65. The South Africans replied with 367, a total that was built on an opening partnership of 84 between Eric Rowan (59) and Ivan Siedle (62). Ken Viljoen then took over. Despite being hit heavily on his right hand and retiring hurt when on 97 he returned to complete an attractive century before retiring for the second time. Altogether his innings of 103 lasted for three and a quarter hours. There was only time left for Norfolk to reach 59 for three to which Barton contributed 39 not out. Altogether, some 10,000 people watched the two days of cricket.

For this game, and the following two, the County Club took the precaution of seeking financial guarantees from its members to guard against the loss of income through bad weather although in the event this proved unnecessary.

## New Zealand (1937)

The New Zealand touring side of 1937 was a young one with only three having toured here in 1931. They won nine and lost nine of their 32 first-class games but despite some encouraging performances in the three Tests their standard of play was considered to be disappointing. Six of their batsmen scored over 1000 runs on the tour although only Mervyn Wallace averaged over 40. The fast right-armer Jack Cowie was far and away their most successful bowler with 114 wickets at an average just under 20. Their visit to Lakenham on 23 and 24 June saw them bowl first, restricting Norfolk to 165. Rodney Rought-Rought top-scored with 26 and Norman Gallichan collected five for 37 in 19 overs of left-arm spin. That score, though, was sufficient to give the hosts a first-innings lead as they bowled out the tourists for 122 with Wilfrid Thompson taking four for 44. Looking to build on their lead, Norfolk were able only to reach 123 in their second innings; this time Cedric Thistleton-Smith offered most resistance before being run out for 33. Set 167 to win, the New Zealanders made light of their task and reached their target losing only two wickets. John Kerr steered them home with 93 not out

### West Indies (1939)

The war clouds were already gathering when the West Indies arrived in England in April 1939 for their sixth tour here. Indeed, the outbreak of hostilities eventually led to the tour's curtailment. After a moderate start, their fortunes improved during the summer and their final record surpassed that of any of their Caribbean predecessors. As in 1933, George Headley took the batting honours, this time scoring 1745 first-class runs at an average of 72.70; the next highest was under 31. Learie Constantine played a full tour and headed their bowling averages with 103 wickets at an average under 18. They played at Lakenham at the end of June when, batting first, they posted an impressive 369. After losing three relatively cheap wickets, Kenneth Weekes, the cousin of his more famous namesake, led the recovery with 123, an attractive innings which included 1 six and 16 fours. 'Foffie' Williams, coming in at the fall of the seventh wicket, then hit a quickfire 78. Norfolk's reply was impressive. Opening the innings, Harold Theobald scored 70 with just one boundary in a three-hour stay at the wicket. The Edrich brothers, Eric and Geoffrey, provided support with 47 and 53 respectively and there were other useful contributions from Desmond Rought-Rought, Falcon (now aged 50), Richard Beresford and Thompson whose short innings of 36 included 4 sixes. 'Bertie' Clarke, the West Indian leg-break bowler, took four for 121 as the home side reached 375 for nine, and a small lead, when time ran out. Norfolk had given an excellent account of themselves. But it was to be the last time for more than 20 years that they would entertain an overseas side.

### West Indies (1950)

When first-class cricket resumed after the war successive touring sides bypassed Norfolk until 1950. Then it was the turn of the West Indians to come to England. They proved to be a formidable team and for the first time established the West Indies as a cricketing power. Their batting was built on the solid opening pair of Allan Rae and Jeffrey Stollmeyer who

The West Indians tourists fielding versus the Minor Counties at Lakenham, 1950.

paved the way for the brilliant trio of Frank Worrell, Clyde Walcott and Everton Weekes. These five and three others each passed 1000 runs for the tour, all at an average of over 37. The bowling was dominated by the 'spin twins' of Sonny Ramadhin and Alf Valentine, each aged 20 at the start of the tour and each with first-class experience amounting to two matches before the tour. Nonetheless, they collected 258 wickets between them during this summer.

They played at Lakenham at the beginning of September after winning a memorable Test series, not to play Norfolk but the Minor Counties in a three-day, first-class game. The Minor Counties, without any local representative, batted first but struggled against the off spin of Ramadhin who took seven for 33. The tourists' response was typical of their batting that summer – 425 for five declared with major contributions from Gerry Gomez (117) and Ken Trestrail (94) who added 170 together for the fourth wicket. Worrell chipped in with 62 not out. Needing 319 to avoid an innings defeat the Minor Counties fared much better in their second innings reaching 312, Yorkshire opener Bill Keighley top-scoring with 92 and five bowlers shared the wickets.

## South Africa (1951)

The 1951 South Africans had a largely disappointing and unsuccessful tour winning only five of their 30 first-class games. Their batting relied largely on Eric Rowan who, with 1852 runs and an average of just above 50, was some way ahead of his colleagues at the end of the tour. The bowlers, too, were generally not as effective as might have been expected, the exception being medium-pace bowler Geoff Chubb with 76 wickets.

Lakenham played host to them at the beginning of September. Again, the Minor Counties were the opposition but on this occasion the game was limited to two days and therefore not treated as first-class. The 'home' side batted first and reached 182 before their last wicket fell. A young Nigel Moore, the only Norfolk player in the side, batted at number six and scored 18. The major innings, of 48, was played by Brian Belle from Suffolk, and Michael Melle took six wickets for 51. The tourists replied with 318 for eight declared to which Jack Cheetham, soon to take over his country's captaincy, contributed 114 not out and Rowan 73. In their second innings the Minor Counties managed only 113 – Moore scored 11 – to lose by an innings and 23 runs. Hugh Tayfield and Percy Mansell, the two spinners, shared nine wickets.

## India (1952)

In the following year the Indians were the tourists. In a summer in which a young Fred Trueman first made his mark in Test cricket and terrorised the Indian batsmen with his fast bowling, the tourists were thoroughly outplayed in the four-match series. Their overall first-class record was equally unimpressive with only four wins in 29 games. Only 'Polly' Umrigar, with 1688 runs, passed 1100 runs; Ghulam Ahmed with his off breaks was the pick of a moderate bowling attack. Early September again saw the Minor Counties take on the touring side at Lakenham, again in a two-day match. The Indians batted first and in miserable conditions compiled a score of 290 with 20 year-old Vijay Manjrekar scoring an attractive 101. Vijay Hazare hit 63 and supported the century maker in a third-wicket partnership of 133. In reply, the Minor Counties lost their first six wickets for 100 but recovered to 200 all out. Only two hours remained in which the tourists reached 168 for three. The opener Pankaj Roy, who in the

Test series had been dismissed for five ducks in seven innings, batted well for 88 not out. It had not been a match to remember which was a shame because, as it turned out, the game marked the end of a period going back to 1923 when, more often than not, Lakenham played host to the overseas tourists.

## South African Fezelas (1961)

It was not until 1961 that an overseas side again came to Norfolk. Even then, they were not the Australian team who were in England that year but a young South African squad known as the Fezelas. Privately funded by a retired Durban sugar planter, E. Stanley Murphy, they were unbeaten in their 21 matches three of which were first-class fixtures. They were skippered by the experienced Test batsman Roy McLean but otherwise comprised largely untried players a number of whom would be leading players on the world stage within a very few years: Eddie Barlow, Colin Bland, Peter Pollock, Denis Lindsay and future Test captain Peter van der Merwe. They played attractive as well as successful cricket that was to be the hallmark of South African cricket for the rest of the decade. Bill Edrich was one of many to express delight at the way they performed, his first-hand experience being gained at Lakenham on 21 and 22 June. In an amazing first day's cricket, Norfolk were first bowled out for 98 with Barlow taking six for 25, and by the end of the day were 78 for one in their second innings. In between, the Fezelas scored 396 for seven declared in 66.5 overs with Barlow hitting 116 in 78 minutes, Bland 81 and Ken Elgie 103 in 48 minutes. The *Eastern Daily Press* reckoned that the only comparable innings was Geoffrey Stevens' innings at Cambridge in 1914 with the nearest at Lakenham being Dick Hoff's 70-minute century against Hertfordshire in 1955. On the second day, Norfolk were dismissed just before lunch for 201 with Edrich hitting 57 and future Test bowler Jack Botten taking four for 41.

## West Indies (1966)

By 1966 the West Indies were established as the leading power in Test cricket. Captained by Garry Sobers and containing other world-class players of the calibre of Conrad Hunte, Rohan Kanhai, Lance Gibbs, Wes

Hall and Charlie Griffiths, they easily defeated England in the Test series. Sobers himself scored most runs (1349) and took most wickets (60) on the tour. Unfortunately for Norfolk cricket lovers he rested himself for the tourists' game at Lakenham on 23 and 24 June against the Minor Counties. The hosts were led by Bill Edrich, now aged 50, and also included Norfolk spinner Billy Rose. Kanhai, leading the tourists for the first time, won the toss and invited the Minor Counties to bat and in less than 24 overs they were bowled out for 65. Wes Hall produced a wonderful display of fast bowling in taking seven for 31 and forcing an eighth to retire with a broken finger. The tourists' reply was led by Peter Lashley who batted for just under three hours for 121 not out. Most support came from Basil Butcher (54) and Kanhai (67) and they eventually declared on 309 for five. In their second innings the Minor Counties were the beneficiaries of some rather generous bowling from the West Indian slow bowlers but, still, their final total of 211 represented a far better showing. Martin Maslin from Lincolnshire batted well for 66 and Bill Edrich hit 61 with 4 sixes and 6 fours.

## India (1971)
By 1971, the practice of 'split' tours to this country by most of the Test playing nations was established. In that year, it was the turn, first, of Pakistan and then India to play a three-Test series. The Indians, in particular, had a very successful tour beating England one-nil and losing only one first-class match. Their success was based on a quartet of spinners – Chandrasekhar, Venkataraghavan, Bedi and Prasanna – but they were also able to boast a number of consistent batsmen including their captain, Ajit Wadekar and a youthful Sunil Gavaskar. Their first-class game against the Minor Counties took place at Lakenham at the end of July immediately after the closely contested First Test. Unfortunately, the first day's play was completely washed out so that when play started nearly an hour late on the second day the Minor Counties sought to make up for lost time with some forceful batting. Martin Maslin with 61 continued where he had left off five years previously and they declared on 203 for five. Chandrasekhar finished with three for 39. The Indians scored freely in their reply with half-centuries from Gavaskar, Ashok Mankad and Abbas Baig enabling them to declare on 252 for three. The Minor Counties were easily able to save the game with

Cheshire's Fred Millett, the captain, scoring 50 not out in a total of 199 for six declared. The Indians then batted out the remaining hour of the game.

## New Zealand (1986)

Following the India game there was a break of 15 years before a first-class touring side returned to Norfolk. On this next occasion it was the New Zealanders, who were sharing a 'split' tour with India, who played at Lakenham early in their tour on 9 to 11 July. They were unbeaten in their 15-match visit and, for the first time, won a Test series in this country. Their star in the Tests was Richard Hadlee but in their other games, as well as the Tests, most players made useful contributions. Notable performers included Martin Crowe and skipper Jeremy Coney with the bat and John Bracewell and Evan Gray with the ball. At Lakenham, they took on a Minor Counties side that included Norfolk's Stephen Plumb and ex-Test batsman Graham Roope. The 'home' team batted first and reached 209, Plumb top-scoring with a patient 69. Gray picked up five wickets for 54 and then followed this up with an innings of 108 in two and three quarter hours. John Wright (65) and Jeff Crowe (69) also made significant contributions. Declaring on 334 for eight, the tourists again encountered resistance from Plumb but after he was dismissed for 29 the innings fell away and the Minor Counties were all out for 141 with Gray completing an excellent personal performance by taking four more wickets for 52. The New Zealanders knocked off the 17 runs required for victory without losing a wicket.

## Sri Lanka (1998)

Twelve years later came the last visit by a Test-playing touring side to Norfolk. On this occasion, it was Sri Lanka who played a one-day game against an ECB eleven at Lakenham on 5 August. The tour was relatively short, with only one Test (which they won) but for this particular fixture the tourists rested many of their senior players. The ECB side was drawn from the Minor Counties and the Second Elevens of first-class counties (but without any Norfolk players) and it turned out to be no match for the visitors. In a one-sided game, the 'home' team managed only 141 in their 50 overs with Sri Lanka reaching their target in only 28.1 overs for the loss of two wickets. The outstanding performance for the tourists came from their captain, Pinnaduwage de Silva, who took three for 12 in his ten overs and then hit an unbeaten 53 at more than a run a ball. The result should not have been a surprise; Sri Lanka were then the reigning world champions in this form of cricket.

# CHAPTER 14

# Looking Back,
# Looking Forward

It is now almost 270 years since that match at the Crown Inn in Stoke Ferry, the first recorded game of cricket in Norfolk. We know from reports and paintings of cricket matches elsewhere in England around that time, and also from the Laws of Cricket drawn up in 1744, that games in the middle of the 18th century are recognisable as the basis of the much more sophisticated game generally now played. They were usually 11-a-side and with umpires, bats, balls and wickets and fielders in broadly the positions we see them today. Of course, there are differences; for instance, in the use of protective equipment and the development of over-arm bowling. But in essence it is the same game.

Locally, and as one would expect, cricket has moved with the times, mirroring developments across the country both on and off the field of play. A good example is the way in which league cricket took root in Norfolk. Following the creation of the first local cricket leagues elsewhere in the late 1880s they began to spring up in Norfolk within a very few years, expanding considerably, in particular, in the years that followed the First World War. For much of the 20th century, the best club sides in the county eschewed league cricket continuing instead to prefer less competitive arrangements. Furthermore, by the 1950s, the minor, generally village-based, leagues were in decline. However, once southern counties 'adopted' league cricket in the 1960s, Norfolk soon followed and within a short space of time a structure was established which, 40 years on, is the basis for Saturday league cricket today.

There are other examples. The introduction, nationally, of sponsorship for competitions – also in the 1960s – very soon spread to Norfolk. Even in these more difficult economic times, those leagues and cups of any size still tend to attract sponsorship, usually by a local business. And advertising boards that have for many years dominated our Test Match grounds can also now be found on many cricket grounds in the county. To illustrate further the adaptability of local cricket, it was extremely rare 40 years ago, except in midweek cup competitions, to limit the number of overs a bowler could send down in an innings. Now, however, it is unheard not to do so except in friendly matches.

It is inevitable in any sport that clubs will rise and fall; indeed, that they will come and go. This can be due to a combination of factors and will at least in part reflect social and economic changes. It is sometimes said that there was a time when every village had its own cricket team, and whilst I have avoided the temptation of recording every settlement that at one time or another fielded a side it is clear beyond doubt that in the first part of the 20th century there were scores of villages who then had a team but no longer do. That is not to say that those teams had as full a fixture list as clubs today or ran more than one team or a junior section or that their facilities were particularly developed, even perhaps by the standards of the day. But the cricket team was, like the village pub and the village school, quite central to the life of the local community.

In more recent times, many players drive several miles to their home ground. As a consequence, the more ambitious clubs, who are generally those that offer most in terms of facilities and opportunities for young players, can develop to the point of having two grounds and running three or four Saturday sides and up to five junior teams. At a time when the costs and bureaucracy of running a cricket club have increased these larger ones have the advantage of an economy of scale.

It is not just the demise of the 'village' team which many bemoan. Compared even with the situation before the Second World War, numerous grounds have been lost, often to development or the plough or even a golf course, although in almost all cases the root cause has been the team's disbanding. Many such grounds were no more than 'meadows kindly lent' by an accommodating farmer and may not in themselves be much missed. But others were an integral part of their community. In some cases, all that there is to show that cricket was played in a particular parish is a derelict pavilion. In most not even that remains.

Also long lost are almost all of the venues associated with country house cricket such as those at Garboldisham Manor, Gunton Park, Middleton Tower, Melton Constable and Didlington. Lost, too, are the grounds within other Norfolk Halls such as those at Merton, Honingham, Heydon, Weston Longville, Keswick and Haveringland.

In addition, the large public recreation facilities at Eaton Park in Norwich and Beaconsfield in Great Yarmouth host only a small proportion of the matches that they accommodated in the past. And Lakenham, the County Club's home for well over a century, witnessed its last County match in 2000. Not only was that the end of an era but in addition the most symbolic element of Norfolk's cricket heritage, with all its history, was lost for ever.

There is, though, a danger in viewing the past through rose-coloured spectacles. One needs only to look at Norfolk cricket at the start of the 20th century to realise that locally the game was not perceived as being in a healthy state. It was, after all, the concerns of the time that led to the initiatives of those such as Revd Ffolkes described in Chapter 3. (Indeed, the *Eastern Daily Press* in April 1902 carried an article under the stark headline 'Village Cricket: Is it decaying?' albeit that, having referred to the gloomy view amongst some that young men were choosing cycling over cricket, it concluded that in fact the future of village cricket was assured). And in the same year the magazine *Cricket* bemoaned the fact that at least on good wickets – although of course these were less common in rural Norfolk – the three or four hours available for an ordinary Saturday afternoon club match was not sufficient to allow everyone an innings and went on to say that this was the reason why ' so many men take to golf and other games in which one is certain to have a fair share of the play' and that it was 'unreasonable to expect a beginner to take a keen interest in a club when he can only get an innings about once a month'. And this in the middle of the period of English cricket known as 'The Golden Age'.

Nonetheless, both nationally and in Norfolk, cricket survived these challenges and the more recent ones after 1945. Indeed, much has happened, not least locally, over the last 30 to 40 years to reinforce cricket as the national summer game. In Norfolk, the commitment of many to youth development and coaching in a way that was not even contemplated in the 1960s has raised standards. Equally, the improvement of facilities within and outside the boundary line has made a positive contribution to the quality of cricket in the county.

It would also be an omission not to recognise the opportunities created by the funding and other support made available by the England and Wales Cricket Board, the Cricket Foundation and the Lord's Taverners as well as those of commercial organisations such as Sky and Nat West Bank. This has enabled the Norfolk Cricket Board in particular to facilitate the introduction of a range of initiatives such as coaching in schools, the rolling out of the Clubmark scheme, the expansion of county age group teams, the development of women and girls' cricket and improving the access of the disabled to the game.

In all of this, one must recognise the pivotal role of the County Club in the history and development of cricket in Norfolk. The county can be proud of past successes in the Minor Counties Championship and the more recent victories in one-day knock-out competitions. It can also reflect on the performances of local cricketers such as the Edriches, Peter Parfitt, Clive Radley, Martin Saggers and, more recently, Jaik Mickleburgh and Robert Newton. Whilst they have made their mark in the first-class and international game others, without that opportunity, have been loyal servants of the County Club.

Similarly, the contribution made by 'imports' has been immense. Herbert Jenner paved the way in the late 1820s. Later, around the end of the 19th century, the likes of Charlie Shore and Edward Gibson made their indelible mark. The middle part of the last century brought Cecil Boswell and Ted Witherden to Norfolk, to be followed by Test players Ken Taylor and Phil Sharpe and others with experience of the first-class game. Then, from

1989, the Derbyshire triumvirate of Roger Finney, Steve Goldsmith and Paul Newman, followed by Lancastrian Chris Brown, took up residence in Norfolk to the great advantage of cricket in the county.

This is not to say that the County Club has only been about its periodic successes and stand-out players. Behind the scenes there has been a succession of hardworking committees and officers. Amongst their contributions were for very many years the holding of youth coaching sessions at a time when no other effective provision was made in the county. Norfolk has also been able to boast a membership and spectator base that has been the envy of other Minor Counties. Whilst county matches no longer attract quite the crowds of the past the County Club can still boast a membership approaching 600 and it is good to see the playing arena at Horsford's Manor Park ringed with the Club's supporters and the tents that were such a feature of the Lakenham Festival.

It is also pleasing to recognise the commitment of the County Club over many years to the nurturing of local talent. Whilst the early 1990s' aim of producing a Minor Counties' team comprised exclusively of Norfolk-based players has not been fully achieved it has been the case that at least eight (and more often nine) of the regular county side in recent years have learned their cricket in Norfolk and that the only exceptions were often only the 'naturalised' County Coach and current Captain Chris Brown and loyal servant Trevor Ward.

None of this is to be complacent about the future of cricket in Norfolk. The last few years have seen a perceptible reduction in the number of clubs and teams operating in the county. There is also no doubt that the administrative burdens that fall on clubs, and particularly their hardworking volunteers, are not getting lighter. Social trends and competition from other leisure activities also mean that cricket, along with other team sports, is not so readily attractive to adults, particularly those in their twenties and thirties, as was the case even a generation ago. Worryingly, the evidence suggests a significant reduction in the commitment to club and league cricket.

The Norfolk Cricket Board are alive to these concerns and their primary activity now centres on player retention and adult participation.

Inevitably, this means reviewing the forms of cricket on offer in Norfolk and understanding players' expectations and the social and economic pressures at work. Whilst Saturday league cricket remains central to the competitive game in Norfolk we need to recognise that not all who might be attracted to play cricket prefer this version of it, at least in its current form. There is also potentially greater scope for midweek evening games that accentuate the game's social side.

It is most likely, too, that the clubs that will flourish in the future will be those who respond positively and imaginatively to the challenges and who are inclusive in terms of both the cricket they offer and those they seek to encourage, regardless of age, gender or ability. Cricket, both nationally and locally, has demonstrated in the past that it can respond positively to changes in society and move with the times. The extent to which the game in Norfolk prospers in the future will depend on its continuing adaptability.

# Statistics:
# Norfolk County
# Cricket Club

## PART 1: MINOR COUNTIES CHAMPIONSHIP (1895–2014)
### TEAM RECORDS

HIGHEST SCORES – FOR

526 for 7 declared   v Kent Seconds at Gravesend, 1937

479 for 8 declared   v Durham at Blackhill, 1939

472 all out   v Bedfordshire at Lakenham, 1920

462 for 9 declared   v Cambridgeshire at Cambridge, 1913

461 for 8 wickets   v Bedfordshire at Horsford, 2005†

459 all out   v Kent Seconds at Tonbridge, 1933

451 for 7 declared   v Hertfordshire at Hertford, 2002

   †: innings closed at 90 overs

LOWEST SCORES – FOR

| | |
|---|---|
| 28 | v Worcestershire at Worcester, 1896 |
| 36 | v Buckinghamshire at Lakenham, 1927 |
| 38 | v Lincolnshire at Lakenham, 1909 |
| 38 | v Hertfordshire at Bishop's Stortford, 1956 |
| 39 | v Durham at Great Yarmouth, 1899 |
| 39 | v Hertfordshire at St Albans, 1909† |
| 39 | v Cambridgeshire at Newmarket, 1909† |
| 39 | v Surrey Seconds at Lakenham, 1930 |

† these two scores were made in successive innings

HIGHEST SCORES – AGAINST

| | |
|---|---|
| 550 for 5 declared | by Surrey Seconds at The Oval, 1925 |
| 503 for 9 declared | by Surrey Seconds at The Oval, 1901 |
| 485 all out | by Northumberland at Jesmond, 2008 |
| 466 all out | by Cambridgeshire at Cambridge, 1911 |
| 452 for 7 declared | by Surrey Seconds at Guildford, 1949 |
| 451 for 4 declared | by Staffordshire at Manor Park, 2003 |

LOWEST SCORES – AGAINST

| | |
|---|---|
| 39 | by Suffolk at Lakenham, 1912† |
| 40 | by Suffolk at Lakenham, 1912† |
| 41 | by Lincolnshire at Gainsborough, 1936 |
| 42 | by Leicestershire Seconds at Loughborough, 1924 |
| 42 | by Lincolnshire at Lakenham, 1931 |
| 45 | by Nottinghamshire Seconds at Lakenham 1958 |
| 46 | by Cambridgeshire at Lakenham, 1914 |

(Cambridgeshire batted two short)

† these two scores were made in the same match

RECORD PARTNERSHIPS FOR EACH WICKET

| | | | |
|---|---|---|---|
| 1st | 335 | C. Amos (180) and C.J. Rogers (153) | |
| | | v Hertfordshire at Hertford, | 2002 |
| 2nd | 223 | C.J. Rogers (133) and J.M. Spelman (121*) | |
| | | v Northumberland at Jesmond, | 2005 |
| 3rd | 290* | S.C. Goldsmith (200*) and R.J. Finney (107*) | |
| | | v Cumberland at Lakenham, | 1993 |
| 4th | 195 | S.C. Goldsmith (157*) and C.J. Rogers (88) | |
| | | v Hertfordshire at Lakenham, | 1998 |
| 5th | 172 | T.R. Ward (123) and C.J. Taylor (127) | |
| | | v Staffordshire at Old Hill CC, | 2013 |
| 6th | 200 | E.F. Penn (133) and L.H. Leman (72*) | |
| | | v Hertfordshire at Watford, | 1905 |
| 7th | 196 | B.W. Rought-Rought (143) and T.G.L. Ballance (107) | |
| | | v Buckinghamshire at Lakenham, | 1937 |
| 8th | 152 | A.K. Watson (83) and R.G. Pilch (88) | |
| | | v Cambridgeshire at Lakenham, | 1905 |
| 9th | 114 | D.C. Rought-Rought (65*) and R.C. Rought-Rought (66) | |
| | | v Kent Seconds at Tonbridge, | 1935 |
| 10th | 101 | D.E. Mattocks (65*) and T.M. Wright (48) | |
| | | v Hertfordshire at Lakenham, | 1963 |

## INDIVIDUAL RECORDS

### TWO CENTURIES IN ONE MATCH
110* and 127* W.J. Edrich v Staffordshire at Lakenham, 1961
102 and 116* S.G. Plumb v Bedfordshire at Dunstable, 1986
111* and 120* S.G. Plumb v Hertfordshire at Lakenham, 1991
105 and 112* T.R. Ward v Staffordshire at Stone, 2010

### DOUBLE CENTURIES
226*  C. Amos v Lincolnshire at Lakenham, 1998
222   G.A. Stevens v Bedfordshire at Lakenham, 1920
217   D.F. Walker v Northumberland at Lakenham, 1939
210   D.F. Walker v Kent Seconds at Hunstanton, 1936
205   M. Falcon v Hertfordshire at Cheshunt, 1920
204*  S.G. Plumb v Cumberland at Millom, 1988
201   G.A. Stevens v Berkshire at Lakenham, 1910 (Challenge Match)
200*  S.C. Goldsmith v Cumberland at Lakenham, 1993

### CARRYING BAT THROUGH A COMPLETED INNINGS
L. H. Leman (44*) v Suffolk at Felixstowe, 1906 (Norfolk batted one short)
B.W. Rought-Rought (52*) v Hertfordshire at Lakenham, 1931
J.A. Donaldson (77*) v Cambridgeshire at Wisbech, 1971
K. Taylor (99*) v Lincolnshire at Grimsby, 1972

MOST RUNS IN A SEASON (800 OR MORE RUNS)

| | |
|---|---|
| 1031 (at 79.30) | E.G. Witherden in 1959 |
| 992 (at 90.18) | S.G. Plumb in 1991 |
| 940 (at 49.47) | G.J. Saville in 1967 |
| 917 (at 70.54) | S.C. Goldsmith in 1993 |
| 908 (at 41.27) | G.A. Stevens in 1911 |
| 902 (at 64.43) | T.J. Boon in 1996 |
| 855 (at 53.43) | E.G. Witherden in 1960 |
| 852 (at 53.25) | W.J. Edrich in 1960 |
| 836 (at 49.18) | Parvez J. Mir in 1981 |
| 831 (at 63.92) | K. Taylor in 1972 |
| 830 (at 55.33) | S.G. Plumb in 1988 |
| 816 (at 58.29) | S.C. Goldsmith in 1995 |
| 808 (at 44.89) | E.G. Witherden in 1958 |
| 801 (at 50.06) | E.G. Witherden in 1957 |

MOST CAREER CENTURIES AND HALF-CENTURIES

| CENTURIES | | HALF-CENTURIES | |
|---|---|---|---|
| 21 | M. Falcon | 67 | S.G. Plumb |
| 19 | C.J. Rogers | 63 | M. Falcon |
| 17 | S.G. Plumb | 61 | C.J. Rogers |
| 15 | G.A. Stevens | 49 | W.J. Edrich |
| 13 | D.F. Walker | 47 | F.L.Q. Handley |
| | E.G. Witherden | 44 | G.A. Stevens |
| 10 | C. Amos | 39 | S.C. Goldsmith |
| | S.C. Goldsmith | 38 | R.D.P. Huggins |
| | F.L.Q. Handley | 35 | C. Amos |
| | T.R. Ward | | |

BEST BOWLING ANALYSES IN AN INNINGS
(EIGHT OR MORE WICKETS)

| | |
|---|---|
| 10–50 | C. Shore v Durham at Lakenham, 1897 |
| 9–24 | Revd G.B. Raikes v Suffolk at Lakenham, 1910 |
| 9–32 | T.G.L. Ballance v Buckinghamshire at High Wycombe, 1936 |
| 9–48 | G.W. Walker v Cambridgeshire at Manor Park, 2009 |
| 9–63 | E.W. Smith v Lincolnshire at Lakenham, 1909 |
| 9–90 | C.S.R. Boswell v Hertfordshire at Lakenham, 1947 |
| 8–24 | W.J. Lingwood v Lincolnshire at Gainsborough, 1932† |
| 8–24 | R.C. Rought-Rought v Hertfordshire at Broxbourne, 1933 |
| 8–40 | P.G. Walmsley v Buckinghamshire at Slough, 1954 |
| 8–41 | M. Falcon v Bedfordshire at Kings Lynn, 1923 |
| 8–41 | W. Rose v Hertfordshire at Watford, 1977 |
| 8–43 | P.G. Walmsley v Middlesex Seconds at Lakenham, 1958 |
| 8–45 | T.H. Barnes v Buckinghamshire at Lakenham, 1977 |
| 8–46 | E. Gibson v Hertfordshire at St Albans, 1908 |
| 8–46 | R.V. Bell v Buckinghamshire at Lakenham, 1967 |
| 8–47 | R. Kingshott v Northumberland at Lakenham, 1990 |
| 8–48 | E.W. Smith v Hertfordshire at Lakenham, 1907 |
| 8–50 | W.J. Lingwood v Lincolnshire at Gainsborough, 1932† |
| 8–50 | C.S.R. Boswell v Buckinghamshire at Lakenham, 1949 |
| 8–53 | J.N. Worman v Suffolk at Lakenham, 1906 |
| 8–59 | W.A. Beadsmoore v Staffordshire at Lakenham, 1923 |
| 8–65 | C. Brown v Bedfordshire at Manor Park, 2005 |
| 8–71 | T.I.Moore v Hertfordshire at Hertford, 1967 |
| 8–102 | A.J. Corran v Buckinghamshire at Lakenham, 1960 |

† these two analyses were returned in the same match

BEST BOWLING ANALYSES IN A MATCH (12 OR MORE WICKETS)

16–72   C. Shore v Durham at Lakenham, 1897

16–74   W.J. Lingwood v Lincolnshire at Gainsborough, 1932

16–96   G.W. Walker v Cambridgeshire at Manor Park, 2009

15–92   E.W. Smith v Hertfordshire at Lakenham, 1907

15–127  C.S.R. Boswell v Buckinghamshire at Lakenham, 1949

14–73   R.C. Rought-Rought v Buckinghamshire at Wing, 1931

13–37   T.G.L. Ballance v Hertfordshire at Cokenach, 1936

13–87   M. Falcon v Buckinghamshire at Lakenham, 1925

13–95   R. Falconer v Suffolk at Bury St Edmunds, 1912

13–103  J.N. Worman v Suffolk at Lakenham, 1906

13–117  C. Shore v Cambridgeshire at Fenner's, 1900

13–118  C. Brown v Bedfordshire at Manor Park, 2005

12–46   R.I. Jefferson v Hertfordshire at Lakenham, 1969

12–68   E. Gibson v Cambridgeshire at Fenner's, 1912

12–75   M. Falcon v Cambridgeshire at Lakenham, 1914

12–79   W.A. Beadsmoore v Staffordshire at Lakenham, 1923

12–80   W.S. Thompson v Kent Seconds at Lakenham, 1933

12–83   R.I. Jefferson v Cambridgeshire at Lakenham, 1968

12–88   R. Falconer v Hertfordshire at St Albans, 1912

12–89   E.W. Smith v Cambridgeshire at Lakenham, 1906

12–91   P.G. Walmsley v Middlesex Seconds at Lakenham, 1958

12–98   M. Falcon v Bedfordshire at Lakenham, 1923

12–100  E.W. Smith v Cambridgeshire at Lakenham, 1908

12–105  R. Kingshott v Northumberland at Lakenham, 1990

12–119  M. Falcon v Kent Seconds at Hythe, 1921

12–127  T.I. Moore v Hertfordshire at Hertford, 1967

12–135  A.J. Corran v Buckinghamshire at Lakenham, 1960

## MOST INSTANCES OF FIVE WICKETS IN AN INNINGS

| | | | |
|---|---|---|---|
| 52 | M. Falcon | 17 | C.S.R. Boswell |
| 28 | R.C. Rought-Rought | | T.I. Moore |
| 25 | E. Gibson | | W. Rose |
| 23 | C. Shore | 15 | H. Watson |
| 19 | W.J. Edrich | 15 | H. Watson |
| 18 | W.A. Beadsmoore | 14 | R. Falconer |
| | C. Brown | | Revd G.B. Raikes |
| | E.W. Smith | | |

## MOST INSTANCES OF TEN WICKETS IN A MATCH

| | | | |
|---|---|---|---|
| 9 | M. Falcon | 3 | W.A. Beadsmoore |
| 7 | C. Shore | | W.J. Edrich |
| 6 | Revd G.B. Raikes | | R. Falconer |
| | E.W. Smith | | R.A. Kingshott |
| 5 | E. Gibson | | P.G. Walmsley |
| 4 | T.H. Barnes | | J.N. Worman |
| | R.I. Jefferson | | |
| | W. Rose | | |
| | R.C. Rought-Rought | | |

## MOST WICKETS IN A SEASON (50 OR MORE WICKETS)

| | |
|---|---|
| 65 (at 7.94) | R. Falconer in 1912 |
| 60 (at 13.23) | M. Falcon in 1922 |
| 60 (at 14.37) | E.W. Smith in 1907 |
| 59 (at 12.37) | R.C. Rought-Rought in 1933 |
| 59 (at 12.95) | R.C. Rought-Rought in 1929 |
| 59 (at 12.68) | Parvez J. Mir in 1984 |
| 58 (at 14.16) | E. Gibson in 1909 |
| 58 (at 9.71) | R.I. Jefferson in 1969 |
| 57 (at 9.05) | C. Shore in 1895 |
| 57 (at 10.67) | Revd G.B. Raikes in 1910 |
| 55 (at 9.49) | R.C. Rought-Rought in 1931 |
| 53 (at 13.96) | M. Falcon in 1921 |
| 53 (at 17.81) | T.I. Moore in 1969 |
| 52 (at 15.56) | C.S.R. Boswell in 1947 |
| 50 (at 12.37) | W.J. Lingwood in 1932 |
| 50 (at 14.42) | P.G. Walmsley in 1958 |

MOST WICKETKEEPING DISMISSALS IN AN INNINGS,
MATCH AND SEASON

Innings: 6 (5ct, 1st)    D.E. Mattocks v Buckinghamshire at Amersham, 1977

    5 (4ct, 1st)    G.R. Pedder v Hertfordshire at Lakenham, 1931

    (5ct)    E.H.Edrich v Northumberland at Lakenham, 1939

    (4ct, 1st)    E.H. Edrich v Hertfordshire at Hertford, 1951

    (3ct, 2st)    H.C. Blofeld v Hertfordshire at Lakenham, 1958

    (5ct)    T. Allcock v Buckinghamshire at Lakenham, 1959

    (4ct, 1st)    C.M. Kenyon v Notts. Seconds at Trent Bridge, 1959

    (4ct, 1st)    E.J. Greatrex v Suffolk at Lakenham, 1969

    (5ct)    D.E. Mattocks v Suffolk at Lakenham, 1982

    (4ct, 1st)    S.C. Crowley v Cambridgeshire at Wisbech, 1993

    (5ct)    S.C. Crowley v Cambridgeshire at Lakenham, 1994

    (4ct, 1st)    M.K.L. Boyden v Lincolnshire at Lincoln in 1997

Match:  9 (7ct, 2st)    S.C. Crowley v Cambridgeshire at Wisbech, 1993

    8 (8ct)    T. Allcock v Buckinghamshire at Lakenham, 1969

    (7ct, 1st)    D.E. Mattocks v Buckinghamshire at Amersham, 1977

    (8ct)    D.E. Mattocks v Suffolk at Lakenham, 1982

    (8ct)    M.K.L. Boyden v Suffolk at Lakenham, 1997

    7 (7ct)    J.E. Nichols v Surrey Seconds at Lakenham, 1926

    (6ct, 1st)    E.H. Edrich v Lincolnshire at Grimsby, 1937

    (7ct)    E.H. Edrich v Northumberland at Lakenham, 1939

    (3ct, 4st)    T. Allcock v Cambridgeshire at Wisbech, 1970

    (7ct)    T. Allcock v Hertfordshire at Hertford, 1973

    (3ct, 4st)    D.E. Mattocks v Cumberland at North Runcton, 1989

Season: 36 (31ct, 5st)   M.K.L. Boyden in 1997

    33 (25ct, 8st)   E.H. Edrich in 1939

    32 (30ct, 2st)   B.J.H. Wood in 1933

    30 (23ct, 7st)   E.J. Greatrex in 1969

    29 (27ct, 2st)   S.C. Crowley in 1994

    28 (24ct, 4st)   D.E. Mattocks in 1977

    27 (21ct, 6st)   B.G.W. Stevens in 1953

    26 (14ct, 12st)  R.W. Thurgar in 1911

    26 (24ct, 2st)   E.H. Edrich in 1938

    24 (20ct, 4st)   E.H. Edrich in 1949

    24 (22ct, 2st)   D.E. Mattocks in 1964

MOST CATCHES AS A FIELDER IN AN INNINGS, MATCH AND SEASON

Innings: 5 Philip J. Sharpe v Cambridgeshire at Papworth Everard, 1980

4 Dr R. Smith v Northumberland at Lakenham, 1897

E. Gibson v Suffolk at Ipswich, 1907

G.A. Stevens v Cambridgeshire at King's Lynn, 1911

G.A. Stevens v Cambridgeshire at Cambridge, 1914

H.F. Low v Hertfordshire at Watford, 1930

R.C. Rought-Rought v Lincolnshire at Grantham, 1933

D.D. Carter v Kent Seconds at Dartford, 1949

P.G. Powell v Hertfordshire at Hertford, 1950

G.J. Saville v Lincolnshire at Lakenham, 1969

Philip J. Sharpe v Cambridgeshire at Lakenham, 1977

C.J. Rogers v Bedfordshire at Southall in 1990

Match: 7 Philip J. Sharpe v Cambridgeshire at Papworth Everard, 1980

6 Revd G.B. Raikes v Oxfordshire at Oxford, 1906

R.C. Rought-Rought v Lincolnshire at Grantham, 1933

Season: 23 G.J. Saville in 1969

21 G.A. Stevens in 1910

16 T. Morley in 1897

I.P. Mercer in 1969

I.P. Mercer in 1970

15 G.A. Stevens in 1911

E.J. Fulcher in 1912

CAREER RECORDS (HIGHEST RUNS AGGREGATES)

| | Matches | Innings | Runs | Highest Score | Average |
|---|---|---|---|---|---|
| M. Falcon | 247 | 379 | 11,538 | 205 | 33.83 |
| C.J. Rogers | 157 | 288 | 10206 | 173 | 38.80 |
| S.G. Plumb | 146 | 265 | 10,067 | 204* | 43.77 |
| G.A. Stevens | 158 | 262 | 8122 | 222 | 33.15 |
| W.J. Edrich | 172 | 276 | 8034 | 152 | 35.08 |
| F.L.Q. Handley | 162 | 295 | 7800 | 122 | 26.99 |
| R.D.P. Huggins | 157 | 282 | 6883 | 110* | 27.64 |
| D.G. Pilch | 225 | 365 | 6333 | 102* | 20.42 |
| S.C. Goldsmith | 90 | 157 | 6063 | 200* | 44.25 |
| C. Amos | 103 | 176 | 5737 | 226* | 35.63 |
| P.G. Powell | 140 | 247 | 5459 | 172 | 23.63 |
| E.G. Witherden | 72 | 128 | 4794 | 134* | 45.65 |
| N.H. Moore | 95 | 162 | 4761 | 163* | 31.95 |
| B.W. Rought-Rought | 140 | 215 | 4665 | 159 | 23.68 |
| J. Spelman | 71 | 123 | 4032 | 181 | 38.04 |
| D.F. Walker | 49 | 72 | 3997 | 217 | 63.44 |
| T.R. Ward | 53 | 89 | 3705 | 149 | 48.12 |
| I.P. Mercer | 74 | 132 | 3688 | 127 | 31.79 |
| D.E. Mattocks | 212 | 279 | 3482 | 104 | 17.32 |
| J.E. Nichols | 100 | 157 | 3263 | 127 | 24.35 |
| D.R. Thomas | 122 | 161 | 3002 | 75* | 27.79 |

## CAREER RECORDS (MOST WICKETS)

| | Overs | Maidens | Runs | Wickets | Average |
|---|---|---|---|---|---|
| M. Falcon | 3981.5 | 872 | 11,395 | 690 | 16.51 |
| | 15.6‡ | 3‡ | | | |
| T.I. Moore | 4000.5 | 925 | 12,001 | 474 | 25.32 |
| R.C. Rought-Rought | 2810.2 | 782 | 6753 | 438 | 15.42 |
| | 153.4‡ | 26 | | | |
| W.J. Edrich | 3200.2 | 856 | 7956 | 415 | 19.17 |
| C. Brown | 3068.2 | 737 | 8720 | 381 | 22.89 |
| H. Watson | 2176.1 | 489 | 5878 | 341 | 17.24 |
| C.S.R. Boswell | 186.5‡ | 26 | 7245 | 329 | 22.02 |
| | 2588.4 | 642 | | | |
| P.G. Walmsley | 2706.4 | 760 | 6972 | 329 | 21.19 |
| E. Gibson | 2114.5 | 593 | 5164 | 307 | 16.82 |
| W.A. Beadsmoore | 1912.4 | 568 | 4200 | 294 | 14.29 |
| W. Rose | 2152.2 | 675 | 5770 | 287 | 20.10 |
| S.G. Plumb | 2854.2 | 696 | 8728 | 283 | 30.84 |
| C. Shore | 1337.2† | 479 | 3696 | 251 | 14.73 |
| | 320.5 | 77 | | | |
| E.W. Smith | 1412 | 356 | 3658 | 226 | 16.19 |
| Revd G.B. Raikes | 271.4† | 91 | 3602 | 224 | 16.08 |
| | 838.2 | 103 | | | |
| J.E. Nichols | 62† | 15 | 4380 | 224 | 19.55 |
| | 1537.3 | 359 | | | |
| D.G. Pilch | 1637 | 280 | 5610 | 222 | 25.27 |
| E. Wright | 1621.4 | 316 | 5460 | 215 | 25.40 |
| T.H. Barnes | 1834.4 | 610 | 4510 | 212 | 21.27 |
| W.S. Thompson | 1244.4 | 252 | 4248 | 203 | 20.93 |
| | 80.3‡ | 12 | | | |
| R.A. Bunting | 1335 | 293 | 4221 | 201 | 21.00 |

† denotes 5-ball over

‡ denotes 8-ball over

CAREER RECORDS (WICKETKEEPERS WITH OVER 100 DISMISSALS)

459 (399 ct and 60 st)  D. E. Mattocks (including a small
number of catches as an outfielder)†

149 (115 ct and 34 st)  E. H. Edrich

143 (122 ct and 21 st)  B.J.H. Wood

113 (83 ct and 30 st)   B.G.W. Stevens

† Mattocks has taken more catches than any other player in
the Minor Counties Championship

CAREER RECORDS (FIELDERS WITH OVER 100 CATCHES)

151  W.J. Edrich

149  C.J. Rogers

145  D.G. Pilch

137  G.A. Stevens (including a small number of
catches as wicketkeeper, plus 1 stumping)

121  F.L.Q. Handley

112  M. Falcon

100  P.G. Powell

# PART 2: MISCELLANEOUS

### 100 OR MORE APPEARANCES IN MINOR COUNTIES CHAMPIONSHIP

| | | | | | |
|---|---|---|---|---|---|
| 247 | M. Falcon | 158 | G.A. Stevens | 122 | D.R. Thomas |
| 225 | D.G. Pilch | 157 | R.D.P. Huggins | 109 | P.G. Walmsley |
| 212 | D.E. Mattocks | 157 | C.J. Rogers | 105 | R.C. Rought-Rought |
| 172 | W.J. Edrich | 146 | S.G. Plumb | 103 | C. Amos |
| 169 | T.I. Moore | 140 | P.G. Powell | 103 | C.S.R. Boswell |
| 162 | F.L.Q. Handley | 140 | B.W. Rought-Rought | 100 | J.E. Nichols |

### APPOINTED CAPTAINS SINCE 1895
### (MINOR COUNTIES CHAMPIONSHIP ONLY)

| | | | |
|---|---|---|---|
| 1895–96 | A. R. Buxton | 1959–68 | W.J. Edrich |
| 1897–98 | Revd W.F.G Sandwith | 1969–70 | R.I. Jefferson |
| 1899 | L.C.V. Bathurst | 1970–71 | I.P. Mercer |
| 1900 | F. Davies | 1972–75 | D.G. Pilch |
| 1901 | G.F. Blake | 1976–78 | T.I. Moore |
| 1904 | L. Barratt | 1979–82 | Philip J. Sharpe |
| 1905–06 | Revd G.B. Raikes | 1983–86 | F.L.Q. Handley |
| 1907–08 | L. Barratt | 1987–90 | S.G. Plumb |
| 1909 | B.K. Wilson | 1991–95 | D.R. Thomas |
| 1910–11 | Revd G.B. Raikes | 1996–2002 | P.G. Newman |
| 1912–46 | M. Falcon | 2003–07 | P.J. Bradshaw |
| 1947–50 | W.S. Thompson | 2008–10 | C.J. Rogers |
| 1951–54 | L.A. Barratt | 2011–12 | G.W. Walker |
| 1955–58 | P.G. Powell | 2013– | C. Brown |

NORFOLK PLAYERS APPEARING FOR MINOR COUNTIES' TEAMS
IN ONE DAY COMPETITIONS

The following players appeared for Minor Counties' teams in the one-day
Benson and Hedges competition

R.A. Bunting – 4 matches (1987)

S.C. Goldsmith – 6 matches
(1995–98)

F.L.Q. Handley – 4 matches
(1979 and 1985)

R.I. Jefferson – 3 matches (1972)

T.I. Moore – 9 matches (1972–1976)

D.G. Pilch – 3 matches (1974–1975)

S.G. Plumb – 47 matches (1980–1992)

M.G. Powell – 2 matches (1996)

C.J. Rogers – 5 matches (1998)

M.J. Saggers – 5 matches (1996)

D.R. Thomas – 8 matches
(1990–1995)

Stephen Plumb captained the side from 1987 to 1990.

In addition, Chris Brown played 3 matches for the Unicorns in the Clydesdale
Bank 40 competition in 2010.

NORFOLK PLAYERS APPEARING IN REPRESENTATIVE MATCHES
AGAINST OVERSEAS TOURISTS

J.N.Worman v West Indians, 1906 (not first-class)

G.A. Stevens v South Africans, 1912; South Africans, 1924

W.A. Beadsmoore v South Africans, 1924

J.M. Coldham v South Africans, 1924

G.R.R. Colman v South Africans, 1924; Australians, 1926 (not first-class)

M. Falcon v South Africans 1924; Australians, 1926 (not first-class)

G.R. Pedder v South Africans, 1924

H. Watson v South Africans, 1924

W.J. Edrich v South Africans, 1935; Indians, 1936; West Indians, 1966 (not
first-class)

B.W. Rought-Rought v New Zealanders, 1937

N.H. Moore v South Africans, 1951 (not first-class); South Africans, 1960;
Australians, 1961 (not first-class)

I.P. Mercer v South Africans, 1965

W. Rose v West Indians, 1966 (not first-class)

G.J. Saville v Australians, 1968 (not first-class); West Indians, 1969; New
Zealanders, 1969

R.I. Jefferson v West Indians, 1969; New Zealanders, 1969

S.G. Plumb v West Indians, 1980 (not first-class); Sri Lankans, 1981; Pakistanis, 1982 (not first-class); Zimbabweans, 1983 (2 games: neither first-class); Indians, 1983 (not first-class); Kenya, 1984 (not first-class); West Indians, 1984 (not first-class); Zimbabweans, 1985; Australians, 1985 (not first-class); New Zealanders, 1986; Pakistanis, 1987 (not first-class); West Indians, 1988 (not first-class); Sri Lankans, 1988 (not first-class); Australians, 1989 (not first-class); West Indians, 1991 (not first-class); Bermuda, 1992 (not first-class)

D.E. Mattocks v Zimbabweans, 1985

R.A. Bunting v Pakistanis, 1987 (not first-class)

D.R. Thomas v Sri Lankans, 1988 (not first-class); Indians, 1990

J.C.M. Lewis v Pakistanis, 1992 (not first-class)

M.J. Saggers v Pakistanis, 1996 (not first-class)

# Bibliography

**Books**

Allen, D.R. (editor) (1987).
*Cricket's silver lining*. London:
Willow Books.

Andrews, W. (1898). *Bygone
Norfolk*. London: William
Andrews and Co.

Arlott, J. (editor) (1949). *The
middle ages of cricket*. London:
Johnson.

Armstrong, D. (1990). *A short
history of Norfolk county cricket*.
Dereham: The Larks Press.

Bailey, P., Thorn, P. and Wynne-
Thomas, P. (1984). *Who's who
of cricketers*. Feltham: Newnes
Books in association with
The Association of Cricket
Statisticians.

Barker, R. (1977). *The cricketing
family Edrich*. Newton Abbot:
Readers Union.

Birley, D. (1999). *A social history
of English cricket*. London:
Aurum Press.

Brodribb, G. (1974). *The Croucher*.
London: London Magazines
Editions.

Brodribb, G. (compiler) (1948).
*The English game*. London:
Hollis and Carter.

Bowen, R. (1970). *Cricket:
a history of its growth and
development throughout the
world*. London: Eyre and
Spottiswoode.

Buckley, G. (1937). *Fresh light
on pre-Victorian cricket*.
Birmingham: Cotterell.

Clark, Sir George. (1987).
*Illustrated history of Great
Britain*. London: Octopus
Books.

Davage, M. (2011). *Knights in whites: major men*. Colchester: Colchester Print Group.

Dennison, W. (1846). *Cricket: sketches of the players*. Simpkin, Marshall.

Driver,T. (1844). *The register of cricket for Hingham*. Printed by Matchett, Stevenson and Matchett.

Edrich, J. (1969). *Runs in the family*. London: Stanley Paul.

Edrich, W.J. (1948). *Cricket heritage*. London: Stanley Paul.

Fogg, J. (1972). *The Haig book of village cricket*. London: Pelham Books.

Forrest, A.J. (1957). *Village cricket*. London: Robert Hale.

Genders, R. (1952). *League cricket in England*. London: T Werner Laurie.

Goulstone, J. (1972). *Early club and village cricket*. Privately published.

Goulstone, J. (2001). *Hambledon: the men and the myths*. Cambridge: Roger Heavens.

Green, B. (1988). *A history of cricket*. London: Barrie and Jenkins.

Guha, R. (2002). *A corner of a foreign field*. London: Picador.

Haygarth, A. (from 1996). *Frederick Lillywhite's Scores and Biographies*. Volumes 1 to 18. Cambridge: Roger Heavens.

Heyhoe,R. and Rheinberg, N. (1976). *Fair play: the story of women's cricket*. London: Angus and Robertson.

Hill, A. (1994). *Bill Edrich: a biography*. London: Andre Deutsch.

Hopkins, E. (1979). *A social history of the English working classes, 1815–1945*. London: Edward Arnold.

Howat, G. (1980). *Village cricket*. Newton Abbot: David and Charles.

Isaacs, R. (2009). *Minor counties List A cricketers*. Cardiff: Association of Cricket Statisticians and Historians.

Joy, N. (1950). *Maiden over: a short history of women's cricket*. London: Sporting Handbooks.

Lonsdale, J. (1992). *The arm's grace: the life of Brigadier General R. M. Poore*. Tunbridge Wells: Spellmount

Major, J. (2007). *More than a game: the story of cricket's early years*. London: Harper Collins.

Martineau, G. (1957). *They made cricket*. London: Sportsmans Book Club.

Mason, R. (1973). *Warwick Armstrong's Australians*.

Newton Abbot: Sportsmans
Book Club.

Midwinter, E. (2010). *The
cricketer's progress: Meadowland
to Mumbai.* London: Third Age
Press.

Midwinter, E. (1987). *The lost
seasons: cricket in wartime,
1939–45.* London: Methuen.

Mote, A. (1997). *The glory days
of cricket: the extraordinary
story of Broadhalfpenny Down.*
London: Robson Books.

Musk, S. (2010). *Michael Falcon:
Norfolk's gentleman cricketer.*
Cardiff: Association of Cricket
Statisticians and Historians.

Narborough Local History Society.
(2004). *The book of Narborough*;
edited by D. Turner. Tiverton:
Halsgrove.

Norridge, J. (2009). *Can we have
our balls back, please?* London:
Penguin Books.

Penny, J. (1979). *Cricketing
references in Norwich
newspapers.* Norwich.

Plumptre, G. (editor) (1986).
*Barclays world of cricket: the
game from A-Z.* 3rd edition.
London.: Willow Books.

Pollock, W. (1934). *The cream of
cricket.* London: Methuen.

Rait Kerr, R.S. (1950). *The laws of
cricket.* London: Longmans,
Green.

Rendell, B. (2010). *Fuller Pilch: a
straightforward man.* Cardiff:
Association of Cricket
Statisticians and Historians.

Scott, J. (1989). *Caught in court.*
London: Andre Deutsch.

Sissons, R. (1988). *The players:
a social history of the
professional cricketer.*
London: Kingswood Press.

Steel, A. and Lyttelton, Hon. R.
(1987). *Cricket.* Shedfield:
Ashford Press Publishing.

Trevelyan, G. (1942). *English social
history.* London: Longman.

Underdown, D. (2000). *Start of
play.* London: Penguin Books.

Wade-Martins, S. (1984). *A
history of Norfolk.* Chichester:
Phillimore.

Webb, A. (editor) (2004–
2012). *The minor counties
championship 1895* (and other
years to 1907). Cardiff:
Association of Cricket
Statisticians and Historians.

West, G. (1988). *The elevens
of England.* London: Darf
Publishers.

Williams, J. (1999). *Cricket in
England: a cultural and social*

*history of the inter-war years.*
London: Frank Cass.

Wynne-Thomas, P. (1989). *The complete history of cricket tours at home and abroad.* London: Hamlyn.

Wynne-Thomas, P. (1997). *The history of cricket from the Weald to the world.* Norwich: H.M.S.O.

Yaxley, P. (1997). *Looking back at Norfolk cricket.* Dereham: Nostalgia Publications.

## Newspapers and Periodicals

*The Cricket Statistician* periodical

*Cricket: A Weekly Record of the Game* periodical

*The Cricketer* magazine

*Dereham and Fakenham Times* newspaper

*Diss Express* newspaper

*Downham Market Gazette* newspaper

*Eastern Daily Press* newspaper

*Great Yarmouth Gazette* newspaper

*Journal of the Cricket Society*

*King's Lynn Advertiser* newspaper

*Minor Counties Annuals*

*The Norfolk Chronicle and Norwich Gazette* newspaper

*Norfolk County Cricket Club Handbooks*

*Norfolk Cricket Association Yearbooks*

*North Norfolk News* newspaper

*Norwich Mercury* newspaper

*Wisden Cricketers' Almanacks*

*Women's Cricket* periodical

## Websites

www.cricketarchive.com
www.norfolkcricket.co.uk

www.measuringworth.com

## Other

White's Norfolk Directories

Minutes of the Norfolk Cricket Association and Norfolk Cricket Board

Minutes of the Norfolk Schools Cricket Association

Norfolk Youth Committee Newsletters

# Index

This Index does not list every reference to every person, place or team referred to in the text. Instead, generally only the more significant of these references are noted